1

¡tango!

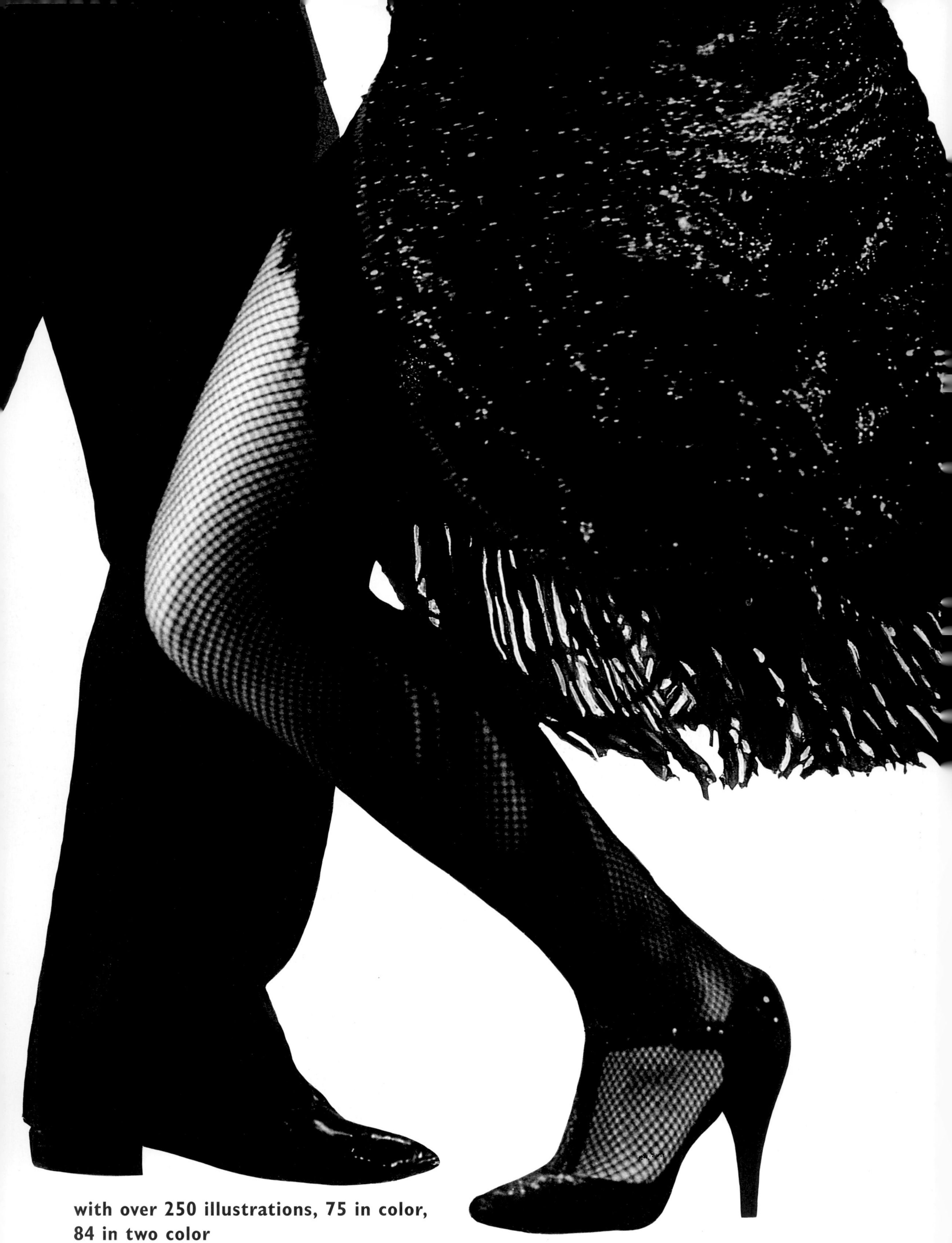

with over 250 illustrations, 75 in color,
84 in two color

SIMON COLLIER

ARTEMIS COOPER

MARÍA SUSANA AZZI

RICHARD MARTIN

¡tango!

The Dance, the Song, the Story

SPECIAL PHOTOGRAPHY BY KEN HAAS

THAMES AND HUDSON

★ **Color portfolio by Ken Haas: pages 1–4: The tango is alive and well on the streets of Buenos Aires, in the cafés of the old neighborhoods and in the finest nightclubs and ballrooms of the city.**

***Half-title:* Natalia Games and Gabriel Angío in *Tango Para Dos* (*Tango X 2*), Sadler's Wells, London, 1993.**

***Title page:* Miguel Angel Zotto and Milena Plebs in *Tango Para Dos* (*Tango X 2*), Sadler's Wells, London, 1993.**

Advisory Editor: Simon Collier

Picture Research: Georgina Bruckner

Ken Haas wishes to acknowledge the support and encouragement of Fuji Photo Film U.S.A., Inc. His tango photographs were shot on Fujichrome film.

First published in the United States of America in 1995 by Thames and Hudson Inc., 500 Fifth Avenue, New York, New York 10110

Library of Congress Catalog Card Number 95-60478
ISBN 0-500-01671-2

Printed and bound in Singapore

CONTENTS

COLOUR PORTFOLIO BY KEN HAAS 13-16

Simon Collier

PART I THE TANGO IS BORN: 1880s–1920s 18

The Birthplace 19

COLOUR PORTFOLIO BY KEN HAAS 25-32

The Birth 40

The Triumph 55

Artemis Cooper

PART II TANGOMANIA IN EUROPE AND NORTH AMERICA: 1913–1914 66

First Tango in Paris 67

The Shock of the Tango 76

The First World War and After 100

COLOUR PORTFOLIO BY KEN HAAS 105-112

María Susana Azzi

PART III THE GOLDEN AGE AND AFTER: 1920s–1990s 114

The Tango Returns Home 115

Carlos Gardel and the Tango Song 122

Tango Lyrics 132

Women Singers 140

The 1930s and 1940s 145

Keeping the Flame Alive 156

COLOUR PORTFOLIO BY KEN HAAS 161-168

Richard Martin

PART IV THE LASTING TANGO 170

Dance of gender, dance of power ★ the tango as image and symbol in literature, theatre and film ★ race, culture and the international tango

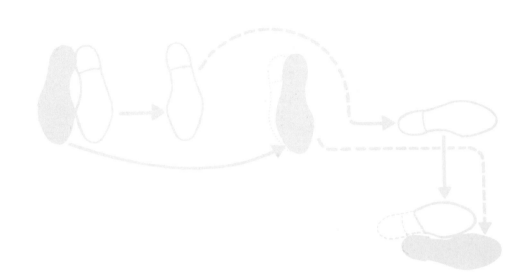

FURTHER INFORMATION 197

The Tango's Family Tree 197

Chart of the History of the Tango 198

Tango Music on Compact Disc 199

International Tango Centres 201

Notes 203

Bibliography 204

Sources of Illustrations 205

Sources of Quotations 206

Acknowledgments 206

Index 207

'The rum, the music, the women, Rosendo with that rough talk pouring out of his mouth and a slap on the back for each of us that I tried to take for a sign of real friendship – the thing is, I was happy as they come. I was lucky too. I had me a partner who could follow my steps just like she knew ahead of time which way I was going to turn. The tango took hold of us, driving us along and then splitting us up and then bringing us back together again. There we were in the middle of all this fun, like in some kind of dream, when all of a sudden I feel the music kind of getting louder. Turns out it was those two guitar pickers riding in the buggy, coming closer and closer, their music getting mixed up with ours. Then the breeze shifted, you couldn't hear them anymore, and my mind went back to my own steps and my partner's, and to the ins and outs of the dance...'

From 'Streetcorner Man'
by Jorge Luis Borges, 1933

★ Pages 13–16: One of the birthplaces of the tango was the colourful waterfront *barrio* of La Boca.

T TANGO
KLORE PROGRAMME
OS AIRES
IR RESERVATION
IR TRAVEL AGENCY
WELCOME
BIENVENU

Underworld song, song of Buenos Aires,
There's something inside you that lives
and is everlasting,
Underworld song, lament of bitterness,
Smile of hope, sob of passion.

This is the tango, the song of Buenos
Aires,
Born in the suburbs, today queen of
the whole world....

From 'Song of Buenos Aires'
Words by Manuel Romero;
music by Azucena Maizani and
Orestes Cúfaro,
1933

I

SIMON COLLIER

THE TANGO IS BORN

1880s–1920s

★THE BIRTHPLACE★

As New World cities go, Buenos Aires has a certain antiquity – founded by a Spanish expedition in 1536, abandoned five years later, and founded again, this time for good, in 1580. For its first three centuries, however, nobody thought much of it as a place. The territory we now call Argentina was a remote, thinly peopled and rather neglected backwater of the huge Spanish-American empire. Its vast Pampa, the mostly level plain stretching inland from the Atlantic and muddy River Plate estuary, provided an ideal setting for ranching and agriculture, and sooner or later this was bound to be recognized. From the later eighteenth century onwards, cattle-hides, salted beef and wool were exported in increasing quantities from Buenos Aires.

The Pampa, still in the 1870s extensively roamed by the Araucanian Indians, was also the natural habitat for independent, nomadic gauchos, the fierce horsemen of the plains, whose harsh way of life had grown up on the edge (when not actually beyond the limits) of organized society, such as it was – and at the time of Argentina's first census in 1869, the population of this enormous land was still only 1,800,000. Much romanticized later on as a noble prototype of Argentine character, the gaucho was regarded as an unruly and 'barbaric' nuisance by the colonial

Opposite: **Carnival at the Pabellón de las Rosas (Rose Pavilion), a popular dance-venue in Buenos Aires, in March 1905.**

Right: **'Soy Tremendo!' (It's Tremendous!) by Angel Villoldo.**

authorities and their republican successors, though he had an outstanding literary defender in the poet José Hernández, author of the epic *Martín Fierro* (1872–79), an Argentine classic.

By the time Hernández wrote his great poem, the gauchos as a group were already doomed. As Argentina gradually moved away from the violent conflicts of early nationhood (the age of the caudillos – the provincial warlords – and their rampaging private armies of gaucho cavalry) and into the era of more settled government, the pressures of civilization and the disciplines of economic growth bore down harshly on the independent gaucho way of life, which had effectively vanished by the end of the nineteenth century, however powerful it may have remained (thanks to Hernández and others) in the Argentine folk-memory.

The year 1880 marked a vital turning point for Argentina. It was then that the port city of Buenos Aires, Argentina's wealthiest city, was made the federal

capital and separated from its rich and powerful province, thus making the two into separate entities with less power over the other thirteen provinces. One year before the federalization law, the man soon to be twice president of Argentina, General Julio Argentino Roca, had, at the head of five divisions of well-armed soldiers, finally cleared the Araucanians from the Pampa, thus opening up an immense new area for ranching and agriculture. With a growing market for beef and cereals in Europe, and with the advent of modern communications (steamships, railways, telegraphs), the country now experienced the most spectacular economic boom any Latin American nation has ever known. It turned Argentina into one of the world's richest nations by the 1920s. Foreign, notably British, capital poured in; a vast railway network (the world's ninth largest in 1914) was constructed, with Buenos Aires as its most important focus; and, seeing Argentina as a promised land second only to the United States, several million European migrants sailed down the Atlantic to Buenos Aires – roughly half of them from Italy and one-third from Spain. In the course of a generation or so, the character of the Argentine population, which by 1914 had reached 8,000,000, was thus radically transformed.

Gauchos, the wandering horsemen of the plains, were celebrated in José Hernandez's epic poem *Martín Fierro*, published in the 1870s (*opposite top*). They are seen *above* branding cattle on the Pampa. The gaucho shown *left centre* is in the process of catching an ostrich with his lasso – ostrich-hunting was a favourite gaucho pastime.

In the 1860s plainsmen's wagons such as those shown *opposite below* were a common sight in Buenos Aires.

In no part of Argentina were economic progress and immigrant influx more clearly visible than in Buenos Aires. The town plausibly described as late as 1884 as *la gran aldea*, 'the big village', suddenly blossomed into the largest and grandest metropolis south of the Equator, by any standard one of the great cities of the early-twentieth-century world. Its population rose from 180,000 in 1869 to 1,500,000 in 1914. Moreover, the rich patrician families who led the republic at this period were eager to make their new federal capital a splendid showcase, an advertisement for Argentine progress. They had a particular model very much in mind: the Paris lately remodelled by Napoleon III and Baron Haussmann. Buenos Aires, the hitherto undistinguished estuarine port, was to become the Paris of South America.

The city fathers cannot be faulted for effort. The docks were modernized; hundreds of thousands of trees were planted; a fine new ceremonial axis (the Avenida de Mayo) was driven through the gridiron of narrow streets inherited

At the turn of the century, Buenos Aires was transformed from a 'big village' into a grand and elegant metropolis – it became known as the Paris of South America. An intensive programme of modernization included the building of splendid tree-lined avenues. The Avenida de Mayo (*opposite*) was the first to be completed, in 1894.

Florida Street, named after a minor battle of the South American wars of independence (*below*), was the city's most fashionable shopping street.

The Federal Capital of Buenos Aires in 1910, superimposed on a contemporary map of Greater London. In fact, the urban area of 'greater' Buenos Aires was already spreading far beyond the boundaries of the federal district proper.

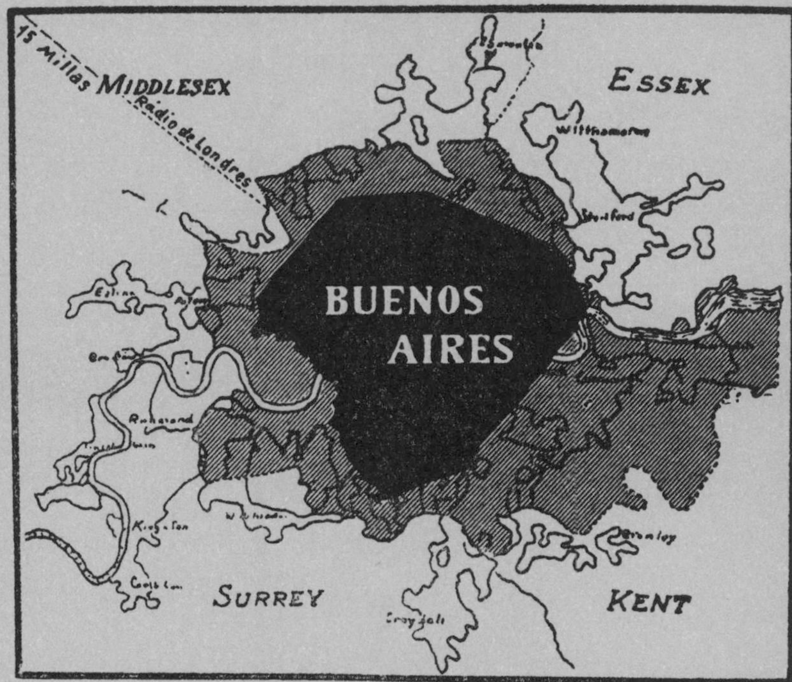

from the colonial era; spacious parks were laid out; a zoo (with some delightfully fanciful animal-houses) was inaugurated; public buildings and private mansions grew increasingly monumental; the world's largest opera house, the Teatro Colón, was opened in 1908; and in 1911 work began on an underground railway – the only underground railway in Latin America before the 1960s, when Mexico City built the second.

By 1910 downtown Buenos Aires – *el Centro*, 'the Centre', in the local term – won extravagant compliments from the foreign visitors who flocked there for Argentina's lavishly celebrated Centenary. R.B. Cunninghame-Graham, the Scottish writer, returned to Buenos Aires during World War I – on a horse-buying mission for the British government – after an absence of thirty-six years. 'How Buenos Aires has changed!' he wrote. 'It is a marvel – Paris with a fine climate. Motors, well-dressed women, restaurants and parks and gardens such as you can see *nowhere* else. It is the cleanest town in the world and beautiful in its own style.'[1]

★ **Pages 25–32: Tango is a world of spiked heels, romantic intrigue and the bandoneon, the quintessential tango instrument which came from Germany to Argentina in the late 19th century.**

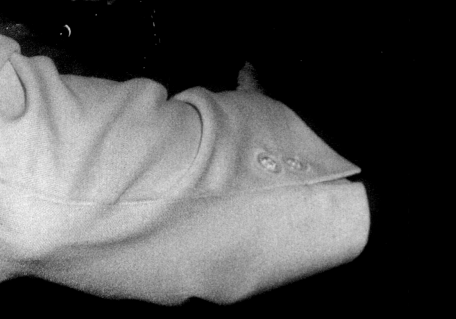

Like all great cities, however, it had its meaner streets. The stylish and monumental Centre was by no means the only face of early-twentieth-century Buenos Aires. As the city grew, the built-up area rapidly expanded outwards, away from the city's historic core along the River Plate shoreline and into the still empty spaces of the newly mapped-out federal capital, new *barrios* (districts) springing up almost overnight with the spread of suburban railways and horse-drawn and (after 1900) electric tramcar routes. The most affluent *barrios*, favoured by the upper class, were those on the northern side of the city, close to the shore of the estuary; the Barrio Norte, which was the closest to the Centre, became the principal upper-class area. A more miscellaneous mixture of social classes occupied the thickly populated area due west of the Centre. Street-paving and tramway routes arrived somewhat later in the generally much poorer districts to the south, where the terrain sloped down to the Riachuelo – the river marking the boundary of the federal district in that direction.

In barbershops, shoeshine boys entertained the clientele by playing music on the gramophone. Opera was popular until the tango took over in the 1910s. Some shoeshine boys remained in the job for the rest of their lives; others worked just for a couple of years. Various well-known tango musicians, including Francisco Canaro and Juan de Dios Filiberto, began as shoeshiners. The photograph *below* was taken in 1905.

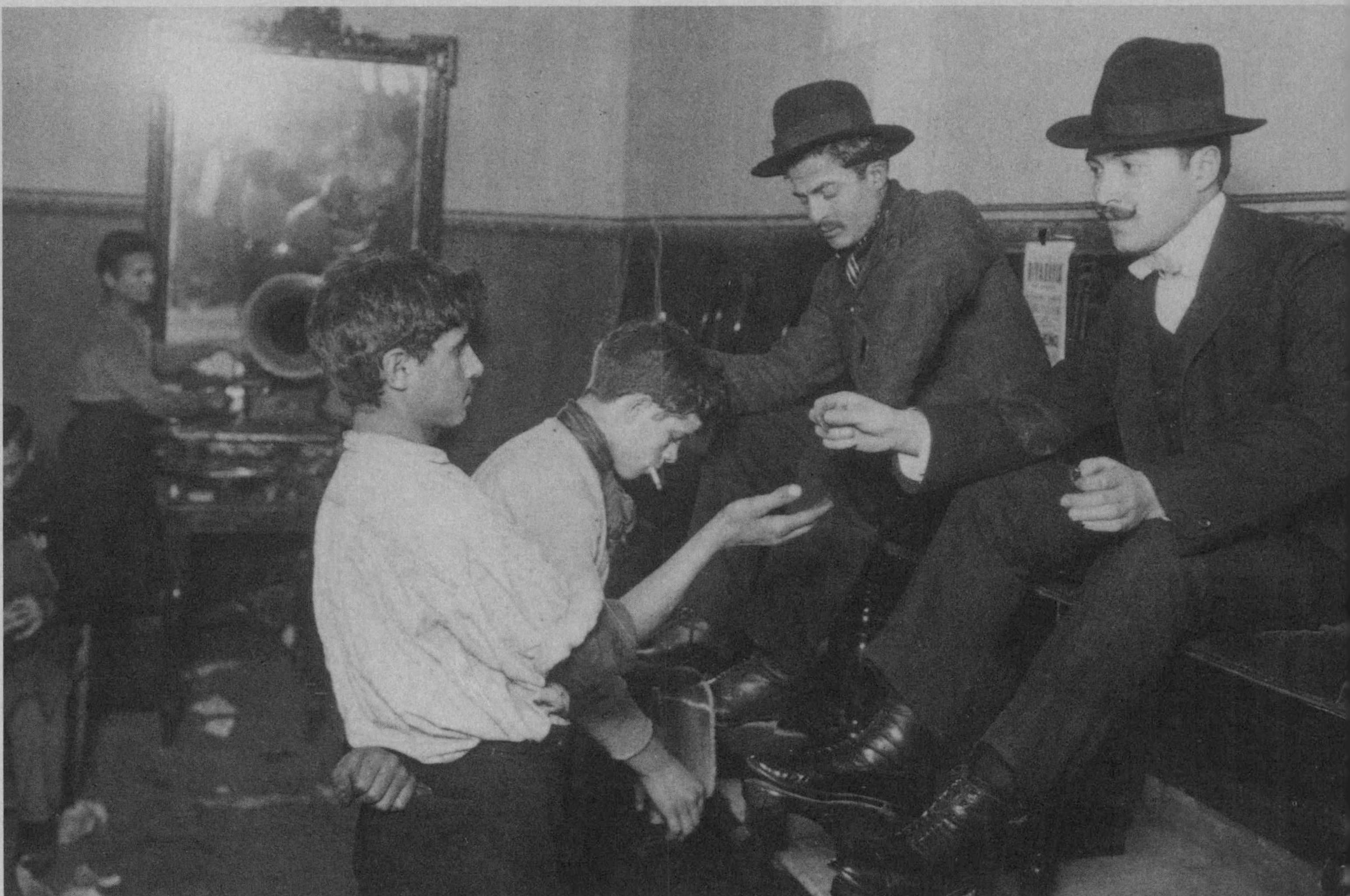

Slaughterhouse, woodcut by Alfredo Bellocq, 1922.

The small-scale industry that was a byproduct of economic expansion was located both here and in the working-class suburb of Barracas al Sur (known from 1904 as Avellaneda) across the river. The outermost areas of the growing city, the so-called *arrabales*, with their muddy streets, modest houses, shacks and workshops, presented the most vivid contrast of all with the magnificent Centre. Corrales Viejos was one such southern *arrabal*, its focal point being the municipal slaughterhouse (located there between 1867 and 1903), at which herds of livestock arrived daily from the nearby countryside of the Pampa. Closer to the Riachuelo, the so-called Pueblo de Ranas ('Frogs' District') surrounded the enormous municipal rubbish dump, which attracted hundreds of human scavengers. The city's underside of poverty, however, was by no means exceptional by the standards of London or New York. There was little long-term unemployment, and wage rates in some trades were often better than those in France or England.

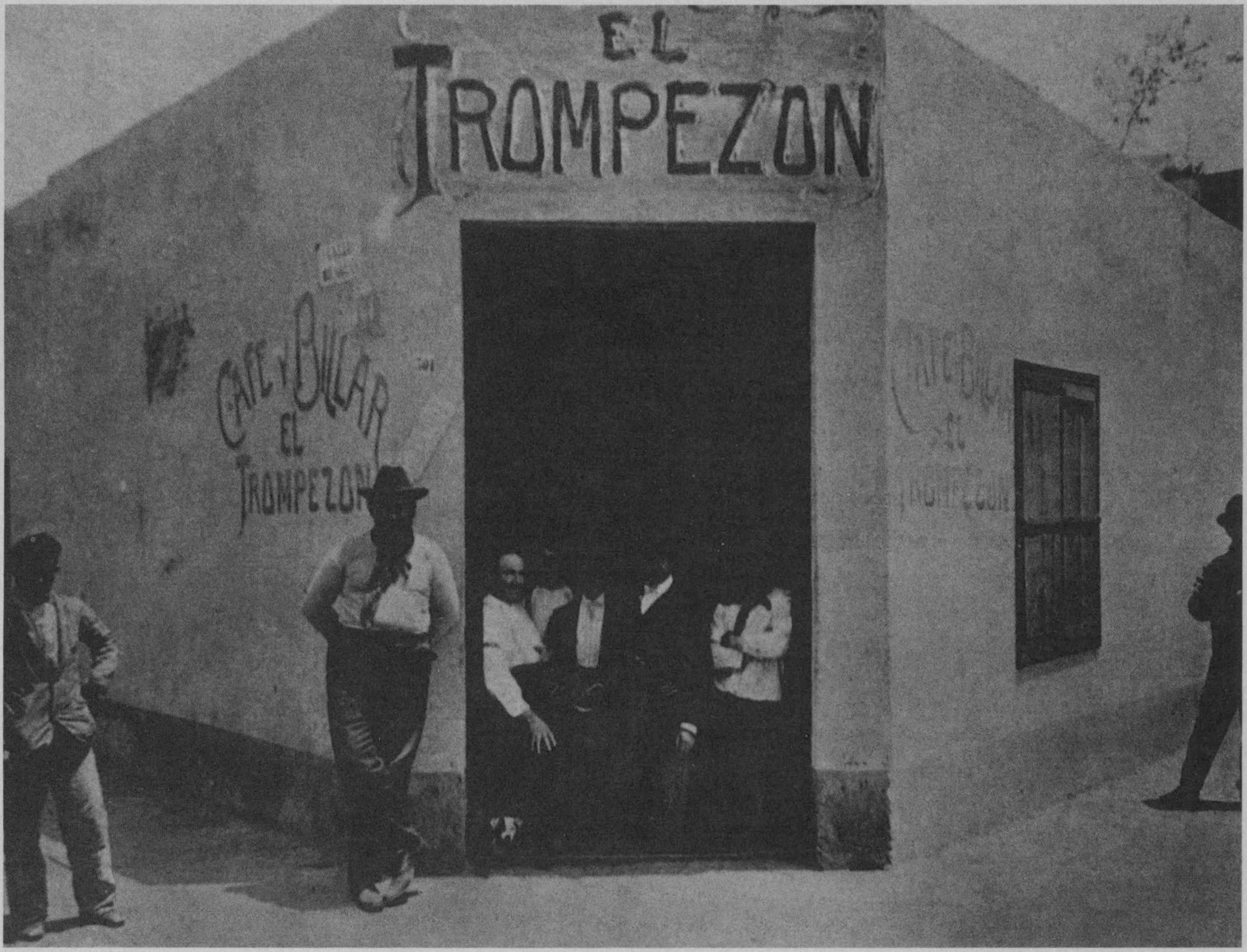

Like turn-of-the-century New York, the burgeoning metropolis of Buenos Aires was a distinctly cosmopolitan place. Some districts, to be sure, became associated with particular immigrant groups, but there were no real ethnic ghettoes in the city. Initially, it is true, there was a heavier concentration of immigrants in the more centrally located districts, where in 1914 immigrant males outnumbered their native-born counterparts three to one. Here Italian and Spanish newcomers often found themselves living in overcrowded tenements, *conventillos*, where families were crammed into narrow rooms surrounding a central patio. Some of the tenements were purpose-built; others were houses vacated by upper-class families with the drift of the better-off into the northern *barrios* – a drift which had got seriously under way after a horrendous yellow-fever epidemic in 1871. As soon as they could, the more enterprising tenement-dwellers made off into the outer districts, often building their own small houses there and helping, over the years, to transform the *arrabales* into ordinary *barrios*.

Opposite below: **The proprietor and some of his customers pose for their photograph outside El Trompezón (The Misfortune) café and billiard parlour in a *barrio* of Buenos Aires in 1907.**

On their arrival in Buenos Aires, many immigrants found themselves forced to live in slum buildings, known as *conventillos*. Conditions were bad, with whole families crowded into one room. The *conventillos* were built around a central patio, which often served as both workshop and playground. The photograph *below* dates from 1908.

From the 1840s to 1940, immigrants poured into Argentina in their millions. About 4 million settled permanently, many in Buenos Aires itself. They came mostly from Italy and Spain, but also from France. Some can be seen *above* disembarking from a French ship in the 1900s.

'The Welcome' (*right*) was published in the popular Buenos Aires magazine *Caras y caretas* in 1906. Founded in 1898, *Caras y caretas* was noted for its early coverage of the newly emerging tango.

In the first decades of the twentieth century, the sheer size of the immigrant influx contributed to a real cultural transformation in Argentina – almost a remaking of the national culture. There was often resentment of the newcomers by native-born 'creole' Argentines, expressed, for the most part, less in acts of violence than in caustic humour. The social and ethnic contrasts of the time were also well-reflected in the *sainetes* – one-act comedies – that became popular on the Buenos Aires stage in the 1890s. But, in general, the immigrants adapted fairly easily to their new surroundings. For the newly arrived Spaniard, of course, there was no language difficulty; the Italian-Spanish interface posed no insuperable problems, though it did produce some interesting linguistic effects including a short-lived hybrid patois called *cocoliche*, and, more permanently, the very expressive and largely Italian-derived local

vocabulary known as *lunfardo*, the strongest influence on the modern colloquial Spanish of Buenos Aires, a vocabulary favoured later on by the writers of tango lyrics, and one still employed by a number of talented poets in the city. Like the tango itself, *lunfardo* became an integral part of the metropolitan identity and culture of Buenos Aires.

This metropolitan identity was still only beginning to form during the tango's period of gestation. In the outer *barrios* and *arrabales*, where city and countryside met, the old 'creole' Argentina perhaps survived longer than in the rapidly swelling inner districts. A familiar figure in the *arrabal* was the usually well-respected *compadre*, a semi-urban type often engaged in herding cattle from the Pampa to the slaughterhouse or in driving carts. It is tempting to see the *compadres* as displaced gauchos, driven to the city's marginal districts by the collapse of their independent way of life with the spread of ranches, railways and barbed-wire fences across the Pampa. For though the gaucho world was dead, certain gaucho attitudes lived on among the suburban *compadres*: fierce independence, masculine pride and a strong inclination to settle affairs of honour with knives.

Children from the *barrios*, early 20th century.

Altogether more numerous than the *compadres* in the closing decades of the nineteenth century were the so-called *compadritos*. The term was not a particularly flattering one. These were young men, mostly native-born and poor, who sought to imitate the manners and attitudes of the *compadres* (some of whom were men of substance in a small way), sometimes in rather exaggerated fashion. Their form of speech seems to have been 'creole' and traditional rather than immigrant-influenced. They can best be described as street toughs, familiar to their contemporaries from their uniform of slouch hat, loosely tied neckerchief, high-heeled boots, and knife casually tucked into belt. For the most part *compadritos*, for all their disdain of the law, were not criminals, though criminals often found a safe refuge in the outer *barrios*. In general the population of such districts was mixed and transient. Soldiers from the nearby barracks, sailors enjoying shore-leave, enterprising immigrant artisans, factory hands, slaughterhouse workers, herdsmen, simple vagrants – these and many other people of relatively modest means made up much of the human world of the ephemeral Buenos Aires *arrabal*.

Above, _below_ and _below right_: Versions of the _compadrito_, the young hoodlum of the Buenos Aires slums, who was responsible for improvising the tango into existence in low-life cafés, bars and brothels. He was immediately recognizable by his rakish outfit of grey hat, neckerchief, high-heeled boots and knife.

It was a world in which there were always more men than women. In Buenos Aires in 1914 the gap was more than 100,000. Both licensed and unlicensed prostitution were rife throughout the city; especially in the outer districts, which were crammed with illegal brothels called *clandestinos*. Many of the city's prostitutes (and their madams) were foreign-born. At this period Buenos Aires had a reputation in Europe as the main destination for the white-slave traffic, and though this reputation was probably somewhat inflated by journalists

and reformers, as a 1992 study by the American historian Donna Guy makes clear, the recruitment of foreign women for prostitution was real enough – masterminded by French, Italian and Jewish organizations, sometimes with the complicity of the Buenos Aires police department.[2]

The motley world of the *arrabal* was situated only a few miles from the sumptuous mansions and ornate restaurants of the Centre and the inner northern *barrios*, but socially it must have seemed another world. There was, perhaps, no special reason why this particular mix of people, this transitory culture, should spark off an internationally renowned dance and a wonderful tradition of popular music. But perhaps it had something to do with the fact that Buenos Aires was (and is) a port – its inhabitants, almost as if to underline the point, are called *porteños*.[3] And it is remarkable how often great ports – from New Orleans to Liverpool – have proved to be the breeding-grounds for new and vital cultural traditions.

Real-life *compadritos:* a group of coachmen in 1906. The one at the *left* is drinking *mate* through a metal tube, known as a *bombilla.* This Paraguayan tea is still popular among Argentines. The coachman at *right* entertains his comrades on his guitar, which was to become the first instrument of the tango.

★ THE BIRTH ★

From well before the start of her great economic boom, Argentina had established close commercial links with Europe and had imported from the Old World not only textiles, machinery and luxury goods, but also a host of new cultural trends, among them fashions in music and dance. It is these, of course, that had a vital bearing on the invention of the tango, so it is essential to ask what was being danced in Buenos Aires in the years before the tango came along?

The first new European dance to reach Argentina in the nineteenth century, roughly at the time of Independence (1816), was the waltz. This was followed in the mid-century years by the polka, the mazurka and the schottische (spelled *chotis* in Spanish). Also in the mid-century came the immensely popular *habanera*, danced to the Spanish-Cuban rhythm perhaps best remembered today from its appearance in Georges Bizet's opera *Carmen* – a *habanera* Bizet borrowed from the Spanish composer Sebastián Yradier.

As its name suggests, the *habanera* evolved in early-nineteenth-century Havana, Cuba, from where it travelled both to Spain and Argentina. (Its mild syncopation was to become altogether less mild in the extraordinary wave of dance rhythms that emanated from Cuba one hundred years later.) On its Spanish side, it derived from the *contradanza*, the Spanish adaptation of the French *contredanse* of the eighteenth century, itself derived in part from the English 'country dances' (few, if any, of which were genuinely rural) of the seventeenth. The *contredanse* was itself introduced into Cuba by French planters fleeing from the slave rebellion in Saint Domingue (Haiti) in the 1790s.

A gaucho fiesta – illustration from the Argentine epic poem, *Martín Fierro*, 1879.

The *habanera* and the polka in particular seem to have played a part in stimulating the emergence of the local Argentine dance known as the *milonga*, a dance evidently very popular by the 1870s among the *compadritos* of Buenos Aires, and which was sometimes referred to, significantly, as 'the poor man's *habanera*'. The *milonga* had originated as a form of song, and was a variant of the lengthy improvisations (with guitar accompaniment)

that were the hallmark of the *payadores*, the folk-singers of the Pampa, who had played an important part in the now vanishing world of the gaucho. Once in the city, the *milonga*, its tempo simplified, acquired steps of its own. We do not know enough to describe them in any detail, but they appear to have been strongly influenced by the new dances imported from overseas.

There has never been any real doubt about the importance of the *milonga* and the *habanera* in the tango's immediate ancestry. It seems fairly clear that the *milonga* actually *was* the embryonic form of the tango before the new dance was finally given a name. It is at this point, however, that the issue becomes complicated, not only because of the lack of precise contemporary descriptions of what was happening in the *arrabales* of Buenos Aires in the 1870s and 1880s, but also because of confusion over the term 'tango' itself. Where, in fact, does this term come from? Answering this question will help us to get closer to the tango's moment of conception and birth.

The etymology cannot be traced completely. It is possible that the word is straightforwardly African in origin, a theory strongly supported by the Argentine historian Ricardo Rodríguez Molas, who notes that in certain African tongues the word 'tango' means 'closed place' or 'reserved ground'.[4] (On the map of Africa today, Tango can be found as a place-name in both Angola and Mali.) An alternative possibility, not to be dismissed too quickly, is that the term derives originally from Portuguese (and therefore from the Latin verb *tangere*, to touch), and that it was incorporated, evidently in some kind of slave-trading connection, into a kind of pidgin Portuguese used on the island of Sao Tomé (in the Gulf of Guinea), an important centre for the slave trade. If this second derivation is correct, the word was picked up by African slaves from their captors. But whether African or Portuguese, it seems highly probable that it reached the Western hemisphere with the slave-ships and on the lips of slaves. A third theory sometimes invoked – that 'tango' is simply onomatopoeic, representing the sound of a drum-beat, *tan-go* – seems on balance to be less convincing.

In many parts of the Spanish-American empire, the word 'tango', whatever its origin, acquired the standard meaning of a *place* where African slaves (or free blacks, of whom there were always more in the Spanish colonies than in the British empire) assembled for the purpose of dancing. In Argentina, as elsewhere in the Spanish-speaking world, 'tango' also sometimes came to be applied, though at a later stage, to black *dances* in general. It was in this sense that the word eventually reached Spain, as a name for African-American or

African-influenced dances of transatlantic provenance. The *habanera* itself was sometimes called a *tango americano*. (Isaac Albéniz's 'Tangos for Piano' are in fact *habaneras*.) A Spanish variation of the *habanera* was given the name *tango andaluz* (Andalusian tango), and this, too, became well-known in Argentina in the second half of the nineteenth century, though as a form of popular song rather than as a dance. In the 1880s and 1890s both the sung *habanera* and the *tango andaluz* (sometimes just called a 'tango') were popularized in Buenos Aires by visiting Spanish theatre troupes. Many *habanera*-songs and *tangos andaluces* became hits, hummed and whistled all over the city, and domestic versions, often with local colour added, soon went the rounds.

It can be seen from this that the name 'tango' had been in use for a long time and was very familiar to the inhabitants of late-nineteenth-century Buenos Aires. It could easily be appropriated by – or attached to – a rising new music-and-dance tradition. And in due course it was.

Quite apart from its availability as a label, the word 'tango' in its earlier meaning – the place where blacks assembled to dance – also had a direct part to play in the spontaneous creation of the Argentine tango proper. The contribution of the Buenos Aires black community to the invention of the tango was indirect but nevertheless fundamental, in the sense that without it there would have been no tango at all. In the eighteenth century, Buenos Aires had been one of the ports of entry for the slave trade, and a sizeable number of its inhabitants had traditionally been black – around one-quarter of the population in the mid-nineteenth century. With the expansion of the city and with European immigration, the black community was now beginning to decline, or at any rate to become much less visible than it had

been in the past. For the most part the African-Argentines had clustered in a number of inner-city parishes; and their distinctive culture had been well-preserved by their communal organizations, not least in the form of enthusiasm for dance festivals. African-Argentine dances, needless to say, bore little resemblance either to those of the Argentine countryside or to the dances imported from Europe. The most prominent was the *candombe*, a local fusion of various African traditions. Its complicated choreography included a final section combining wild rhythms, freely improvised steps and energetic, semi-athletic movements.

After the middle of the nineteenth century – according to George Reid Andrews, the historian of Buenos Aires's black communities – younger blacks in particular abandoned the *candombe* in favour of European imports such as the polka and the mazurka – perhaps as a means of winning greater social acceptance. While blacks began dancing white dances, some whites reciprocated by imitating the steps and movements of African-Argentine dancers, though it may be doubted whether this was really a case of imitation proving the sincerest form of flattery. In the 1860s and 1870s, and for some

Some of the roots of the tango can be seen in the *candombe*, a wild, rhythmic, often improvised dance, popular among African-Argentines in the *barrios* of Buenos Aires as well as in other parts of South America. The drawings *above* and *opposite* are by the Uruguayan artist Pedro Figari and depict scenes from the 1860s and 1870s.

time after, upper-class *porteños* blacked their faces and, calling themselves Los Negros, formed one of the carnival processions each year.[5] This is a good illustration of what seems to have been a common trend, but it had no direct influence on the creation of the tango. Far more interesting from the viewpoint of the tango story were the contacts between African-Argentines and *compadritos*. For it was the *compadritos* who provided the vital spark, the spark that set off the explosion, and what specifically prompted them to provide it was the example of the African-Argentines.

Around the late 1870s, African-Argentines in Buenos Aires improvised a new dance – with some similarities to the *candombe* – which they called a 'tango'. The *compadritos*, in a spirit of mockery, took elements of this dance, parodied them, and incorporated them in their own favourite dance of the time, the *milonga*. It was the *milonga* that would eventually develop into the tango as we know it today.

The caricature *below*, showing an African-Argentine couple dancing 'el tango,' appeared in an Argentine magazine in 1882.

At this critical point in the story, it is necessary to take account of what seems to be the only coherent eyewitness description of the birth of the tango. This striking piece of evidence was brought to light by José Gobello, one of the wisest and most knowledgeable writers on the history of the tango and *lunfardo*, and the moving spirit of the Academia Porteña del Lunfardo (the main body that studies the traditional popular culture of Buenos Aires) since its creation in 1962. It is contained in an article printed on 22 September 1913 in *Crítica* – Buenos Aires's first mass-circulation popular newspaper, itself founded only a few days earlier. The author signed himself Viejo Tanguero, (Old Tangoer): he has never been definitely identified, but on the evidence of the piece he was an educated man who knew what he was talking about. Although the article was written thirty years after the events it describes, its testimony is impossible to ignore.

Viejo Tanguero's most serious claim is that in the year 1877 the African-Argentines of Mondongo (an area on the western side of the centrally located *barrio* of Monserrat) improvised a new dance, which they called a 'tango' – that name again! – and which embodied something of the style and the movement of the *candombe*. Couples danced it apart rather than in an embrace. Groups of *compadritos*, who apparently had the habit of visiting African-Argentine dance venues and then parodying the gestures and movements they saw there, took this 'tango' to Corrales Viejos – the slaughterhouse district – and introduced it to the various low-life establishments where dancing took place, incorporating its most conspicuous features into the *milonga*. From Corrales Viejos, according to Viejo Tanguero, this new way of dancing the *milonga* spread rapidly to other districts. At this distance in time, we have no way of corroborating his claim, but an interesting confirmation that something like this *was* going on may be found in a book by Ventura Lynch (1850-88) – a noted *contemporary* student of the

Gauchos Dancing, by Pedro Figari.

dances and folklore of Buenos Aires Province – published in 1883. According to Lynch, 'the *milonga* is danced only by the *compadritos* of the city, who have created it *as a mockery of the dances the blacks hold in their own places*' (author's italics). Moreover, Lynch further testifies to the popularity of the *milonga* at the time when it was undergoing this obviously important modification.

> The *milonga* is so universal in the environs of the city that it is an obligatory piece at all the lower-class dances (*bailecitos de medio pelo*), and it is now heard on guitars, on paper-combs, and from the itinerant musicians with their flutes, harps and violins. It has also been taken up by the organ-grinders, who have arranged it so as to sound like the habanera dance. It is danced too in the low-life clubs around the . . . [main] markets, and also at the dances and wakes of cart-drivers, the soldiery and *compadres* and *compadritos*.[6]

So at the beginning, what was soon to become the tango was simply a new way of dancing the *milonga* – and probably, José Gobello suggests, also the mazurka in districts closer to the docks. It was not yet a new dance as such. The distinctive features of the new dance-form came entirely from the *compadritos'* parodistic borrowings from the African-Argentine tradition – in particular the so-called *quebradas* and *cortes*. The *quebrada* was simply an improvised, jerky, semi-athletic contortion, the more dramatic the better, while the *corte* was a sudden, suggestive pause, a break in the standard figures of the dance, not in itself a particular movement so much as the prelude to a *quebrada*. The true novelty, as the embryonic tango slowly took shape, was that *cortes* and *quebradas* were incorporated into dances in which the partners danced *together*, not, as in the African-Argentine 'tango', apart. It is understandable that high society in Argentina, some sections of which frowned on dances like the mazurka and *habanera* as inherently lascivious, should have found the 'Africanized' *milonga*-tango wholly unacceptable. Its lower-class, semi-delinquent origins made it doubly so.

For the social milieu in which the tango was gradually improvised into existence by the *compadritos* and their women (and the many who were drawn

Dance at the Patio de las Malevas, Buenos Aires, in the 1900s. The imposing central figure is probably a *compadre*. He wears the characteristic white neckerchief, known as a *lengue*.

into their world) was essentially that of the outer *barrios* and *arrabales*. It is possible only to sketch the kind of places where the vital experiments occurred – at impromptu Sunday gatherings under the trees, in rudimentary dance-halls (some with earth floors, some in tents) and, above all, in and around the brothels, and in those other, more numerous, establishments which were probably often no more than thinly disguised brothels: the so-called *academias* ('academies', from 'dance academy') and *perigundines*. (There is some dispute about which term was used first.) These were shady cafés, bars or dance-venues where the 'waitresses' could also be hired as dancing partners and in many cases, no doubt, as whores. Drunkenness and casual violence (typically in the form of knifing) were common in the *academias* – which ran the constant risk of being closed down by the police.

The *compadritos* were not criminals as such, but were often in trouble with the police for fighting and drunkenness. This cartoon from 1909 shows a *compadrito* – rather the worse for wear – being arrested by a policeman.

It was in such places, mostly on the poor southern side of Buenos Aires, that the tango's murky and unchronicled prehistory was lived out. Both the dance and its music were gradually refined through improvisation, by trial and error. It seems fair to assume that there was constant interaction between the music and the dance – the musicians fitting rhythm and melody (rather less in the way of harmony: that came later) to the complex and often unpredictable movements invented and repeated by the dancers themselves. The music, at this early stage, was entirely improvised, the musicians themselves untrained. The first instruments to accompany the dance seem to have been the flute, violin and harp, with guitars and clarinets soon making an appearance.

The first generation of tango musicians – not to mention tango dancers – is extremely shadowy. Viejo Tanguero's article assigns a place of honour to a talented mulatto violinist, El Negro Casimiro, a legendary figure in the *academias* and *perigundines*. His surname (that of a distinguished jurist who employed Casimiro's mother as a cook) may have been Alcorta. His dates are unknown, though he was still alive in 1913. We have no clues at all to the real name of El Mulato Sinforoso, an apparently notable clarinettist of the period. A similarly obscure figure (though it is known that he worked as a conductor on the tramways) is El Pardo (The Mulatto), Sebastián Ramos Mejía, the first real exponent of the bandoneon – the German-made cousin of the accordion that was soon to become the quintessential tango instrument. What is interesting is that all three musicians were of African-Argentine background.

As for the first dancers – men and (especially) women who made a reputation for themselves in the various tango venues – they have survived as nicknames only: El Flaco Saúl, La Parda Refucilo, Pepa la Chata, La Mondonguito, Pepita (she was Casimiro's girlfriend or wife), and so on. Of one such, Rubia (Blonde) Mireya, we *do* know that her real name was Margarita Verdier, and that she was nostalgically evoked in a tango lyric of 1926.

As with jazz in New Orleans a few years later, the connection between the tango and the brothel is inescapable. But prostitution ran right through the social scale, and the tango soon found its way into high-class bordellos (some close to the Centre itself) as well as into those of the outer *barrios*. Two legendary upmarket *clandestinos* at the end of the nineteenth century, and for some years beyond, were those of María la Vasca (María Rongalla) – the house was still standing in the 1970s – and Laura (Laurentina Montserrat), the latter virtually in the Centre itself, and an establishment, by all accounts, of some luxuriousness. As Mario Battistella's tango lyric of 1931 has it:

> You were king of the dances
> at Laura's and La Vasca's . . .

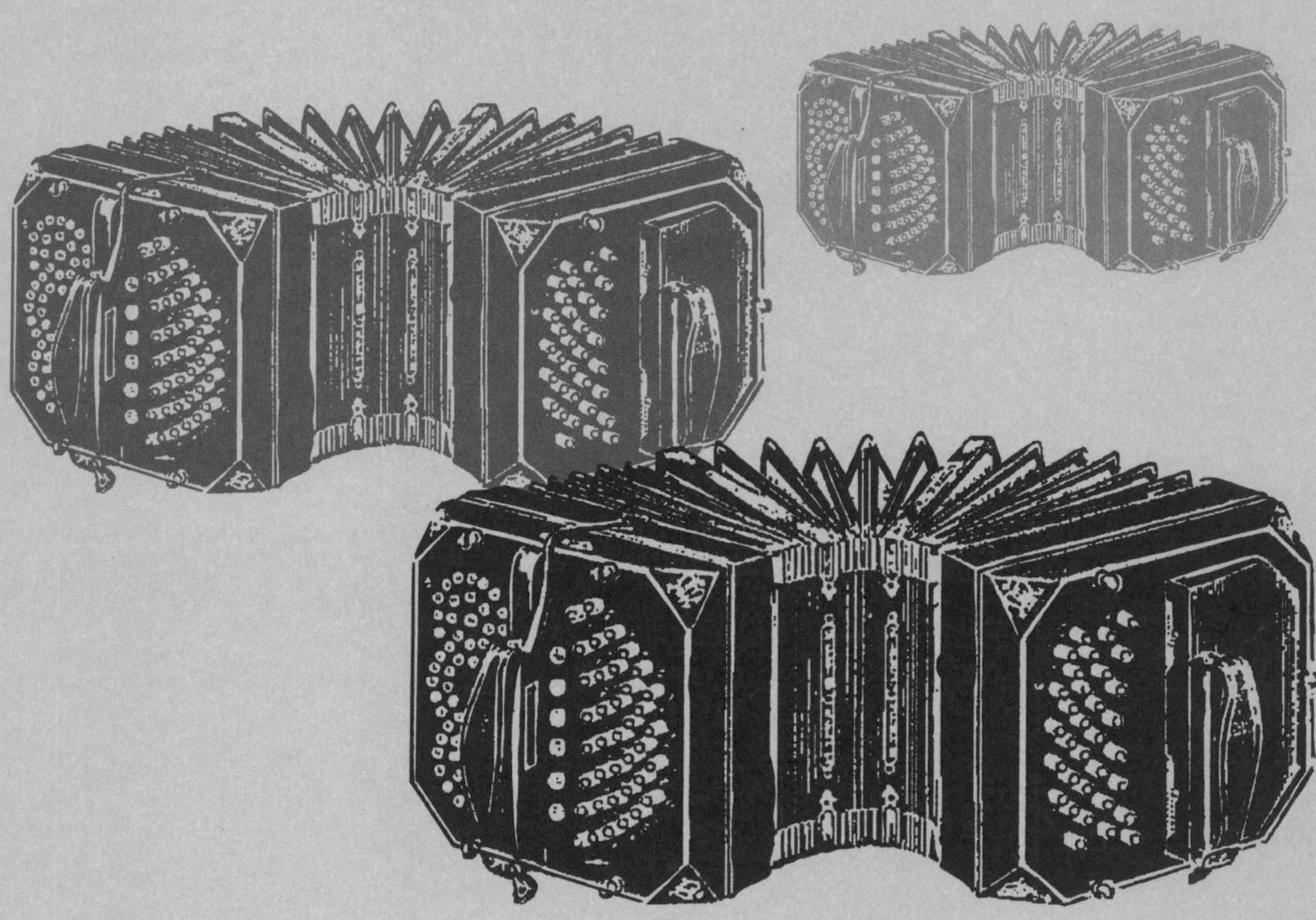

The bandoneon, introduced to Argentina from Germany in the late 19th century, is the fundamental instrument of tango groups. The one shown *below* is the 71-button variety, which came into widespread use after 1900. This fully developed instrument has 38 buttons for the right hand and 33 for the left. Each button can produce two notes, depending on inflation or deflation of the squeezebox.

The wild, jerky movements of the African-Argentine dance the *candombe* (*below*) offer an interesting contrast with the more sedate tango (*right*). Both scenes took place in the 1860s/1870s, when the tango was at a very early stage of its development. The pictures themselves were not painted until the 1920s, but represent childhood memories of the artist, Pedro Figari, who was born in Uruguay in 1861.

The local police chief was always a welcome visitor at Laura's and had a tango written in his honour by the *clandestino*'s celebrated pianist, Rosendo Mendizábal – a key figure in the early musical development of the tango, and another African-Argentine.

There were many other ways in which the new dance moved outwards from its original base in the *arrabal*. The well-heeled sons of the *porteño* oligarchy, like their counterparts all round the world, were not averse to 'slumming' – or to taking part in the occasionally bloody skirmish with *compadritos*, a tradition that extended itself into the early twentieth century. Viejo Tanguero, thirty years later, could remember 'many young men with well-known surnames', dedicated frequenters of the brothels, who by 1913 occupied 'high positions in the national government'. These fun-loving young bloods of the 1880s took the new dance from its disreputable surroundings and introduced it into their *garconnières* – the apartments they rented for their amorous ventures. Though the upper class – like the respectable middle class and much of the respectable immigrant working class – might disapprove strongly of the 'reptile from the brothel', as the writer Leopoldo Lugones was later to call the tango, it harboured a subversive fifth column within its own ranks almost from the beginning.

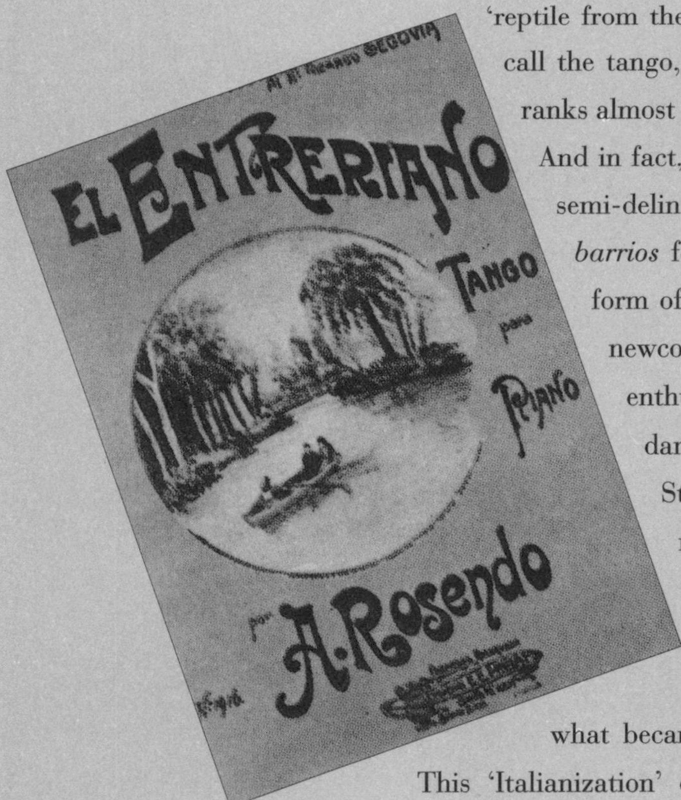

And in fact, though the tango was long tarred with the brush of its semi-delinquent origins, it did not remain confined to the outer *barrios* for long. The new dance has sometimes been seen as a form of 'creole' protest against the immigrant influx – but the newcomers themselves, or some of them, soon took it up with enthusiasm. In the course of time, it became popular in dance halls patronized by Italian immigrants, such as the Stella de Italia and later the Scudo de Italia, which were more centrally located than many of the *academias* and which catered to a relatively poor but much less raffish clientele. Here the wilder and more aggressive *cortes* and *quebradas* were somewhat toned down, and what became known as the *tango liso* (smooth tango) emerged. This 'Italianization' of the tango, as it has been called, also meant the introduction of new instruments – accordions and mandolins complementing the harps, violins and flutes of the earlier groups. Professional dancers are known to have worked in these dance halls – a further sign that the tango was taking on a life of its own, gradually disconnecting itself from the world of pimps, ruffians and whores.

This early division of dancing styles was fraught with significance for the future: the 'smooth' tango was undoubtedly the forerunner of the ballroom tango of the twentieth century, while the fierce, lubricious aggressiveness favoured in the outer *barrios* eventually faded away – though reconstructions of it, in 'performance tangos', can still be seen to spectacular effect in shows such as the *Tango Argentino* of the 1980s.

It is in the closing years of the nineteenth century that the mists of obscurity begin to dissolve and the tango's prehistory shades into something more closely resembling history. The musicians and dancers acquire biographies; the tango's growing presence can be documented. By now it was beginning to show up regularly at dances organized by various theatres at carnival time. Organ-grinders throughout the city added primitive tango tunes to their stock selection of *habaneras*, mazurkas and operatic numbers. Night-spots such as Hansen's, El Tambo and El Velódromo seem to have become redoubts of the dance – all three located, significantly, in the Palermo district, near the city's two main racetracks. Before the end of the 1890s tangos had been performed on stage in a handful of plays and musical comedies.

The celebrated pianist Rosendo Mendizábal (*below*) composed some of the first true tangos. In 1897 he wrote the music for 'El entrerriano' (*opposite*) under the pseudonym A. Rosendo. An 'entrerriano' is a person from the interior, the countryside.

Most important of all, the music now started to move away from the ragged improvisation of the earliest times, as musicians began writing tangos for publication – usually under the label *tango criollo para piano* ('creole tango for piano'). The oldest 'creole tangos' to have survived, all written in the 1880s, still have much of the *milonga* or the *tango andaluz* in them, and this was to remain true for many 'tangos' until the music acquired definitive shape and form after 1910.

But in the 1890s a number of talented musicians wrote pieces which were something more than thinly disguised *milongas* or *tangos andaluces*, and which were structured in a form that was to evolve directly, later on, into the mature, fully developed tango. 'El Talar' (*c.*1894), by the precocious Prudencio (El Johnny) Aragón (1886-1963) is in three sections (of 12, 16 and 16 bars), while 'El entrerriano' (1897) by Rosendo Mendizábal (1868-1913) – composed and first performed at Laura's, where, as mentioned, Mendizábal played the piano – is also in three sections (of 16, 32 and 16 bars). Pieces such as these are the first true tangos.

The covers of published tangos (often described in the early years as 'creole tangos for piano') are picturesque and colourful and have long since become collectors' items (***above and left***). Creole tangos reached the height of their popularity in the 1900s, when some sold as many as 20,000 to 30,000 copies. 'Alma de Bohemio' (Heart of a Bohemian: ***left***) was one of the bandleader Roberto Firpo's hits in the 1910s.

Above: From the cover of 'Imitando' (Imitating), a tango for piano.

The cover *right* pays tribute to El Cachafaz (José Ovidio Bianquet), the most famous dancer of the early years, whose skills in the tango were spectacular. His nickname means 'barefaced cheek' and was given to him by his father when he was a child. El Cachafaz is still thought of as the finest of all tango dancers. Born in 1879, he started his career dancing in the street and ended it in a dance salon at the age of 63 – he had just finished one tango and was getting up to dance another when he died.

Right: **The corner of Corrientes Street (now Avenue) and Reconquista Street in downtown Buenos Aires, around 1910. Corrientes Street was famous for its cafés and nightspots – it was (and still is) called 'The street that never sleeps'.**

The dancing figures *this page and opposite* are taken from the sheet music of 'El maco', a 'creole tango'. The man is Arturo de Nava, well-known at the turn of the century as both a dancer and a *payador* (folk singer). He later became a friend and teacher of the tango's most celebrated singer, Carlos Gardel.

The formula 'creole tango for piano' – obviously used to distinguish the music of the transformed *milonga* from the still-popular *tango andaluz* – remained standard for some years on the often picturesque covers of published tango pieces. In reality it soon ceased to be necessary. From the turn of the century on, with the fading away of dances like the *habanera*, the polka and the mazurka, and the decline of the *tango andaluz* in the theatre, there was only one real tango: *the* tango.

By the beginning of the twentieth century, the tango both as a dance and as an embryonic form of popular music had established a firm foothold in the fast-expanding city of its birth. It had also spread to provincial towns in Argentina and across the estuary to Montevideo, the capital of Uruguay, where it became as much a part of the urban culture as in Buenos Aires. The strange inner vitality of the tradition need not be doubted. Over the next twenty years it would finally conquer its own city – and much of the world beyond.

In the early years of the 20th century the tango began to find its way out of the shady cafés and brothels in which it had been born and into the more respectable dance halls – though it was still strongly disapproved of by the upper classes.

The organ grinders of Buenos Aires (*below*) played a key role in popularizing tango music and were a common sight on the city's streets at the turn of the century.

★ THE TRIUMPH ★

After 1900 the tango's story is an upward curve of triumph. The main battle for social acceptability still had to be won in its native city, where upper-class disapproval remained strong and unyielding. By now, however, the tango was being danced at a great variety of more or less respectable venues around the city, occasionally on the stage, and in the night-spots of Palermo. It was no longer the preserve of the *compadritos*. Perhaps drawn to it by the insistent melodies of the street-organs, the *conventillo* population began to dance the tango in the patios of their tenement houses. Popular, well-run dance-salons opened, the most celebrated being the San Martín in Rodríguez Peña Street – hence the title of the classic tango 'Rodríguez Peña', written in honour of the salon by Vicente Greco. Moving inexorably towards the Centre in the years just before the Centenary,

'Woman who left me
in the prime of my life,
wounding my soul
and driving thorns into my heart . . .
Nothing can console me now,
so I'm drowning my sorrows
to try to forget your love . . .'

'Mi noche triste' (My Sorrowful Night) was written around 1917. It is one of the earliest tango songs and the first ever to be performed by the great Carlos Gardel. The lyrics are by Pascual Contursi, who was to bring an entirely new mood to the tango song. Earlier lyrics had been joyful, if somewhat simpleminded. With Contursi came a more robust language and a new note of pessimism, melancholy and nostalgia. 'Mi noche triste' expressed what became an archetypal tango theme – the abandoned lover finding consolation in drink.

'Lagrimas' (Tears), by the legendary bandoneonist Eduardo Arolas, tells another familiar tango story – the mother weeps from the shame of having a drunkard for a son.

the tango increasingly found a congenial home in cafés which were simply cafés, rather than undeclared brothels, although the *café con camareras* (café with waitresses) preserved the traditional role of the old *academias* and *perigundines* in a new form. Genuine dance-academies now also operated, where the 'smoother' tango continued its evolution into a ballroom dance.

There were many signs of the tango's growing appeal, the most obvious being the fact that talented musicians (still for the most part self-taught and earning their livings as railway workers, factory hands, shop assistants and so on) were joining the primitive tango bands. With the new century the musical tradition took on a definite life of its own. In fact, while the dance lost much of its original fierce, aggressive, erotic character (as it more or less had to do in order to be accepted in the ballrooms of the world), the music that went with it became gradually richer and more sophisticated – became, in fact, a tradition of popular music in its own right. This tradition was to achieve its full flowering in the 1920s, with the onset of the Golden Age of the tango, yet its roots were here, in the formative phase tango historians refer to as the *Guardia Vieja*, or 'Old Guard'. The Old Guard musicians were the true pioneers.

From the turn of the century, with the consolidation of more or less stable ensembles (mostly trios), the musicians themselves gradually hit on the best combinations of instruments for playing the new dance-music. The fundamental innovation in the first years of the century was the incorporation of the bandoneon, a German-made squeezebox instrument which, above all others, was to give the distinctive sonority of the great tango bands of the future its marvellous edge. The bandoneon was and is a formidably difficult instrument to play, but it somehow became indispensable to tango music, so much so that many of the early 'stars' of tango music were bandoneon-players, and this remained true later.

In the years leading up to Argentina's much-celebrated Centenary, the ramshackle waterfront district of La Boca, with its heavily Genoese population, briefly became the focus of the nascent musical tradition. Tango trios began playing in the cafés around the intersection of Suárez and Necochea Streets, to deliriously enthusiastic, and often rowdy, audiences. Here the music was listened to rather than danced. The young Uruguayan violinist Francisco Canaro – a former house-painter who had started working with a trio in provincial *academias* in 1906 – has left a description of the scene:

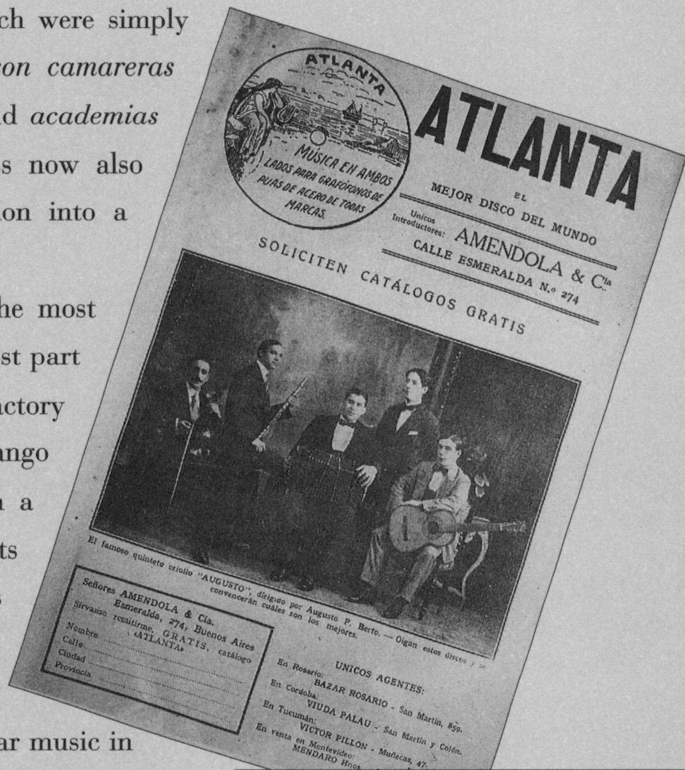

Top: **Catalogue of the Atlanta record label, Buenos Aires, 1910s.**

Above: **'The Wind', a tango by Francisco Canaro and his brother, Juan.**

Opposite top: **'El choclo' (The Corncob), written by Angel Villoldo around 1903 and still one of the most popular of all tangos.** ***Below:*** **Early tango music covers.**

Opposite below: **Eduardo Arolas called himself 'Tiger of the Bandoneon' – a nickname he earned by being perhaps the finest bandoneonist of the 'Old Guard' tango.**

> We played on a narrow stage where there was barely room for the three of us and a piano.... The Café Royal, like similar establishments, was served by 'waitresses' dressed in black, with white aprons, and they were much in demand by the customers . . . . The boss of the Royal was a Greek with grimy, curly hair and, as was common in those days, he had long, thick moustaches. From his picturesque waistcoat there hung a thick watch-chain, suspended from which was a huge gold medallion, which the Greek showed off with pride, perhaps as a sign of his opulence. Opposite the Royal was a café of similar style and importance, where the brothers Vicente and Domingo Greco played. Round the corner, in Suárez Street, about thirty metres away, was the 'La Marina' café, where Genaro Espósito performed. Roberto Firpo was playing at another café opposite 'La Marina'. Along Necochea Street, at a similar establishment, was Bernstein 'the German', who, while playing, was accustomed to having an enormous number of half-litre glasses of beer at his side, since he claimed that without 'moistening the old throat' every so often he could not play – and he was continually half-smashed.[7]

To read Canaro's account of this phase of his career – a career which was to continue with increasing glory until his death in 1964 – is to appreciate two things: first, the relative modesty (and, as the inverted commas round 'waitresses' indicate, loucheness) of the surroundings in which tango music was still often being played, and second, and far more important, the way in which the first great generation of tango musicians was suddenly crystallizing. All the names mentioned by Canaro can be heard on recordings: one or two were to become important figures over the next few years. It is probably not an exaggeration to say that La Boca, in the first few years of the century, was the true musical birthplace of the tango.

It was now, in fact, that the first real 'stars' of the tango began appearing – pianists like Rosendo Mendizábal, mentioned earlier, or Samuel Castriota (1885-1932); violinists like Ernesto Ponzio (1885-1934), who later spent many years in prison for homicide, or David (Tito) Roccatagliatta (1891-1925); and, above all, bandoneon-players: Juan Maglio (1880-1934); Arturo Hermán Bernstein (1882-1935), 'the German' (in fact born in Brazil), who was the earliest of the musicians at La Boca (1903); Genaro Espósito (1886-1944); and the self-styled 'Tiger of the Bandoneón', Eduardo Arolas (1892-1924). Nor must we forget the rising bandleaders Vicente Greco (1888-1924, bandoneon-player), Roberto Firpo (1884-1969, pianist) and Canaro himself.

Dancers as well as musicians became stars in the years around the Centenary, including many individual *porteños* – the madam María la Vasca and her bad-tempered husband Carlos Kern ('the Englishman'), the musician Enrique Saborido, and the well-known actor Elías Alippi. But far and away the most celebrated professional dancer of the time was the great Ovidio Bianquet (1879-1942), known as El Cachafaz (Barefaced Cheek) or more simply Cacha. El Cachafaz was an impeccable ballroom dancer, but one who could still dance the fiercer tango to spectacular effect – never quite able to forget the squalid surroundings from which his dance had sprung. He has always been taken as the paragon, the all-time master. He died as he lived – in a dance-salon at Mar del Plata, having just danced one tango and preparing to dance another.

Writing in the early 1960s, Jorge Luis Borges could still easily remember

> ...the echo
> Of those tangos of Arolas and Greco
> I have seen danced on the sidewalks.[8]

The classic tangos of Eduardo Arolas and Vicente Greco really belong to the 1910s. Yet when Borges was still a boy (he was born in 1899), the repertoire was growing fast. The first decade of the century saw the writing of many tango numbers which have since become permanent classics. Angel Villoldo (1868-1919) composed his 'El choclo' around 1903: in the restaurant where it was first played it was announced as a 'creole dance'. Ernesto Ponzio gave the world his 'Don Juan' around 1905. 'El irresistible' by Lorenzo Logatti (1872-1961), an Italian immigrant, appeared in 1907. Enrique Saborido (1876-1941) wrote two notable tangos in these years: 'La morocha' (1905) and 'Felicia' (*c.* 1910). It is said that 'La morocha' sold more than 100,000 copies, making it by far the greatest hit of the period. Yet other 'creole tangos for piano' (increasingly known just as 'tangos for piano') often sold as many as 20,000 or 30,000 copies.

Most revealing of all, perhaps, was the interest shown in the new dance-music by recording companies, then setting up in business in Buenos Aires, as in every other major city round the world. The phonograph was to play a notable part in boosting the tango's fortunes. The earliest recordings of tangos,

using brass bands, seem to have taken place around 1902. But a decisive moment came in 1911, when the local agent for the Columbia label asked the bandleader Vicente Greco to record some tango numbers. Greco, a true pioneer, had gradually enlarged his original trio of 1906, consisting of bandoneon, violin and guitar into a sextet comprising two bandoneons, two violins, piano and flute. (He made his 1911 recordings with this combination, though dispensing with the piano and bringing back the guitar.) Greco also came up with a label for bands specializing in tango music: *orquesta típica criolla* ('creole traditional band'). The adjective *criolla* soon dropped out, but tango bands from then on were invariably known as *orquestas típicas*.

Ironically, Greco's records (he made ten in the Columbia batch) proved less popular than those of Juan Maglio, who headed a quartet (bandoneon, violin, flute, guitar) which was, in comparison with Greco's band, slightly behind the times. His nickname was Pacho, and his discs (with his picture and signature prominently displayed on the labels) were so sought-after that purchasers simply asked for *Pachos* in the shops. If his versions sound slight and anaemic today, that is simply an indication of the musical richness of Argentina between his time and ours. For modern listeners they have the same fascination as, say, the very earliest jazz recordings – which came only ten years later.

The success of Maglio's records and the copious flood of printed 'tangos for piano' indicate that by the early 1910s the dance and its music were sweeping the city. By this stage they were entrenching themselves in cafés and dance-salons in the Centre itself, not least along Corrientes Street (now Corrientes Avenue). In terms of urban geography, the conquest was complete. Socially, however, the fortress of upper-class prejudice remained intact, despite the fact that young members of the *porteño* oligarchy were dancing the tango more enthusiastically than ever, not only in their *garconnières* and in the better-class bordellos but also in opulent night-spots such as the Armenonville in Palermo – inaugurated in 1912 by Vicente Greco's band, no less – which was a forerunner of the plush cabarets of the 1920s.

It was at this point that something entirely unexpected occurred, far from Buenos Aires: in 1913-14 the tango suddenly invaded the dance-floors of Paris and London and was taken up by high society – that same high society admired and respected by Argentina's own social elite.

The effect of this European craze was gradually to soften the harsh attitudes of the Argentine upper class. If European high society was tangoing, surely Argentine high society could safely follow suit, especially since the 'Parisian' tango, daring as it seemed to Europeans, had little of the dance's original ferocity. And, as we have seen, the tango had never entirely lacked allies in *porteño* high society. In 1912, a notable man-about-town, Baron Antonio de Marchi, the Italian son-in-law of former president Julio Argentino Roca, arranged a tango night at the Palais de Glace, a skating-rink that had been converted into a dance-hall that same year.

In September 1913 he went further, organizing a three-day tango festival at the Palace Theatre in Corrientes Street, and making sure that it was sponsored by a committee of ladies with impeccable upper-class credentials. The Baron cautioned the dancers (not with complete success, it seems) to avoid wild and erotic figures. The first evening, according to contemporary accounts, was distinctly monotonous; on the two remaining evenings, when the price of admission was lowered, proceedings grew altogether more animated.

Records did much to popularize the tango. In the shoeshine parlour *opposite*, patrons could listen to tango and other recordings on the gramophone. The advertisement *opposite below* lists tango records released by the Columbia label in the 1910s.

In the mid-1910s, the tango's success in Paris began to have an impact in its home country. The Armenonville (*below*) was a ritzy nightclub named after the famous cabaret on the Bois de Boulogne in Paris. It became a well-known tango venue for young men from upper-class Buenos Aires families. This tango was by the very popular Juan Maglio, known as Pacho.

The first decades of the 20th century produced many exceptionally talented tango musicians. Roberto Firpo (*right*) led the finest *orquesta típica* of the period.

It cannot be claimed that all social disapproval vanished overnight – there are a few Argentines, even today, who still hold the tango's murky origins against it. But the great Buenos Aires public now so manifestly wanted the dance and its music that in the end high society (undermined from within by de Marchi and his subversive following) was bound to yield. Was there an element of class conflict here? Perhaps. The great Buenos Aires public, so much larger, and better educated, in the 1910s than it had been in the 1880s, may consciously or unconsciously have championed the tango *because* it was despised by the elite. Whether this is true or not, ordinary *porteños* clearly saw no good reason to reject what was after all a genuinely local and popular creation – in a real sense, *their* creation.

Linda Thelma (*below*) was known as 'the Queen of Creole Song' but also had a great success as a tango singer in France and Spain. She often appeared on stage dressed as a man.

Thus, in the years after Baron de Marchi's festival, the tango finally moved openly into middle-class households and into the opulent mansions of the Barrio Norte. There was, of course, some initial nervousness in the households in question. Francisco Canaro's memoirs recall the first time he and his band were hired to provide the music at a dance in one of the most splendid of the Buenos Aires mansions. He was firmly told to make certain that his musicians did not ogle the girls or get drunk. Canaro's musicians, in their uncomfortable new dinner-jackets, were so well-behaved that the band was promptly recommended to other affluent households.[9]

The tango as a dance was now more or less tolerated by all sections of Buenos Aires society, and with acceptance lending new strength to the tradition, the music of the tango made its final leap into the Golden Age, slowing down, with the consolidation of the ballroom dance. Two other musical developments of great importance took place in the second half of the 1910s. The first was the appearance of the standard tango sextet, the second the first sign that the tango was about to turn into a form of popular song.

In the mid-1910s, the bandleaders Francisco Canaro and Roberto Firpo – the latter the leader of the most notable *orquesta típica* of the moment – made what turned out to be the vital innovation in the instrumental line-up. They took Vicente Greco's sextet of 1911 – two bandoneons, two violins, a piano and a flute – and substituted a double-bass for the flute, so giving the *orquesta típica* that distinctive sonority, a depth combined with sharpness, which it was to retain over the next twenty years, and which continued even in the larger ensembles that became common after the mid-1930s.

The repertoire of tango bands like Firpo's and Canaro's expanded so fast in the 1910s that it would be futile to attempt a representative list of numbers from that decade which are still regularly played. There is one title, however, which demands to be singled out. In 1917 the young Uruguayan Gerardo Hernán Matos Rodríguez composed a marching tune for the student federation of which he was a member and discovered that it could easily be turned into a tango. He and his friends took the piece to Roberto Firpo, then performing with his band at a Montevideo café. A few deft touches, and the tune became 'La cumparsita', the most famous tango of all time.

The tango song as such did not fully emerge much before the early 1920s, yet once again the vital innovation was made in the mid-1910s. Words had been fitted to tango melodies from the earliest times, with many of the verses reflecting the shady origins of the dance, and some covertly obscene, as in the case of the early tango 'Bartolo', which begins:

> Bartolo had a flute
> with a single little hole,
> and his mother said to him:
> Stop playing the flute, Bartolo!

Most of the tango verses written in the 1890s and 1900s were lighthearted in tone and undemanding in content. A number of singers, the forerunners of the wonderful vocalists of the Golden Age, made limited reputations during the Guardia Vieja, among them Pepita Avellaneda, Linda Thelma and Flora Rodríguez de Gobbi.

The outstanding figure of this early period, however, was Angel Villoldo, who sang his songs in cafés, at dances and on the variety stage. Mostly written in the first person, they evoke a world of ruffians and pimps – very much the tango's own original world. But they have no great depth or sophistication. It was left to Pascual Contursi (1888-1932) to bring these qualities to the tango lyric. Like nearly all the figures in the early history of the tango, his background was poor. As a young man he worked in a shoe shop, though his interests were theatrical and artistic. In the mid-1910s Contursi was living in Montevideo, where he frequented cabarets like the Moulin Rouge and Royal Pigall. He started to write fully developed lyrics for fitting to existing tango tunes, and may even have sung a few of the resulting

Angel Villoldo, composer of the tango song *above*, was the outstanding singer of the early years. He also wrote the words of 'El entrerriano', which begins: 'They call me Pepita, jai, jai...', especially for the singer Pepita Avellaneda. Avellaneda is shown (*below*) dressed as a gaucho, a role she adopted for many of her performances.

songs himself. One tango which obsessed him was 'Lita', by the pianist Sạmuel Castriota. The verses Contursi attached to this piece described the sadness of an abandoned lover drowning his sorrows in a lonely room. The text was salted with expressions from *lunfardo*. Here at last was a fully rounded tango lyric, and a model for the lyrics of the future.

> Woman who left me
> in the prime of my life,
> wounding my soul
> and driving thorns into my heart . . .
> Nothing can console me now,
> so I'm drowning my sorrows
> to try to forget your love . . .

Among those Contursi bumped into in Montevideo – probably in January 1917, though conceivably a year earlier – were two folk-singers, Carlos Gardel and José Razzano, whose duo had recently become the most popular act on the Argentine variety stage. Gardel liked Contursi's lyric, and later in 1917 he sang it – with the new title 'Mi noche triste' (My Sorrowful Night) – both onstage in Buenos Aires and in the recording studio. The rest, as they say, is history.

In fact, this particular history did not start quite as abruptly as is often supposed. Gardel was well-satisfied with the folk repertoire which had brought him local fame, and had no way of knowing that it would be the tango song which would make him Latin America's greatest popular singer of the twentieth century, and the tango's supreme legend. He did not make the tango his speciality until the early 1920s. Yet Contursi's example was soon followed by other lyricists, a handful at first and many more later. By the time Carlos Gardel became a tango-singer, there was no shortage of tangos for him to perform and record.

Yet the tango's final triumph in its own homeland was not inevitable. In the 1910s, the tradition of folk and country music so spectacularly taken to the Buenos Aires stage by the Gardel-Razzano Duo and other artists might well have become the city's main popular music over the ensuing decades. As it was, Argentine 'neo-folklore' had to wait until the 1940s and 1950s for its second wind. Its place was taken by the tango, that insidious rhythm that had risen from the *arrabal* and the brothel to the mansions of the rich. With its local fortunes bolstered by overseas triumph, with its music now settling into its mature shape and form, with its transformation into a popular song, the long-reviled tango was ready for its unforgettable Golden Age.

This is how to dance the tango!
Feel the blood
rise to your face
with every beat;
while an arm
winds like a snake
around a waist
that is about to break.
This is how to dance the tango!

From 'This Is How to Dance the Tango . . .'
Words by 'Marvil' (Elizardo Martinez Vilas);
music by Elias Randal, 1942

EDOUARD
HALOUZE
1919

ARTEMIS COOPER

II

TANGOMANIA IN EUROPE AND NORTH AMERICA

1913–1914

★ FIRST TANGO IN PARIS ★

In 1910, very few people in Paris had ever heard of the tango. By 1913, it was the most hotly debated subject in the capital. Its effect on morals was as fiercely contested as the supposedly degenerative effect of its racial origins. Some Frenchmen, curiously enough, believed that the word tango came from their own verb 'tanguer' – to pitch, as of a boat. They could not agree whether the dance's origins lay in the slums of Buenos Aires or in Uruguay, or whether its music was in origin a cross between the Hispanicized Berber of the flamenco and South American Indian music.

The first genuine *tangueros* to come to Paris from Buenos Aires were Angel Villoldo and Alfredo Gobbi, the latter accompanied by his wife, the singer Flora Rodríguez de Gobbi. They arrived in 1907 to make records, for at that time Paris was reputed to have the most modern recording techniques then available. It is interesting that the rise of the tango coincided with great technical improvements in recording: no longer did voices and music sound as if they were coming from beyond the grave. Villoldo and Gobbi recorded some of the best-known early tangos, including Villoldo's 'El choclo' and Enrique Saborido's 'La morocha'. The accompaniment was provided, most improbably, by the band of the Republican Guard, hired for the occasion.

Opposite: **The Parisian tango, by Edouard Malouze, 1919: a more refined affair than the tango of the Argentine slums.**

Right: **Detail from a design by Fish, *c.* 1925.**

Le Tango

The tango was first danced in a Parisian theatrical review in 1908, and there is some evidence that the first demonstration of a tango was given in 1910, performed by the cabaret star Mistinguett and a certain Professor Bottallo. In the same year an *orquesta típica criolla* came to Paris to make a record for Columbia Phonograph entitled 'La Infanta', in honour of the Spanish Princess Isabel de Borbón, who had been invited to Buenos Aires for the centenary of Argentine independence. Yet the tango was still not in a position to make much impact, for it had not come to the attention of smart society, without whose enthusiasm no new fashion could be launched.

Parisian society before the First World War was rigidly compartmentalized. The monde, demi-monde and the bourgeoisie had all flourished since the financial boom of the 1890s, though the distinctions between them extended even to public entertainments. For example, the *gratin* and the *cosmopolites* went to the Opéra on Monday nights, while the grande bourgeoisie and the judiciary showed a preference for Fridays.

Even within le grand monde there were many gradations and nuances. There was the arch-reactionary *gratin*, which was so pious and obsessed with petty points of genealogy that cosmopolitan dandies like Gabriel-Louis Pringué regarded it as provincial. In his autobiography, *Trente Ans de dîners en ville*, Pringué said of it: 'This locked, chained and triple-bolted society had unreservedly married the past and poured scorn equally unreservedly on the present.'[1]

This '*gratin provincial à Paris*' looked down on the government, which was not only republican and anti-clerical, but in their view reeked of the corruption of liberalism. Politics was not even considered a proper subject of conversation. According to Pringué, 'One spoke of it only in whispers, in the intimacy of boudoirs.'[2] The *gratin* also shuddered at the 'déclassement' of those ancient families who had allowed their sons to marry American heiresses, although most European aristocrats now considered this a acceptable way of rejuvenating their family fortunes.

'The tango', wrote Maurice Rostand, son of the author of *Cyrano de Bergerac* and one of the most flamboyant men of his day, 'produced a real upheaval in society and introduced . . . its own Trojan Horse within the most closed milieux'.[3] The entry of this 'Trojan Horse' was made easier by a strong thirst for the new, which was already opening gates in the ramparts of society. A literary salon, for example, could hardly be limited to the *gratin*, and that of the Duchesse de Rohan's, the most important in Paris, attracted the young prodigy Jean Cocteau. His relentless verbal firework display reduced her husband the duke to a flabbergasted silence behind his monocle. Cocteau observed the changes taking place: corsets were becoming less rigid, while dresses became looser and more fanciful. He noted that even duchesses were allowing Paul Poiret to dress them up in exotic costumes.[4]

Then, in 1909, came Sergei Diaghilev's Ballets Russes: an explosion of talent, sensuality, vibrant music and exotic colour, which left its mark on almost every branch of fashion and the arts. The impact of the first night of the Ballets Russes was recorded by the poet Anna de Noailles:

> When I reached my box – and I arrived a little late, for I did not believe it could possibly be as sensational as people had told me – I realized that I was faced by a miracle. I could see things that had never been seen before. Everything dazzling, intoxicating, enchanting, seductive, had been brought together and put onto that stage . . .[5]

The Ballets Russes awakened a craving for all things rare and exotic, not least among Parisian hostesses. In 1912 Princess Jacques de Broglie gave a Bal des Pierreries, in which costumes had to evoke the magic of precious and semi-precious stones. She herself appeared in a dress completely encrusted in pearls. *Bals persans* were given by the Comtesse de Chabrillan and Comtesse Blanche de Clermont-Tonnerre. Their town houses were transformed into Persian palaces, with fountains and rose-garlanded pillars, while Léon Bakst – the great designer of the Ballets Russes – turned their halls into his vision of Isfahan.

Fashion followed this newly awakened taste for the Thousand and One Nights. Colours became rich and vibrant, and a whole range of 'exotic' perfumes appeared on the market. Hitherto, respectable women had restricted themselves to floral scents – only courtesans wore sandalwood and patchouli; but now that the aim of fashionable beauties was to look as much like an odalisque as possible, they experimented with intoxicating scents with names such as 'Sakountala', 'Le Fruit Défendu' and 'Nirvana'.

***Above:* Music cover of 'The Last Tango', Paris, 1912.**

Mistinguett (*opposite below*), one of France's greatest and most glamorous music-hall stars, was known for her skill in the tango and is thought to have given the first ever demonstration of the dance in France as early as 1910. Her partner then was probably Professor Bottallo, director of the Academy of Dance and Deportment at the Sorbonne. He is shown *opposite above left* performing tango steps with Mme Bottallo and *opposite above right* demonstrating another popular dance of the time, the maxixe. He guaranteed to teach anyone, of any age, the genuine 'Tango Argentin'.

The tango took fashionable Paris by storm. Tangomania was used to sell every kind of product, from gowns to gateaux. Postcards on the tango theme were immensely popular – the illustrations *below* and *opposite* are from a postcard series around 1910-13. The charming artificiality of the poses derives from the inability of photographers of the time to photograph motion without blurring.

By putting poetry and passion back into classical dancing, which had been moribund for many years, the Ballets Russes also freed ordinary people to dance again – not as a set of rigidly controlled movements, but as a form of exhilarating self-expression. Freedom of movement was made easier by the new, sensuously draped fashions.

While all this was happening, new dances were coming in from America, with the syncopated rhythms of jazz. Among the first to appear were the Boston and the turkey trot.

In their study of dance, published in 1914, Troy and Margaret Kinney describe how the turkey trot, which was relatively easy to learn, 'raced eastward from San Francisco in a form to which the word "dancing" could only be applied by exercise of courtesy'. They note its 'negroid origins' and describe its practitioners as being 'in an exhilaration of rediscovery . . . happily, beneficially mad with varied rhythm, marked by the free movements of their own bodies'.[6] The turkey trot was a dance which left most dancers laughing, red in the face and out of breath, whereas the Boston and the Brazilian maxixe, other fashionable American dances of the time, were more genteel and proper, being essentially no more than variations of the waltz to different music.

In the long debate over who started 'Tangomania' in Europe, many claims are made on behalf of different individuals. Probably no single person was responsible, but there is no doubt that the most influential force in fashionable society was the Argentine writer and poet Ricardo Güiraldes. Tall and broad-shouldered,

The poet and writer Ricardo Güiraldes (1887-1927) was the archetypal Buenos Aires playboy – rich, handsome and debonair. He came to Paris in 1910 as part of his grand tour of Europe, and it was he more than anyone who was responsible for championing the tango in the French capital. In 1911 he wrote a famous poem in honour of the dance, and the following year gave a dazzling impromptu performance of tango dancing in front of astonished guests at a fashionable Paris salon. During the First World War Güiraldes published *Raucho*, a semi-autobiographical novel set in pre-war Paris. An illustration from this is shown *opposite*.

with a high forehead, swept-back hair and patrician moustache, Güiraldes was in some ways the archetype of Buenos Aires playboys known as *los niños bien*. Born in 1887, he came from a rich cosmopolitan family and had been brought up in Saint-Cloud on the edge of Paris at the time the Eiffel Tower was being built, as well as on the family *estancia* 'La Porteña' at San Antonio de Areco. He was one of the many rich young men in Buenos Aires who adored the vibrant night life of the waterfront district of La Boca and who often went out in a group together – known as a *patota* – and found themselves involved in fights with local *compadritos*.

In 1910 Güiraldes's father, Don Manuel Güiraldes, with whom he had a stormy relationship, was Mayor of Buenos Aires and performed the official welcome of the Infanta Isabel on her visit to the Argentine capital to celebrate the centenary of the 25 May revolution. Ricardo was not present. He had left for Europe, taking with him the guitar given to him by his mother. Later in life he is said to have regretted missing this great occasion, but at the time the twenty-four year old had been overcome by an urge to travel.

From Paris, he went as far as India and Japan before returning via Russia and Germany. He was back in Paris in 1911 to enjoy himself with three close friends, Roberto Leviller, Hermenegildo Anglada Camarassa and Alberto López Buchardo. They threw themselves into the night-life of the capital, revelling in everything from the Opéra to the brothel. These young Argentines were all tango amateurs and all from the upper classes of Buenos Aires: they had learnt the dance in brothels and *conventillos*, but, unlike the poor, they could afford to travel. Thus the tango came to Paris as part of the cultural baggage of elite young men during their grand tour of Europe.

In 1912, Güiraldes and his circle made friends with the singer Jean de Reske, whose wife held a salon. One evening, guests were asked to sing the song or perform the dance which best represented the culture of a particular country. Alberto Buchardo seated himself at the piano and exploded into the beat of 'El entrerriano', Rosendo Mendizábal's famous and well-loved tango of 1897. Güiraldes took the hand of another guest, Yvette Gueté, and pulled her to him, causing a gasp of astonishment in the room. Gueté, finding herself in the arms of an expert dancer, found that she could follow him instinctively, even though the music and the dance were unknown to her. Güiraldes took her through the whole repertoire – while the audience looked on, in amazed silence.

Whether or not Güiraldes was the man who first launched the tango craze in Paris, he was certainly the one who contributed most to its sensual and morbid glamour. He published a semi-autobiographical novella, *Raucho*, set in Paris just before the First World War. It evokes a truly tango mood of coital sadness, fatalistic about both death and sex. It is also an intriguing mixture, juxtaposing a fascination with Parisian corruption with a longing for the simplicity of the Pampa, an expression of Güiraldes's own longing for San Antonio de Areco, '*su tierra de siempre*' – his own eternal homeland.

In one passage, which contains a heavy sexual charge, he describes an evening at Maxim's. Soon after one in the morning the tzigane orchestra starts to play a tango. At the suggestion of one of his friends, Raucho goes over to a beautiful blonde woman. As he arrives she is saying, 'as a shamelessly amorous confession – "Oh! I adore the tango."'

They dance. 'Her body bent pliantly with his. Timorous at first, he made single steps; then, seeing the skill of his partner, he took courage and danced without thinking, letting himself go to the dedicated rhythm. She followed him, bent to his will, anticipating the special movements . . . Her eyes were concentrated in a sad smile, voraciously sensual.' After another dance half an hour later, she asks him to go with her to the powder-room, where she shows off her body while he watches her in the mirror. 'Am I ugly?' she asks. Then she returns to her partner, and he goes off to a brothel with his friends.

Güiraldes's most beautiful homage to the tango was written in 1911, in a poem called simply 'Tango'. Here the dance is seen as a distillation of the beauty and tragedy of life itself – painful, yet irresistibly compelling. At the same time, he imbues the tango with all the dark magic traditionally invested in that arch-enemy of the social order: the handsome seducer, whom the tango was to turn into the 'Latin lover'.

'It has spread all over Paris... There are tango tea parties, tango exhibitions, tango lectures. Half of Paris rubs against the other half. The whole city jerks: it's got the tango under the skin.'

What the caricaturist Sem wrote about the French capital was true also of other European cities. The tango was everywhere. Tango teas, in particular, proliferated. These were no doubt a way of making the dance respectable and acceptable to the middle classes. But as a London minister of the Church remarked in 1913: 'It is not what happens *at* a tango tea that so much matters as what happens *after* it.'

Left: **E.L. Kirchner, *Tango*, 1925, from the series 'Tanzcafé'.**

Below: **'Tango Tea', from the album *Tango Rausch*, 1913.**

Above: 'Tango', postcard by Xavier Sager, 1913.

Top right: 'Tango Tea', Paris, 1914.

Right: 'Tango Tea', Munich, 1913.

. . . Creator of silhouettes that glide by silently
as if hypnotized by a blood-filled dream,
hats tilted over sardonic sneers.
The all-absorbing love of a tyrant,
jealously guarding his dominion
over women who have surrendered submissively,
like obedient beasts . . .
Sad, severe tango . . .
Dance of love and death . . .[7]

Dances for couples are always designed to enhance the masculinity of one partner and the femininity of the other; but not until the tango had Paris seen a dance which gave so much scope for overt sexuality. The tango had other advantages too: it was sufficiently picturesque to cover up the faults of a bad dancer, and dramatic enough to show off a really good one. With such a history, such a launch, and such credentials, it could not fail.

★THE SHOCK OF THE TANGO★

On first seeing the tango danced, the Comtesse Mélanie de Pourtalès leaned towards the distinguished académicien seated next to her and murmured, 'Is one supposed to dance it standing up?'[8] In 1913, tangomania had reached even the most fashionable salons, causing shockwaves in French society. The ballet-master of the Opéra, among many others, condemned it as an atrocity.

The tango was everywhere' that summer, taken up by almost everyone – beau monde, demi-monde, bourgeoisie and petite bourgeoisie – but the working class was a notable exception. There were tea-tangos held between four in the afternoon and seven, where the public, for an entry fee of up to five francs including tea and sandwiches, could dance to their heart's content. There were also champagne-tangos, surprise-tangos, charity tangos, dinner-tangos, and of course tangos in nightclubs, then spreading like wildfire to cater to the dance craze. Many were on the Champs Elysées, where grand town houses were being rapidly converted. There were tangos on ice at the Palais de Glace on the rond-point des Champs Elysées, which also staged a huge tango competition. The winning couple had to dance sixty-two tangos, an idea which crossed the Atlantic to Buenos Aires where the same number of tangos were performed before a jury. There was even a 'Tango Train', which plied its way between Paris and Deauville during the summer season.

One of the men most in demand for demonstrations of the dance was Ludovic de Portalou, Marquis de Sénas. An ex-Hussar, he had been instrumental, with the Prince de Sagan, in the 1895 launch of Maxim's, a rest… ch came to be known as 'reserved for the cream of the demi-… arquis was one of the few Frenchmen to have learnt the tango … long before it became fashionable; for this distinction he was … du Tango'.

… t school were, of course, forbidden to learn the tango; but … iece, Adry de Carbuccia, begged him to teach her. He did, … ment came at a tea-dance in the Casino at Deauville in … of the main events was a tango competition, and the … nd young Adry – wearing a white dress of broderie … bow in her hair – won first prize. In her autobiography … – and everyone who defended the dance agreed – that … re was nothing improper about the tango'.[9]

… as undeniable. According to Carbuccia:

> … rmed conventions and scruples: women who, a …, would not have left the house unaccompanied, lost the fear instilled by their mothers; and allowed themselves to be closely embraced by dancing partners who were often unknown to them . . . *Thés dansants* were the rage . . . Women of all classes attended. One paid for lessons from 'danseurs mondains', Argentines, South Americans, Frenchmen. Mature women also paid for a little love afterwards, in some discreet garçonnière![10]

Perhaps this was why the mythical 'Latin lover', though irresistible to his female victim, was seen by everyone else as little better than a gigolo.

The tango gave its name to any number of commercial products, from perfume to corsets; but it became most closely associated with a colour, known as 'couleur tango'. The story was that a certain silk manufacturer found himself left with a large stock of satin, dyed such a garish orange-yellow that it proved unsellable. Since the fabric was now badly shop-soiled as well, it was put on sale at a bargain price, and given the name 'Satin-Tango'. The trick worked like magic. The stock sold out within days and people clamoured for more but the manufacturer had, to his dismay, lost the formula for that particular shade. This gave his competitors the chance to leap into the market,

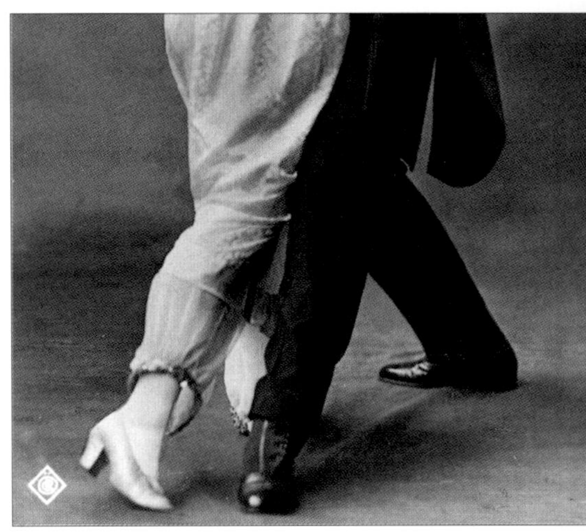

From a series of French postcards on the tango, 1913.

and sell every variation from pale lemon to the deepest saffron as 'la véritable couleur tango'.

The next craze was for the 'blouse-tango', a light, full-sleeved blouse of tango-coloured silk or satin trimmed with black fur or swansdown. The

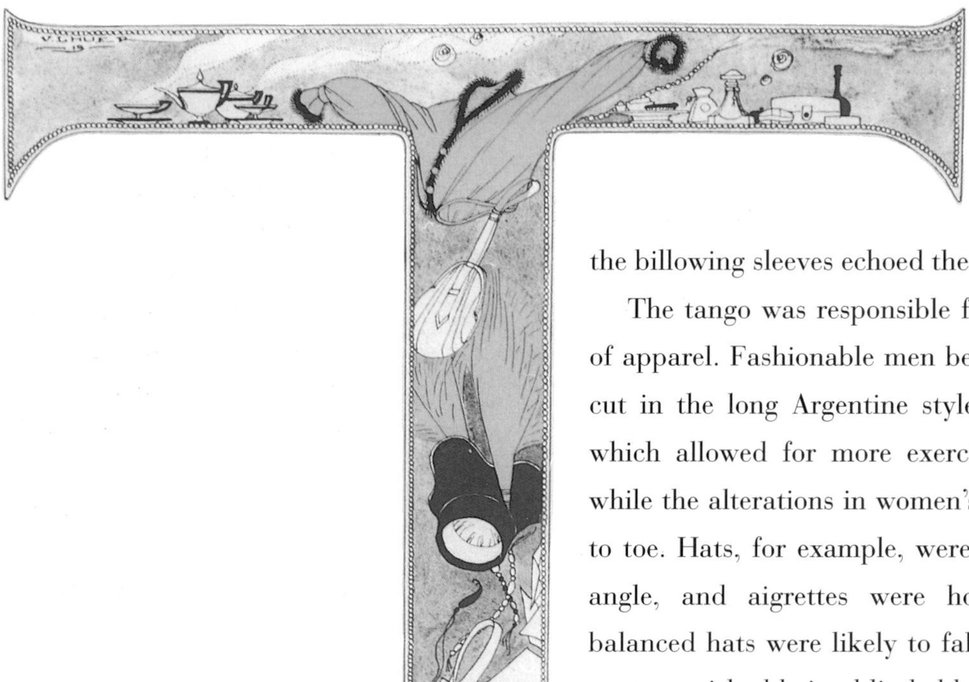

garment was made in one piece, the only seams being from shoulder to wrist. It was a cut which gave the upper body far more freedom, and the billowing sleeves echoed the movements of the dance.

The tango was responsible for changes in almost every item of apparel. Fashionable men began to have their dinner jackets cut in the long Argentine style known as 'fumadero tango' – which allowed for more exercise of the arms and shoulders; while the alterations in women's costume were evident from top to toe. Hats, for example, were at the time usually worn at an angle, and aigrettes were horizontal. But since insecurely balanced hats were likely to fall off during the tango and male partners risked being blinded by feathers at sudden, swift turns of the dance, the fashion in headgear had to be changed. Aigrettes became vertical and were usually restricted to only one, sticking straight up out of a hat. Hats themselves – often small tricornes – were planted firmly in the middle of the head. Long dangling necklaces and heavy, cumbersome trains were also out, as were evening bags in the form of small silver or gold boxes suspended by strings, which could bruise the hips of both partners. The waists of dancing gowns grew higher, giving maximum length and freedom of action to the draped skirt; while the already-fashionable knee-length overskirt accentuated the hips and made the tango strides more modest. Shoes, previously kept short in the toe, were lengthened to exaggerate the long, deliberate steps.

To allow even more freedom of movement, some very daring women wore divided skirts, known in Paris as 'jupes culottes'. These had first been forecast as 'fashions for the future' in 1911 by Paul Poiret. They caused a sensation when seen in 1913, either at tango dances or at the races, though to modern eyes they look modest enough. The culottes were very full and gathered at the ankles, and often a knee-length overskirt or tunic covered the rest.

Cooks and patissiers also jumped on the tango bandwagon. The humble banana, by virtue of its tango-evoking colour, was transformed into La Banane Tango, and took its place on smart menus beside La Peche Melba; while Le Gateau Tango first appeared at tea-dances. This last confection could be anything from an elaborate chocolate cake topped with port-wine icing to a tiny sablé biscuit, hastily nibbled between one dance and the next. Artists exploited the craze, with paintings on the theme such as *Au Cours du tango* by Albert Guillaume, which was exhibited during May 1913 in the Salon de la Société des Artistes Français. Apollinaire wrote a poem to Picabia called 'The Tango', the last couplet of which ran,

> And if you dance the tango,
> *Noli me tangere*!

'Dancing', wrote the Duchesse de Clermont-Tonnerre, 'spread from the ground floor to every floor. People who *hated* dancing gave dances. Mme Boas de Jouvenel replaced her politician guests with tangoing couples.'[11] Comte Etienne de Beaumont, Paris's most famous host for the first half of the century, gave tango dances in the white and gilt salons of his family's eighteenth-century palace.

'Still caught up in my old habits', continued the Duchesse (later the lesbian lover of the American hostess, Natalie Clifford Barney),

> I went to the rue de Varenne to an old lady who traditionally gave quiet little parties at which orangeade was served. But when I arrived the racket of the music made the portraits of her ancestors vibrate on the walls. Young women were wandering around cigarette in hand, and gauchos, their hair awry from sweat,

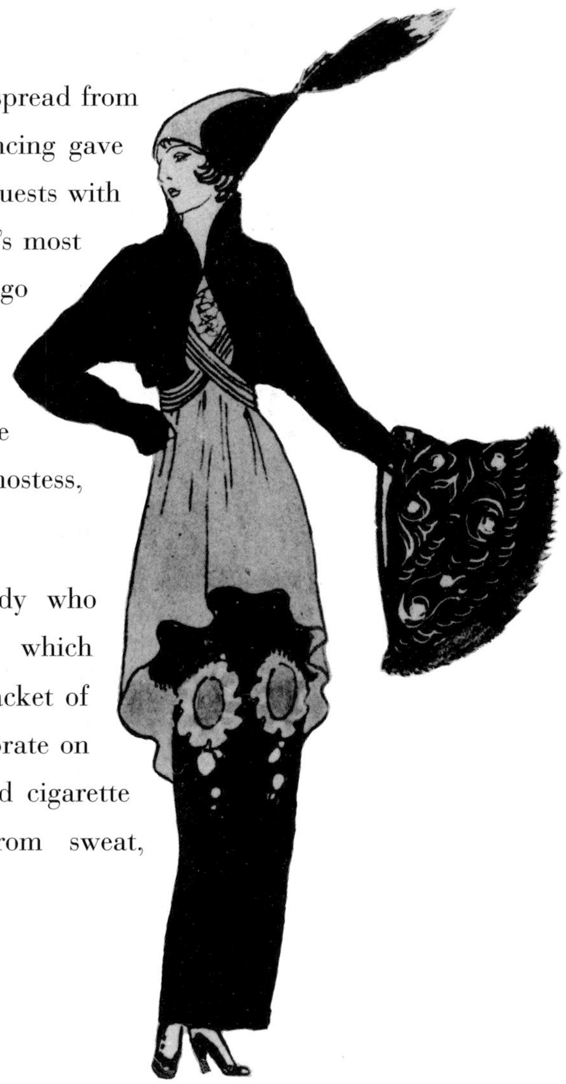

The tango brought changes to many items of dress: hats became smaller; waistlines were raised and sleeves were cut more loosely to allow for extra freedom of movement. Slits appeared down the front of now slightly shorter dresses. Some women wore the new tango slipper, designed with ribbons criss-crossing over the instep and tied around the ankle.

The dance had its impact too on women's underwear: a special 'tango corset' was produced, shorter and more elastic than earlier corsetry.

The tango also became closely linked to a particular colour spectrum, ranging from yellow to reddish-orange.

grasped their partners, whose calves were visible. 'Where are the usual guests from the *gratin*?' I asked a friend. 'They must have sought refuge elsewhere, came the reply'.[12]

According to others, the *gratin* were just as eager to learn as everyone else. Madame Mainchin, who organized tango classes for the Faubourg de Saint-Germain, was one of many to profit from the craze. Drawn by reports of the tango's popularity, young Argentines had come to seek their fortune in Paris as tango teachers. Among those who became fashionable were Casimiro Aín and Bernabé Simara. Simara, who was known as El Indio, attracted a very fashionable crowd. He refused to wear the white tie and tails normally demanded of dancing masters, but this did not hinder him from making a great deal of money in Paris. Certainly, men who danced the tango were much in demand, though the Duchesse de Clermont-Tonnerre was perhaps exaggerating when she claimed that at Magic-City, one of the larger dance-halls in Paris, 'respectable women danced the tango sometimes with their valets or hairdressers'.[13] At his own request, she took the savant Dr Gustave Le Bon to the Ritz to see the famous dance about which everyone was talking. She explained that the star of the tango in Paris was the Infanta Eulalia of Spain, who had an entourage of Argentines, one of whom had apparently had the gall to remark: 'We love dancing with this ruined old French nobility.'

Paul Poiret, the greatest couturier of the pre-war period, designed the costumes for Jean Richepin's play *Le Tango*, which opened in Paris in 1913. The illustrations on *this page* and *opposite* show a scene from the play and some of the costumes. Poiret's famous harem trousers, which were worn with an overskirt, proved to be perfect tango wear.

Cocteau described Soto and Martínez, two members of this entourage, arriving with a portable gramophone, to play the tango, as if it were a basket for a picnic:

> From the villa Montmorency (between Bergson and Gide) the tango was set to invade Europe. Knotted couples, their shoulders immobile, performed the slow Argentine promenade. Fat gentlemen advanced on sliding little steps, squarely in front of their partners. From time to time they halted, turned, lifted a foot and inspected the sole, as if they had just trodden in something horrible.[14]

At one point, the tango even spawned a breed of petty criminals, many of whom passed themselves off at fashionable dance halls as Russian princesses or Italian counts. The *New York Times* reported early in 1914 that 'police have discovered that these pseudo-aristocrats have taken full advantage of the complicated attitudes which the tango . . . involves to pick pockets and purloin jewellery'.[15]

From Paris, the craze swept to London, and also spread to Germany, Russia and Italy. It seems likely that the first English people to be exposed to the tango were visitors to the French Channel resorts in the summer of 1911, and it was in the same year that photographs of the tango being danced first appeared in England, in the *Dancing Times*. What actually sparked off the craze,

however, was the show *The Sunshine Girl*, which opened in London's Gaiety Theatre in February 1912 and ran for a year. Starring George Grossmith and Phyllis Dare, it included one tango routine. Grossmith had learned the steps in Paris in the winter of 1911-12 and the expert and dazzling display given by both him and his partner inspired a host of imitators, both on stage and off.

By spring of 1913 the craze was in full spate – tango teas had become as popular in London as they were in Paris and were held not only in hotels and restaurants but in the homes of the middle and upper classes. The Savoy Hotel began to host regular tango dinners.

Not everyone approved, however. The attack on the tango in England was launched on 20 May 1913 by a letter in *The Times* from 'A Peeress':

THE TANGO:
AND
HOW TO DANCE IT

I am one of the many matrons upon whom devolves the task of guiding a girl through the mazes of the London season, and I am face to face with a state of affairs in most, but not all, of the ballrooms calling for the immediate attention of those in like case. My grandmother has often told me of the shock she experienced on first beholding the polka, but I wonder what she would have said had she been asked to introduce a well-brought-up girl of eighteen to the scandalous travesties of dancing which are, for the first time in my recollection, bringing more young men to parties than are needed. I need not describe the various horrors of American and South American negroid origin. I would only ask hostesses to let one know what houses to avoid by indicating in some way on their invitation-card whether the 'Turkey Trot', the 'Boston' (the beginner of the evil) and the 'Tango' will be permitted.

The *Dancing Times* defended the tango stoutly against the Peeress, who soon became synonymous with all that was most reactionary in British society. 'We can all guess what her grandmother would have said, because we know exactly how our grandmothers fought tooth and nail against the introduction of the

***The Tango and How to Dance It* (*opposite below*), by Mrs Gladys Beattie Crozier, included not only instructions on the steps themselves but also advice on how to host a successful tango tea 'in any ordinary-sized drawing room'.**

The *Dancing Times* advertisement *below* invites readers to a week in Le Touquet, one of France's most fashionable resorts, from 12 to 19 September 1913. On Wednesday the Tennis Tournament and the final of the Golf Tournament are followed in the evening by the Grand Tango Competition.

***Opposite top:* From *La Vie heureuse*, 1913.**

THE DANCING TIMES 739

"The Jolliest Week of the Summer Season."

Le Touquet's Invitation to "Dancing Times" Readers to Visit their Delightful :: Arcady beside the Silver Sea. ::

…YTHING is becoming Inter…ional. Dancing is essentially …rnational, and Le Touquet …hat most enchanting of all …ide resorts—sends us and our …ecial invitation to the dances …rm so prominent a feature of … Week that will be held from …12th to 19th.

…ure of special interest to … the DANCING TIMES is that …e a Grand Tango Competi-

…nce at the following tentative … will show, lovers of dancing … to enjoy themselves to the …r the supervision of Miss …he grand ball, cotillion, and … dances will go with that irresistible swing and air of good fellowship that makes one keen to begin and reluctant to stop, nor does the evening's

PROGRAMME FOR WEEK—
SEPTEMBER 12TH-19TH.

Friday.

Leave Charing Cross at 2.5 p.m.
Arrive at Le Touquet 7.27 p.m. in time for Dinner.
Evening: *Impromptu Concert.*

Saturday.

Morning free for the general pleasures of the place.
Afternoon: *Introductory Tea.*
Evening: *Impromptu Dance du Casino.*

Sunday.

Morning free.
Afternoon: 4 o'clock *Children's Ball at Casino.*
Evening: *Grand Concert.* "*Souper Dansant*" after 12.

Monday.

Morning and Afternoon: Opening of *Golf Tournament.*
Evening: *Grand Ball with Cotillion and Souvenirs.*

Tuesday.

Morning free.
Afternoon: Opening of *Tennis Tournament.*

In Great Britain controversy raged. Was the tango a suitable dance for young women, or was it a scandalous pastime unfit for Anglo-Saxon ballrooms? A famous correspondence took place in *The Times* in which passionate letters both for and against appeared daily for two weeks.

The humorous magazine *Punch* also made numerous allusions to the tango craze throughout 1913 and 1914, including the cartoon *right*. (Upper Tooting was a prosperous middle-class suburb of South London.)

STAMPING OUT REVOLT IN UPPER TOOTING.

Mother (to daughter with yearnings for the higher life). "USE WHAT ARGUMENTS YOU LIKE, CHILD; NO TANGO-TEAS SHALL BE GIVEN IN *THIS* DRAWING-ROOM."

polka and the valse into England. Nowadays, the valse, however badly it may be danced, is tolerated, even, I presume, by "A Peeress" . . .'[16] The journal went on to fire a broadside at the noblewoman by suggesting that if she was so shocked, she must have been 'moving in a very curious stratum of society, where the antics of the Montmartre Cabarets . . . have been tolerated.'[17]

The actor George Grossmith rose to the tango's aid in the *Daily Graphic*, calling it a most 'graceful and beautiful dance'.[18] The correspondence in *The Times* lasted for two weeks, and during the summer many magazines joined in the discussion of whether or not it was the done thing to do the tango. The general consensus was that it was quite acceptable if danced with decorum.

'In a previous incarnation', wrote the Kinneys (who had frowned on the turkey trot), 'the Tango did, in all likelihood, fall short of the requirements for acceptance in Anglo-Saxon ballrooms. [But] the Tango is now, and has been for a year or more, a beautiful and irreproachable dance – assuming, of course, its performance in the clean spirit usually found in good society'.[19]

By late 1913 the tango craze had become so widespread that in November the illustrated magazine *The Sketch* chose the tango as its cover story and reported: 'Everybody's doing the Tango, learning the Tango, talking the Tango, watching the Tango'.[20] In the summer of the following year the tango finally received the royal seal of approval. P.J.S. Richardson tells the story in his *History of English Ballroom Dancing*.[21] That summer the Grand Duke Michael

By mid-1914 the tango battle had been decisively won. In the summer of that year, by special request of the usually strait-laced Queen Mary, Maurice and Florence Walton gave a 7-minute tango display at a ball held in London by the Grand Duke Michael of Russia. The Waltons (Maurice was American) were two of many exhibition dancers who flourished during the tango craze. They are shown *left* on the cover of a tango number called, somewhat confusingly, 'La Rumba'.

of Russia gave a ball at Kenwood in Hampstead, which was attended by Queen Mary. Rumour had it that the Queen strongly disapproved of the tango, so in deference to her feelings it was left out of the demonstration of new dances given during the ball by two well-known professional dancers, Maurice and Florence Walton. As it happened, the Queen was not so much pleased as disappointed by this omission and quickly made her feelings known to her hostess. Then followed a seven-minute tango, which was by all accounts highly appreciated by her majesty, who is reported to have described the dance as 'charming'.

Although the German upper classes were in two minds about the tango – the Kaiser forbade his officers from dancing it in uniform – people in general were enthusiastic. The show *Tango Princessin* (*top*) was the hit of the season at the Thalia Theatre, Berlin, in 1913. Those who wanted to learn all the currently popular dances, including the tango, could turn to the teach-yourself-to-dance handbook *above*.

***Opposite:* From the weekly illustrated magazine *Jugend*, Munich, 1920.**

In German royal circles, things were rather different. Kaiser Wilhelm II ruled German society with a rod of iron, and held views on dancing which even A Peeress might have thought old-fashioned. He did not like 'modern' dances, by which he meant the polka and the waltz; and at court balls, the minuet and the gavotte were the only dances permitted. He was therefore outraged to learn in the summer of 1913 that Countess Schwerin-Löwitz, wife of the Speaker of the Prussian Parliament, had used the official parliamentary reception rooms to give a 'tango' tea which was attended by diplomats and high officials. The Kaiser declared that officers in uniform were forbidden to dance the tango; and since uniforms were always worn at balls, and no ball was complete without a large contingent of officers, this effectively banned the dance for the rest of high society. He was also seriously annoyed with his son, the Crown Prince, who was a well-known tango enthusiast. Nevertheless, outside of court circles, the tango was proving to be as popular in Germany as it was elsewhere in Europe. Tango teas proliferated and tango shows were immensely successful.

Tsar Nicholas II was perhaps the first monarch to see the tango danced. In 1911, he was informed by his Minister of the Interior that two young grand-dukes, nephews of the Tsar, had been involved in an incident in a fashionable nightclub in St Petersburg, 'where a new perturbing dance was revealed' – not a can-can, but a South American dance called the Tango Argentino. The Tsar ordered his two young nephews to give him a demonstration, and – perhaps surprisingly – he liked it.

One of the nephews in question was the Grand Duke Dimitri who was at the time serving as an unwilling escort to his fifty-six-year-old aunt the Grand Duchess Anastasia, who though entirely without talent, had an overwhelming desire to dance. The Grand Duke eventually passed her over to Vernon Castle, one half of the most famous dancing duo of the time, who taught her to do both the one-step and the tango. In her autobiography, *Castles in the Air*, Irene Castle, Vernon's wife and dancing partner, relates how she 'always longed to see the Grand Duchess do the tango. It would have been like watching an elephant waltz.'[22]

In Spain, the frivolous Alfonso XIII adored the tango, even though it shocked his more conservative courtiers. This was a curious repetition of the battle at the Spanish court under Charles IV, in the late eighteenth century, when a powerful faction tried to ban the fandango until the King decided in its favour.

In Rome the tango became as popular as it was in Paris. Impoverished young aristocrats, whose noble blood made them disdainful of more useful employment, suddenly found their vocation as tango partners. 'It was diverting to watch them,' wrote Harold Acton in *Memoirs of an Aesthete*, 'so conscious of their mastery of adventurous side-steps, twining and twisting in and out of those gliding, dragging measures with a sharp click at the end . . . their impassive virility contrasting sharply with a flashing wrist-watch, a sparkle of rings and a silk handkerchief reeking of Coty . . .'[23]

By late 1913 the tango was also all the rage in Russia. 'Everybody's dancing the tango', ran the headline in the St Petersburg magazine *Argos* (*above*). 'The highlight of the Christmas season will be the tango, which has penetrated all drawing rooms,' the article began. The magazine also included instruction by Phyllis Dare, the English tango star, on the proper method of performing the dance.

In Paris, where the flame burned the fiercest, the tango controversy was even more hotly contested between '*tanguistes*' and '*anti-tanguistes*'. In the *Mercure de France* of 16 February 1914, the antis argued that the tango was 'une danse de filles publiques' (a whores' dance), and, quoting the Scottish writer R. B. Cunninghame-Graham, who claimed to have seen dreadful scenes in Buenos Aires, said that it led to drunkenness and murderous brawls. At the very least it was a 'sure path to indecency, authorizing poses and movements which make the body of the purest woman look infamous'. At the *bals publics* the young were acting like 'monkeys from the Andes'. The dance was a bastard, miscegenated progeny of Europe and the Americas,

On Joue "le Tango" de Mr et Mme Jean Richepin

NOS LECTRICES trouveront encarté dans ce numéro, en un fascicule spécial, les deux premiers actes du Tango *de M. et Mme Jean Richepin, dont nous publierons la fin dans notre prochain numéro. Ci-dessous, elles liront une interview de Mme Jean Richepin sur la pièce qui marque ses débuts dans la littérature aux côtés du grand poète depuis longtemps glorieux — ainsi qu'une chronique de modes détaillée sur les toilettes du* Tango, *toilettes dont l'originalité, parfois hardie mais toujours artistique, s'harmonise plus qu'en toute autre œuvre theâtrale avec le fond même du sujet, d'un modernisme d'« avant-garde »... Elles verront aussi en ces pages des croquis et des dessins d'après ces costumes et, pour compléter cette documentation, quelques aperçus d'ensemble des scènes principales.*

Nous sommes heureux de donner à notre public, qui a accueilli et qui suit avec une si grande faveur notre transformation, la primeur de cette actualité sensationnelle ; nous avons pensé que nous devions à cette bienveillance, à ce succès, et à notre programme même, d'accomplir un effort spécial à propos d'une œuvre dont, pour tant de raisons, on a tant parlé, avant et après la première représentation.

Les origines du "Tango"

and France itself was as demeaned as Argentina by its exhibition. Of course, many upper-class Argentines had already said similar things. The diplomat Don Carlos Ibarguren even went so far as to disown the tango: '[It] is not really Argentinian, but a hybrid of mixed blood, born in the slums.'[24]

The writer Jean Richepin was known for his bohemian lifestyle and strong views. His first book of poems was judged so scandalous that it earned him a one-month prison sentence. Richepin was one of France's most ardent tangoists. In December 1913 his play *The Tango,* on which Madame Richepin (the actress Cora Laparcerie) collaborated, opened at the Athénée Theatre in Paris. The play tells the story of a young couple who fail to consummate their marriage until they unlock their sexuality by dancing the tango. This rather risqué theme, plus the fact that both hero and heroine were played by actresses, may explain the play's chilly reception by the critics.

One of the most celebrated 'tanguistes' was the writer and dramatist Jean Richepin. He had once been the lover of the great actress Sarah Bernhardt and his plays, which were often in verse, celebrated instinct and tempestuous passions. It is surprising that such a colourful character, whose work was written for a popular audience, should have been a member of the French Académie des Beaux Arts – an institution usually noted for its high intellectual seriousness. Yet he was, and on 25 October 1913, at the annual public gathering of the five Academies of the Institut de France, he made an oration in the dance's defence entitled 'A propos du Tango'.

The speech took place in the Institut, and the rotunda under the great cupola was filled with women of fashion – which was in itself unusual. Lucile Dubois, a journalist for the *anti-tanguiste Mercure de France*, described the hall as being 'packed like a barrel of herrings, except that the elegant ladies who made up the major part of the audience gave it the air of an enormous bouquet'.[25] They were, she reported in her newspaper, eagerly awaiting the famous *académicien* to introduce 'the aesthetic of the bordello to the Cupola, to which Zola was never admitted on grounds of modesty.'[26] Richepin's fellow Academicians, however, were conspicuous by their absence: only four attended.

Richepin defended the tango's humble origins by pointing out that all dances enjoyed by royal courts had plebeian ancestry of one sort or another; while many of them – the English country dance, the German waltz, the Polish mazurka, the Hungarian polka and the American Boston – had caused a stir when first danced in polite society.

Everything depended on the way it was danced. 'I have had the pleasure', declaimed Richepin, 'of seeing tangos danced by princesses which were models of elegant distinction, and I have also seen the insipid polka and the honest lancers danced in a manner that, to use the phrase of one of our illustrious predecessors, would have made a monkey blush.'

'Fierce moralists' were now attacking the tango, and so were nationalists, who saw it as a symptom of moral decline, but what did the tango's original appearance and character matter? 'We Gallicize everything, and the dance we love to dance becomes French.'

This curious patriotic turn was taken to further heights in Richepin's conclusion. 'France is like ancient Greece,' he cried, 'She is a country where dance is necessary to life.' This was a great national strength. The French army

The title page of Richepin's play *Le Tango* is shown *left*, published in the magazine *La Vie heureuse* in 1914. The illustration *opposite* is from an article on the play in the same magazine.

Given the Church's strong condemnation of the tango, the event shown *above* seems highly unlikely. Yet it does seem to have taken place. Early in 1914 two members of the Roman nobility demonstrated the tango for Pope Pius X. Apparently the Pope was not impressed – he described the dance as 'barbarian contortions'. In Argentina a verse soon circulated: *Dicen que el tango tiene gran languidez/ Por eso lo ha prohibido el Papa Pío Diez.* (The tango's languorous, we understand/ And so the Pope has had it banned.)

fought to music. He invoked the 'twenty-five thousand whistling a rigadoon.' The image unintentionally conjured up, of moustachioed *grognards* from the Imperial Guard tangoing into the attack, must have made the Napoleonic ghosts of the Institut de France shudder.

Richepin's play *The Tango* opened on 30 December 1913. The plot centred on a young couple who, to their family's dismay, have failed to consummate their marriage. It is not until they dance the tango that they discover their sexuality (a message in sharp contrast to Richepin's defence of the tango in the Academy, in which he stressed that there was nothing intrinsically arousing about the dance). Despite the lavish sets and costumes by Paul Poiret, the play was not a success and in the following months the *Mercure de France* accused Richepin of merely cashing in on the tango craze.

Since by the end of 1913 the tango had not only been danced for an entire summer but had also been defended that autumn in the Academy, it might be thought that it had finally achieved respectability; yet in the first days of 1914, perhaps as a result of Richepin's play, the Catholic Church in France began attacking the dance with renewed ferocity. Several Church dignitaries thundered against it from the pulpit. On 11 January Monsignor Amette, the Primate of France, published a solemn exhortation to his flock to 'observe the rules of Christian modesty'. He condemned 'the dance of foreign origin, known as the tango' for being 'by its nature wanton and offensive to morals', and he urged priests to emphasize its sinfulness when hearing the confessions of their parishioners.[27] President and Madame Poincaré banned the dance from the Elysée Palace.[28]

After this severe admonition, readers of the Parisian review *L'Illustration* must have been astonished to see, in the issue of 7 February, a picture of Pope Pius X actually watching the tango being performed in his presence. The drawing was admittedly entitled *Se non è vero, è bene* [sic] *trovato* (It may not be true, but it's a good story); but the story itself, according to *L'Illustration*'s correspondent, was all over Rome and widely corroborated.

The prelude to this unlikely scene was the work of a tango-loving Italian Prince, who approached one of the Pope's most trusted advisers, Cardinal Merry de Val. The Prince pointed out that the tango had been 'revised and corrected' by the celebrated dancing master Professor Pichetti; and, as performed in Roman salons, was now irreproachable. Yet it was not only condemned by the Pope, but the Minister of War was about to issue an order forbidding officers to dance it in uniform. The Prince begged the Cardinal to bring this to the attention of His Holiness, particularly since carnival time was approaching and the most resplendent balls of the season were about to begin.

The following day, Cardinal Merry de Val took this news to the Pope, who was then in private audience with a brother and sister of the Roman nobility. They were fashionable people, no doubt familiar with the tango; and, on a whim, the Pope asked them to dance it for him. The brother and sister were amazed by the request, but could hardly disobey. And given the solemnity of the occasion, plus the fact that women in the presence of the Pontiff had to wear an ankle-length black dress and a mantilla covering head and shoulders, one may assume that the tango they danced was restrained to say the least.

The Pope, who came from the Veneto, was not impressed. He teased them for being such slaves to fashion that they should put so much effort into such an unamusing dance, and added, 'I understand that you love dancing; it is carnival time, and you are young . . . But why adopt these barbarian contortions of Negroes and Indians? Why not choose the pretty Venetian dance, so elegant and graceful, the *furlana*?' The brother and sister had never heard of it, so the Pope called in one of his Venetian servants, who danced it for the young aristocrats.

In the winter of 1913-14 tangomania reached the United States. ALL NEW YORK NOW MADLY WHIRLING IN THE TANGO ran the headline in the *New York Times* early in the New Year. The craze spread quickly across the country – so many dance halls sprang up in a section of the French Quarter of New Orleans that it was given the nickname 'The Tango Belt'.

8 THE NEW YORK TIMES, SUNDAY, JANUARY 1, 1914.

ALL NEW YORK NOW MADLY WHIRLING IN THE TANGO

Every Day New Places Where You May Dance Are Springing Up and Older Establishments Yielding to the Craze, Which Apparently, Has Come to Stay.

The tango craze reached New York in the winter of 1913-14, and the ability of the dance to shock and delight lost nothing on the transatlantic journey. Dance halls and tango teas sprang up in its wake, just as they had in Paris, Rome and London; and on 4 January the *New York Times* reported: ALL NEW YORK NOW MADLY WHIRLING IN THE TANGO. To its devotees, the dance had much in its favour. It bridged social distinctions: in Newport, Rhode Island, houses which had hitherto welcomed only senior officers of the U.S. Navy now opened their doors to officers of all ranks, and a young officer who danced well was tipped as a man who would go far. It also proved to the French and the English, who could never understand the strength of the temperance movement in America, that Americans did know how to enjoy themselves.[29] The fashionable interior decorator Elsie de Wolfe was quoted in the *New York Times* as saying 'To me [the tango] is the greatest

rest, because there is in it so much repose, after the violence of the One-Step.'[30] Some people even claimed it cured indigestion. Mrs Charles H. Israels, who headed the Committee on Amusement Resources for Working Girls, also approved of the tango – if danced properly; and her organization sent model dancers to its meetings to ensure it was correctly taught.[31]

Teaching the tango, and the other fashionable dances of the time, was providing many with a new means of livelihood. 'Since the tango became popular,' reported the *New York Times*, 'an extraordinary number of dark-skinned young men have appeared in New York as teachers of the Argentine dance, and who claim to have come from south of the Rio de la Plata.' Sceptics said that the arrival of these 'dusky young tango-ists' dated from the first of the recent revolutions in Mexico.[32]

Yet because the dance was undeniably risqué and provoked gasps of horror from the ultra-respectable, the tango-loving New Yorkers felt the need for moral support. They were constantly looking over their shoulders to see who was dancing the tango in Europe, and the *New York Times* assiduously supplied its readers with their names – the Earl and Countess of Drogheda in London, Princess Lucien Murat in Paris, and – best of all – the Queen of Denmark, who attended tango teas with her mother, the Grand Duchess Anastasia of Mecklenburg-Schwering, the very same Grand Duchess who was being taught the tango by Vernon Castle.

The *New York Times* also carried reports throughout January of 1914 on the controversy over whether or not the tango was a suitable dance for right-thinking persons. The Catholic Church in New York had been the first to voice its vehement opposition to the tango, which it saw as the worst of a whole series of wild and shameless modern dances. In late 1913, Cardinal Farley inaugurated the crusade by cancelling the annual Cotillion of the Junior Auxillary of the Roman Catholic Institute for the Blind, which was to have taken place at Delmonico's in the New Year. Six hundred invitations had to be recalled, and the ladies organizing the event made it clear that this action had been taken at the express wish of His Eminence. The Cardinal's office announced that 'all Catholic societies in this city have been notified of the Cardinal's opposition to dancing in the present mode.'[33] A certain Father Phelan of St Louis, Missouri, made himself notorious for taking the opposite view. He wrote an editorial supporting the tango in a Roman Catholic journal called the *Western Watchman*, and by so doing disconcerted his flock and infuriated his archbishop. Father Phelan was made to retract his views in the next issue.

Various Protestant and Jewish elders joined in praise of the Catholic Church's lead. One rabbi remarked that 'Certainly the rage which seems to have taken hold of people so that some of them dance at luncheon . . . is prejudicial to a sane view of life, to moral responsibility and the performance of duty.'[34] A Baptist minister accused those mothers who allowed their girls to dance the tango of 'throwing their daughters to the crocodiles' in the cause of social advancement.[35]

Irene and Vernon Castle (*opposite*) were instrumental in popularizing the tango in the USA. Cleancut, clean-living and married, they danced a tango which, in Irene's words, 'had nothing suggestive about it'. She wrote: 'If Vernon had ever looked into my eyes with smouldering passion during the tango, we would have both burst out laughing.'

***Left:* An American tangoing couple, with plenty of distance between them, drawn by Elie Nadelman in 1917/18.**

Under pressure, a group of fashionable New York matrons did band together to oppose the tango in society; but part of the unease among the older generation was due to the fact that they themselves had been the first to adopt the 'objectionable dances', which were then taken up so enthusiastically by their children. One fashionable dancing master, T. George Dodworth, pointed out that the tango itself was not to blame. Young people had taken to clasping each other much too close in a number of dances, 'so close', he complained, 'that it would be impossible even to get a sheet of paper between them.'[36]

The tango's success caused great embarrassment in Argentine communities abroad, especially in Paris. In the 1890s, Argentine expatriates had been famous for their bouts of extravagance which were inevitably followed by periods of penury – until the next banker's draft arrived. A decade later, however, they had become staider and more conscious of their respectability. Their parties, though still magnificent, were far more decorous, and designed to attract the cream of international society. In May 1912, the Iturbe family gave a Hungarian party with dancing in the garden of their splendid palace on the Avenue du Bois de Boulogne. Among their guests were Princess Stephanie of Belgium, a couple of Russian grand-dukes, the Ducs de Gramont, Morny and Clermont-Tonnerre, Prince Murat, Prince Radziwill, the Baron Maurice de Rothschild and the wife of ex-President Porfirio Díaz of Mexico.

‘Every year in the month of April’, wrote Baron Marcel Fouquier, ‘liners from South America arrived in our ports to unload the elite of Argentine society, including the richest landowners of the Pampas’.[37] These visitors usually stayed for two or three months, and took home with them French tastes and styles, especially that of eighteenth-century French architecture for their town houses in Buenos Aires. Even if the French were patronizing, they were well aware of the benefits of such slavish imitation; it swelled exports of French furnishings, to say nothing of scent and fashion jewellery. Certain establishments on the rue de la Paix and the Place Vendôme even sent representatives to meet the liners on their arrival. Shops close to South American consulates and embassies changed hands at inflated prices.

The South American colony in Paris had its own society magazine, *Elegancias*, edited by the poet Ruben Darío, with a social diary written by ‘Lady Mayfair’. It catered to every aspect of the fashionable life, proffering advice on subjects ranging from table decoration to the right automobile to be seen in.

The Argentine Minister Plenipotentiary to France, the novelist Enrique Larreta, came from a family well-known in Argentine political life. An earnest looking man with a carefully curled moustache and hair brushed sideways, he took his social duties seriously. The legation in the rue de la Faisanderie saw ‘an endless procession of beauty and elegance’, as the always respectful gush of

There is a saying about the people of Buenos Aires which runs: The *porteños* are Italians who speak Spanish, think they are British and wish they were French. Certainly in the early decades of the 20th century upper-class Argentines drew heavily on French style for their architecture, household furnishings and, of course, fashion. And it was *de rigueur* to make a long visit to Paris. The photograph *opposite* shows a celebration given by the Argentine Minister Plenipotentiary to France, the novelist Enrique Larreta, on the Argentine national holiday, 25 May 1913. Larreta is thought to be the figure right of centre, with curled moustache. He banned the tango at the Argentine embassy, calling it ‘a dance exclusive to houses of ill-repute and bars of the lowest class’.

In less formal mood, Argentine regulars pose for their photograph at the ‘Dancing Palace’ (*above*). Both pictures appeared in 1913 in *Elegancias*, the society magazine of the South American colony in Paris.

Elegancias put it. The most important event of the year for the Argentine colony in Paris was 25 May, the national holiday, when the greatest number of Argentine visitors happened to be in France.

In Paris, members of the rich Argentine community saw the tango as symbolic of that strong anarchistic streak in their own society which was a threat to the established order. ('The Argentine', wrote Borges, 'does not identify with the soldier, but with rebels – the gaucho and the *compadre*.'[38]) And fear of anarchism was almost hysterical at that time. On 12 November 1912, the Spanish prime minister, Canalejas, had been assassinated in Madrid as he paused to glance in a bookshop window on the way to his office. These upper-class Argentines, so keen to be accepted as equals by Parisian society, were also deeply embarrassed by the tango's reputation of sexual and aggressive machismo, with its strong suggestion of tainted blood and prostitution. (The tango was even associated with the white slave trade, largely by mothers keen to discourage their daughters from taking up the dance.) Argentine reaction can be imagined when the *Mercure de France* announced that a country 'which has such a national dance must really be a collective of monkeys', and that 'only somebody with the temperament of a negro can face such a spectacle without repugnance.'[39] The good impression achieved by Argentina's Centenary of Independence celebrations should have marked the country's coming of age as a state to be taken seriously; yet to Argentine diplomats this had been almost ruined by the tango. When the Argentine Ambassador in St Petersburg was presented to Tsar Nicholas II in 1913, the Tsar was heard simply to remark: 'Argentina . . . Oh yes, the tango!'

No wonder the dance was banned at the Argentine embassy in Paris. Enrique Larreta explained why: 'The tango in Buenos Aires is a dance exclusive to houses of ill-repute and bars of the lowest class. It is never danced in the best salons or by people of distinction. Tango music arouses truly disagreeable feelings in Argentine ears. I see no difference whatsoever between the tango as it is danced in elegant Parisian dance halls and that which is danced in the most base night spots in Buenos Aires.'[40]

This distaste for the tango was not confined to the Argentine Minister and members of his circle, but was also widespread among South American intellectuals and writers in Paris, many of whom were diplomats. The Mexican writer Alfonso Reyes, a second secretary in his country's embassy, wrote at the time of the tango's 'lamentable influence', and was still complaining a quarter of a century later that as a result of the tango, Parisians looked on South Americans as 'half monkeys and half parrots.'[41]

In Buenos Aires, *porteños* looked with a mixture of amusement and horror at what Paris was doing to their tango. In 1914 an article appeared on the subject in the magazine *Caras y caretas* (*above*). The headline reads: 'The Tango Caricaturized'.

***Opposite above:* Illustration from Manuel Galvez's novel *Historia de Arrabal*, 1922. This tells the tragic story of a prostitute, Roselinda, who stabs her lover to death on the orders of her pimp. Galvez later wrote: 'Nothing in my novel is invented. Everything was as I described it – the sadness, the poverty, the desolation, and the bitter poetry.'**

***Opposite below:* 'Tango delle Capinere' (Tango of the Black Caps), Italian music cover, 1928.**

Astonishment was expressed that Parisian and Roman salons should encourage a dance that was not only proletarian but – even worse – a creole mixture of gaucho and Andalucian Moorish. The newspaper *El Hogar* could only explain it on the grounds that 'Paris was so capricious in its fashions.'[42] The English language newspaper of Buenos Aires wrote: 'It is really impossible to give an exact description of what is to be seen in Paris. However, one can say that the Tango appears as a double belly dance whose lasciviousness is accentuated by exaggerated contortions. One would think one was seeing a couple of Arabs under the influence of opium.'[43]

Yet for Ricardo Güiraldes and other Argentine poets devoted to the *gaucho* tradition, the tango's earthy quality was its strength and fascination. The poet Silva Valdés said that it 'heated the blood and intoxicated' those who danced it.[44] Manuel Gálvez wrote of it as '*un perfume turbadoramente delicioso*'.[45] Few of them, however, were pleased by the tango's astonishing success in Europe. 'For the public in Paris or London', wrote José María Salaverría, 'the tango is nothing more than an exotic dance, vaguely sinful, that they dance for its sensual, perverted and slightly barbarian context.'[46]

Despite the furore it had caused, however, despite the condemnations of the clergy and the outrage of the great and good, despite the fact that it had left all Europe with a zest for dancing which has scarcely been paralleled, the tango became Frenchified in Paris, just as Richepin had predicted. It went back to Argentina looking much tamer than when it had left; and in this form, it became known as the '*tango a la francesa* – the Tango that Paris sent back to us after 1913'.[47]

The English writer H. G. Wells called 1913 'the year of the tango'. Its impact was felt not only on dancefloors but also in art, in music, in opera. In that year the Hungarian composer Franz Lehár featured the tango in his operetta *The Ideal Wife* (*opposite below*), which was rewritten after the war and presented in 1920 as *Tangokönigin* (Tango Queen). The tangoing couple *left* are also Hungarian, from a 1913 music cover 'Oly pompás a tango!' (The Tango Is So Wonderful!).

In Berlin the satirical weekly *Lustige Blätter* brought out a special album of tango drawings by German artists (*above*) – *Tango Rausch* (High on Tango). Even Russian Futurist poets were not immune: 'Tango with Cows' was the title given by Vladimir Mayakovsky to one of his poems (*above left*).

'El irresistible' (*above*), one of the earliest tango songs, was written in 1907 by an Italian immigrant to Buenos Aires, Lorenzo Logatti, and was arranged for piano and song by the composer Angel Villoldo. In 1913, when the tango craze had reached its zenith internationally, it was being danced to by the 'irresistible' Max Linder at the Alhambra and by Vernon and Irene Castle at Olympia and Deauville.

THE FIRST WORLD WAR ★AND AFTER★

In 1912, President Raymond Poincaré of France had confessed to Enrique Larreta, the Argentine Minister, that the French were indifferent to the threat of war. Two years later, in August 1914, when war fever suddenly gripped the country, Ricardo Güiraldes was shaken by the patriotic frenzy in Paris; he felt that all his respect for Europe had been destroyed. 'What a great word is civilization', he said bitterly, 'and what a crushing reality is instinct'.[48] On the outbreak of war Ruben Darío's magazine *Elegancias* had to close down since virtually its entire readership promptly left for home.

The exodus of South Americans accelerated during the German invasion of France. As the Government prepared to withdraw to Bordeaux, and Marshall Joffre tried to assemble troops for a counter-attack on the Marne, a large block of the Hispano-American community left Paris on the Irún train from the Gare d'Orléans. A number, however, stayed behind, having volunteered to fight for France: the artist José García Calderón died at Verdun two years later. In that autumn of 1914, even the tango was swept up for patriotic service. Back in Argentina, Eduardo Arolas rapidly composed the tango 'El Marne' during Joffe's great defensive battle.

The horrors of the Great War made leisure of every kind more urgent and febrile. Young men coming back on leave tried to forget the trenches in a few dizzy hours at a nightclub or dance hall, while the women who danced with them were only too aware that they might never see their partners again. In the fashionable London circle led by Lady Diana Cooper, the parties of the war years became known as the 'dances of death'.

It was during the war that the first films featuring the tango appeared, all made in Argentina. In 1915 came *Nobleza gaucha*, part of which was filmed in the Armenonville – the Buenos Aires cabaret club named after a well-known establishment in the Bois de Boulogne. The following year, the great Carlos Gardel featured in *Flor de Durazno*, a silent film in which he appeared dressed as a sailor. In 1917 came the first film devoted entirely to the tango – and appropriately called *El tango de la muerte*. After the war, Rudolph Valentino acted in a film adaptation of a novel by Blasco Ibáñez called *Los cuatro jinetes del apocalipsis* (The Four Horsemen of the Apocalypse). Valentino appeared as a gaucho in an Aztec poncho and Andalucian hat, and in the film he danced the first Hollywood tango.

By 1920, life had more or less returned to normal, and a new craze for dancing swept Paris. The Apollo and Magic-City dance halls were packed day and night, and by the following year the Argentines, richer than ever after the war, were flocking back to Paris. For Argentina, the war had brought considerable advantages, and its economic situation was transformed with a hefty balance of payments surplus – largely due to the millions of tins of bully beef consumed by the British and French armies (the French called it '*singe*', or monkey.)

The tango enjoyed a revival in France, as it did in England. The *orquestas típicas* in Paris included those of Francisco Canaro, Osvaldo Fresedo, and the Pizarro brothers (who were friends of Gardel's), playing in nightspots such as El Garrón and El Abasto. French law decreed that foreign musicians could

***Opposite:* Rudolph Valentino dances with Beatrice Domínguez in a scene from *The Four Horsemen of the Apocalypse* (1921), the film which catapulted him to fame. Valentino had previously worked as a dancer in night-clubs and in this scene he performed the first ever Hollywood tango, though his exaggerated style has never won the approval of real tango enthusiasts.**

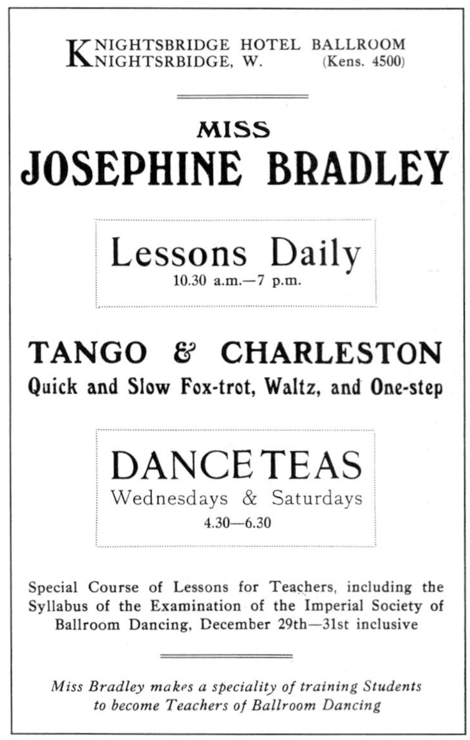
KNIGHTSBRIDGE HOTEL BALLROOM
KNIGHTSRBIDGE, W. (Kens. 4500)

MISS
JOSEPHINE BRADLEY

Lessons Daily
10.30 a.m.—7 p.m.

TANGO & CHARLESTON
Quick and Slow Fox-trot, Waltz, and One-step

DANCE TEAS
Wednesdays & Saturdays
4.30—6.30

Special Course of Lessons for Teachers, including the Syllabus of the Examination of the Imperial Society of Ballroom Dancing, December 29th—31st inclusive

Miss Bradley makes a speciality of training Students to become Teachers of Ballroom Dancing

In the mid-1920s, the tango enjoyed a revival in Europe. Miss Josephine Bradley offered lessons in both the tango and the newly popular Charleston (*above*).

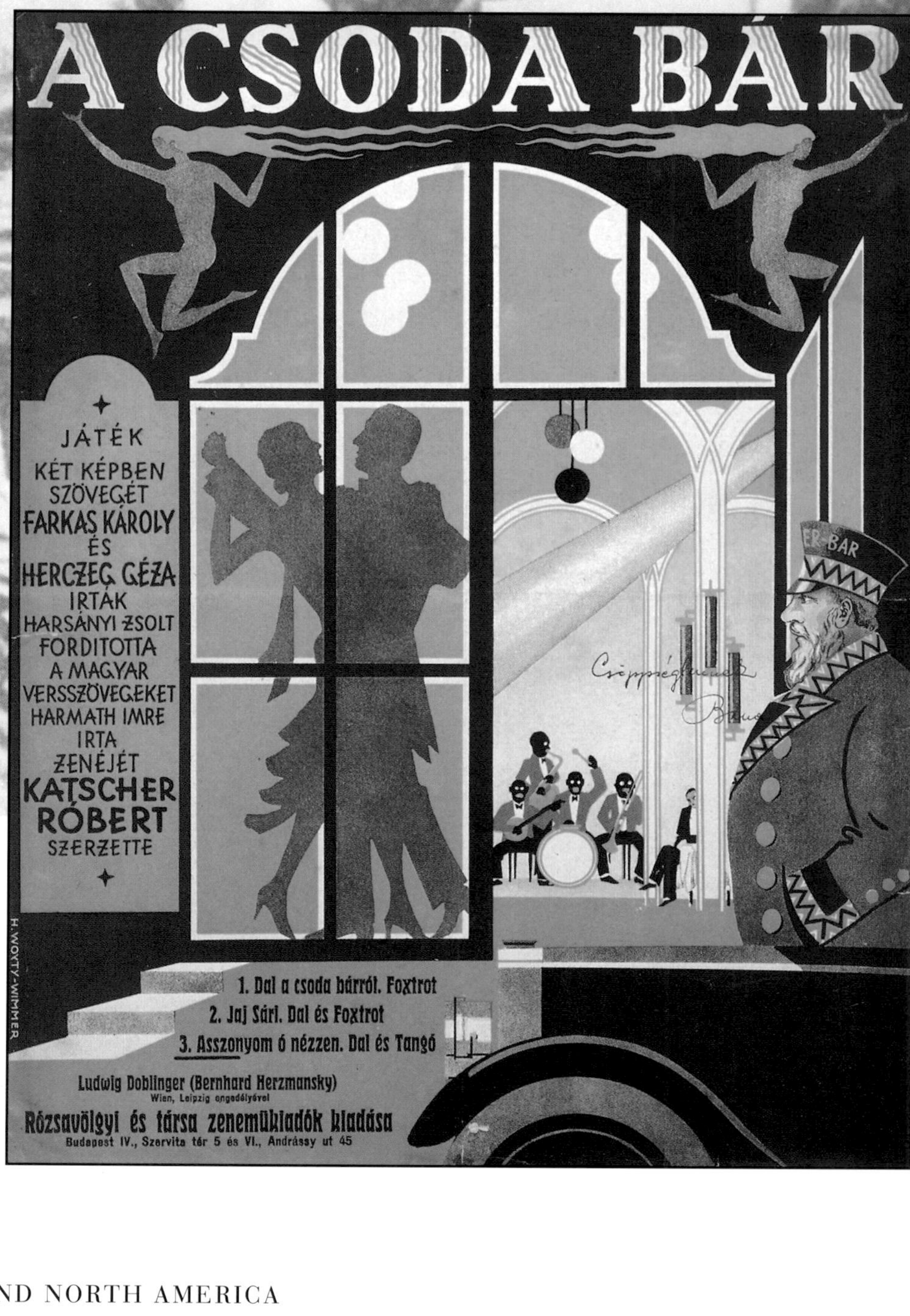

After the war the tango made a comeback across Europe, fastening its hold on much of Eastern Europe in the 1920s and 1930s.

Above: **Dancing in St Jean de Luz, near Biarritz, France, 1920s.**

Left: **Hungarian tango song from the play *A Csoda Bar* (The Miraculous Bar), 1930s.**

Above right: **Italian tango song 'Serenata malandrina' (Bewitching Serenade), 1929.**

Right: **Spanish tango 'Sparta', 1920s.**

Quintin Verdu's tango orchestra. Foreign musicians performing in Paris in the 1920s were compelled to wear national costume, which explains the loose tops, baggy trousers and neckerchiefs.

only perform in Paris in their national dress – so tango players were obliged to dress up as gauchos wearing baggy *bombacha* trousers. This suited dance-hall owners who, in their desire for publicity, wrote into contracts that the musicians had to make the journey from home already dressed in their gaucho costumes so as to attract as much attention as possible. The tango was also popular in Germany, where the singer Juan Llosas enjoyed a great success. He wrote and dedicated a tango to Greta Garbo, entitled 'Oh! Fraulein Greta!'

As time went on and other dances came into fashion, people began to forget all but the most basic steps of the tango and it was seen more in dance competitions than in nightclubs. By the 1930s, in Paris, it was rather out of date, but in Argentina it was entering the full flowering of its Golden Age.

★ **Pages 105–112: The origins of the tango were in the *arrabales,* where immigrants feuded, drank, played the card game *truco* and, above all, nurtured both the longings and wounded spirits of the New World. Carlos Gardel smiles from a café wall on pages 110–111. Lavalle Street, page 112, is lively both during the day and at night.**

Paddy
Smuggler

CAFÉ
TÉ
GRAN VISIR
BOEDO 510
T.E. 97-4763
Bs. As.
PINERAL
CITIBANK

Crush
250

OCEAN
AMBASSADOR
PARIS
PAPA
PALACIO
DE LA
PAPA

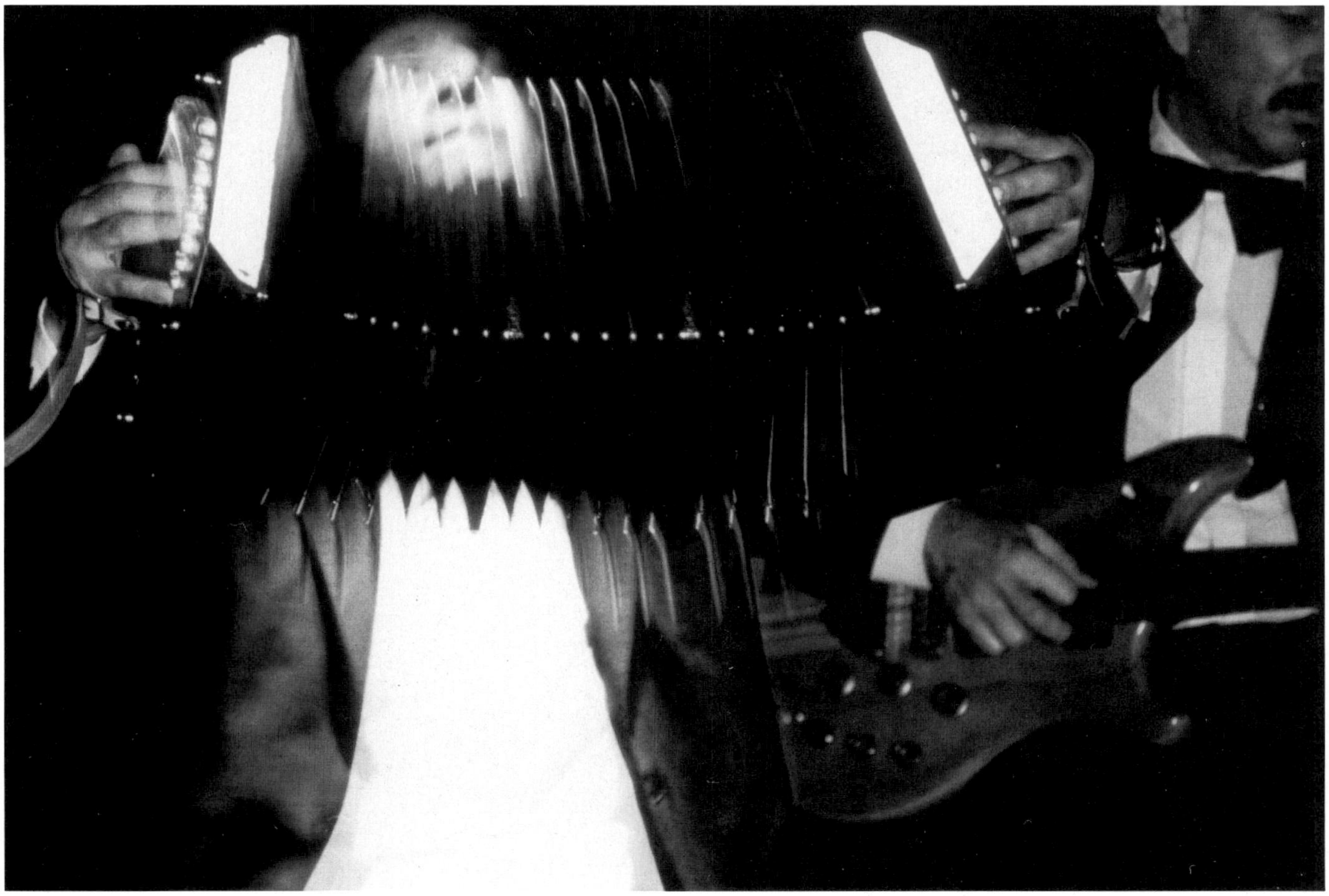

‘The bandoneon is a hellish instrument. It was made and developed in Germany, at a time when things were meant to last, a time when plastic didn’t exist. The materials were noble: wood, metal, leather, mother-of-pearl – they were all used in its construction.

For a bandoneonist, the instrument becomes one’s alter-ego – it is partly oneself, partly one’s wife. There’s even a homosexual element to it. One feels possessed and possessor, one caresses it, is aware of its temperature…’

Rodolfo Mederos, bandoneon player

‘When I walk around the city with my bandoneon case, when I get on a bus, I can see the surprise in the driver’s eyes. The case looks familiar, he knows it’s a bandoneon, but, in the hands of a woman… “No, it can't be.” Actually, this reaction makes me feel good. Also, when men look at me, they make me feel as if I’ve stolen something. What is a woman doing carrying that case? I like the look on the faces of the ticket collectors, the bus conductors. I put my bandoneon to one side and the bus driver says to me, “I used to play, I played with De Caro’s brother. I used to go to his house.” He’s steering and collecting tickets… There are a lot of bandoneon-playing bus drivers.’

Susana Ratcliff, bandoneon player

MARÍA SUSANA AZZI

THE GOLDEN AGE AND AFTER

1920S–1990S

★ THE TANGO RETURNS HOME ★

While the tango was conquering a large part of the outside world, its development in the country of its birth was little short of spectacular. By the 1920s it had gained acceptance at almost every level of Argentine society. It was a time when the country was enjoying a period of unprecedented prosperity and was still welcoming immigrants in huge numbers: during the 1920s two million arrived, mainly from Italy, Spain and France. In Buenos Aires tango venues multiplied in the Centre and spread rapidly to every district of the city. People flocked to bars, cafés, cinemas and theatres to listen to their favourite groups. Tango lovers who wanted to dance went out to what were called the *dancings* (dance halls), as well as to the somewhat more elegant *salones de baile* and cabarets. More and more dance venues sprang up every year.

One of the most famous tango centres was the Nacional café, next to the Nacional theatre in Corrientes Street. Set up in 1916 – a women's orchestra played on its opening night – the café was host to all the key figures of the tango for nearly four decades and was known as the Cathedral of the Tango.

The best tango bands performed at the cabarets, which mushroomed in the Centre in the 1920s. The influence of Paris is

Opposite: **Tango street party in Buenos Aires on 6 September 1936, the 400th anniversary of the founding of the city.**

Right: **Illustration from the cover of the tango 'De amor propio' (Vanity) by Juan Canaro, 1920s.**

After its gentrification in Paris the tango arrived back in Buenos Aires – now rendered acceptable to the upper classes. No longer the dance of the *compadritos*, it had become the smooth *tango de salón*. The picture *below* shows a couple dancing a tango in a Buenos Aires nightclub in 1924.

evident in their names: the Abbaye, Maxim, Montmartre, the Petit Parisien, the Pigall, the Tabarís and the Folies-Bergère. A connection with France was thought to add sophistication: 'I'm from Paris, you know,' was often a Buenos Aires prostitute's opening gambit, and prostitutes and madams often took French names. At this time the cabaret was the social and musical centre of Buenos Aires life. It was a microcosm of a society which, unlike Paris, was a melting pot. And whereas in Paris the tango was an intra-class phenomenon – men and women who danced the tango together belonged to the same social class – on Buenos Aires dancefloors class barriers disappeared. Society men,

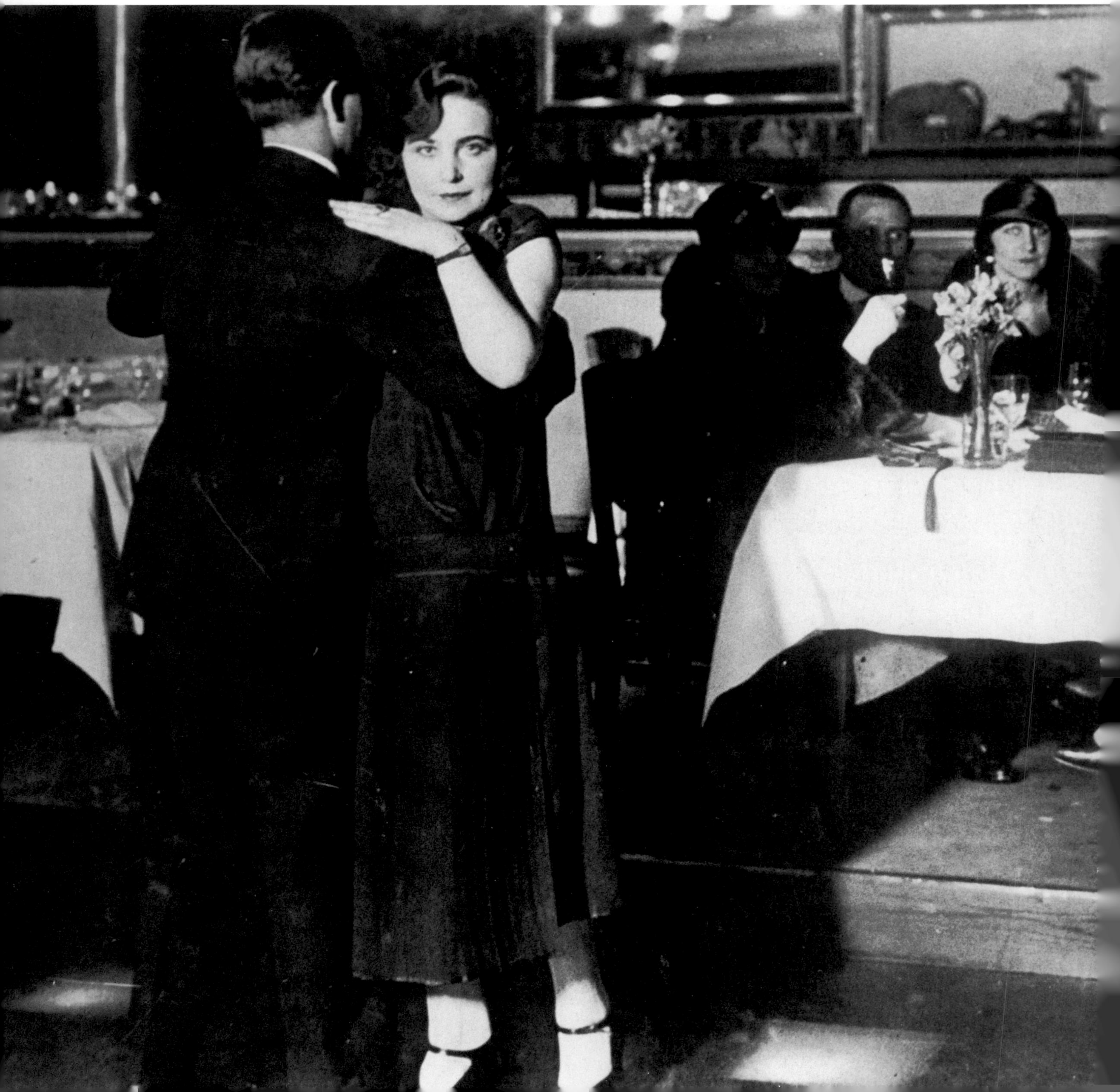

property owners and little rich boys took the floor with women of poor backgrounds, who were now, by virtue of their skill in the tango, transformed into glamorous cabaret dancers. Many tango lyrics reflect the character of the *milonguita* – the woman who was paid to dance with clients. Dazzled by jewels, silk, furs, champagne and the bright lights of Corrientes Street, she dreams of becoming rich and leaving behind the hard life of the *conventillo*. And perhaps those dreams were sometimes realized. Tania (Ana Luciana Devis), lifelong companion of the famous tango musician and lyricist Enrique Santos Discépolo, remembers the atmosphere of cabaret in the 1920s:

> The patrons were all men of leisure – they had never worked. They drank bottle after bottle of champagne and consumed vast quantities of caviar. They were nice, generous, but irresponsible people. It was not unknown for one of them to give a dancer a country house as a present. The nights passed slowly – they didn't have to rush off anywhere. Even love affairs where money changed hands were subject to a lengthy, patient ceremony: from the time the gentlemen approached the *milonguera*, plying her with drinks, four days would often pass before the adventure actually took place.[1]

Top: **The lyrics of 'Milonguita' (Cabaret Girl) were written by Samuel Linnig in a Buenos Aires restaurant in 1920. Legend has it that the real-life *milonguita* who inspired the song worked at the Pigall cabaret in Corrientes Street and died of tuberculosis at the age of 18.**

Above: **'Mentira' (Lie), 1932.**

Left: **'Picardía' (Wantonness) by Samuel Castriota, 1930.**

Despite the new Paris-led gentrification of the tango, however, it retained its association with the brothel and was still seen as the dance of prostitution, which of course it was. Men who wished to dance the tango with the most desirable prostitutes had to be skilled dancers. They practised among themselves during the week and there was great competition and rivalry. The ability to dance the tango well was viewed as a sign of masculinity – a macho credential. The dance was a prelude to sex, which took place after about three tangos. Some brothels hired a trio or a quartet to accompany the dancers, though more modest establishments had to make do with a pianola.

Illegal brothels in Buenos Aires were often protected by the patronage of affluent politicians, whose representatives would be paid every week by both the prostitutes and the madams. On Mondays the prostitutes had a day off; they were allowed to go out shopping or to the hairdresser. Their public behaviour was strictly regulated – provocative behaviour in the street was forbidden. Every week the municipal medical staff visited the brothels and examined the women in order to protect the local men from venereal disease, but the system was far from perfect – several tango musicians died syphilitic, some of them blind. Legal prostitution was eventually abolished in Buenos Aires in 1936.[2]

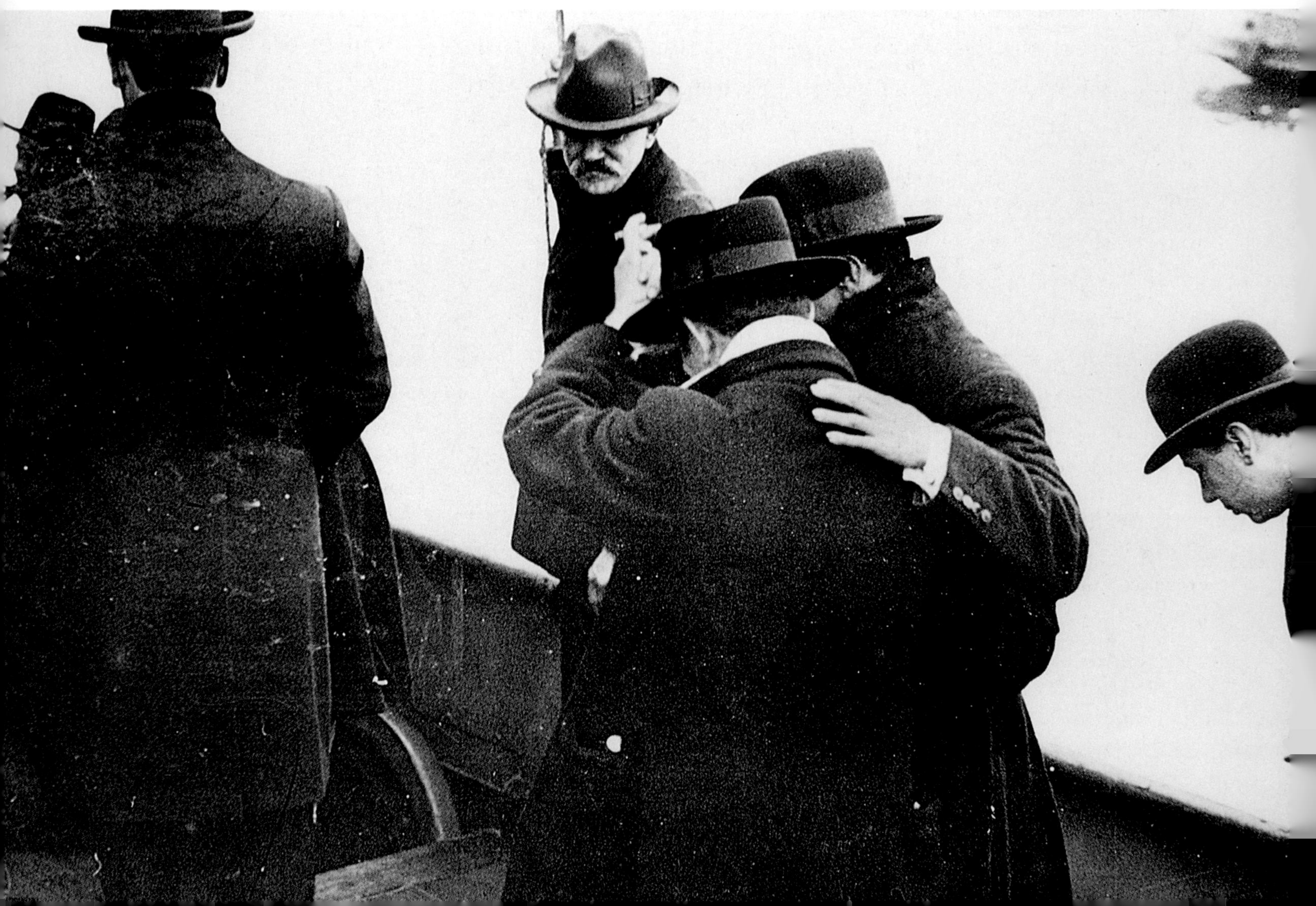

A group of male tango dancers make their way to a dance in the neighbourhood of La Boca in 1926. This rundown waterfront *barrio*, south of the Centre, was home to most of the Genoese immigrants – it was a kind of Little Italy.

The man in the centre, turning to watch the impromptu sidewalk display, is Juan Filiberti, known as Mascarilla (Little Mask), one of the best and most admired tango dancers of his district. He was the father of the well-known tango musician and composer Juan de Dios Filiberto, who is shown on page 120.

The 1920s saw an aesthetic and technical evolution both in the composition and performance of tango music. Among tango musicians morale was high – the then president of Argentina, Marcelo T. de Alvear, was a strong supporter of the tango – and musicians were motivated to struggle for social advancement of the genre. An element of competition among themselves speeded up the creative process. The result was a division of the tango into two schools, each with its own musical structure and style: the 'evolutionary' school and the 'traditional' school.

The members of the 'evolutionary' school were committed to the improvement of the tango through the study of melody, harmony and interpretative techniques, a process which they felt sure would result in a more complex and refined tango. Among the 'evolutionists' were Julio De Caro, Osvaldo Fresedo, Juan Carlos Cobián, Pedro Maffia and Cayetano Puglisi. The 'traditional' school stressed rhythm, and produced an infinitely more danceable tango. Its members included Roberto Firpo, Francisco Canaro, Francisco Lomuto, Anselmo Aieta, Edgardo Donato, Roberto Zerrillo and Juan de Dios Filiberto. The difference between the two schools lay not only in the interpretation but also in the number of musicians featuring in the ensembles.

Julio De Caro and his sextet, 1926. *Left to right:* José Nieso (violin), Armando Blasco (bandoneon), Vicente Sciarreta (double-bass), Francisco De Caro (piano), Julio De Caro (violin cornet), Pedro Laurenz (bandoneon).

De Caro was a leading member of the 'evolutionary' school of the tango, and his 1920s sextet was widely thought to be the finest band of the period.

The violin cornet that he is playing here, which became his trademark, was given to him in 1925 by the Victor Talking Machine Company, at the suggestion of the bandleader Paul Whiteman.

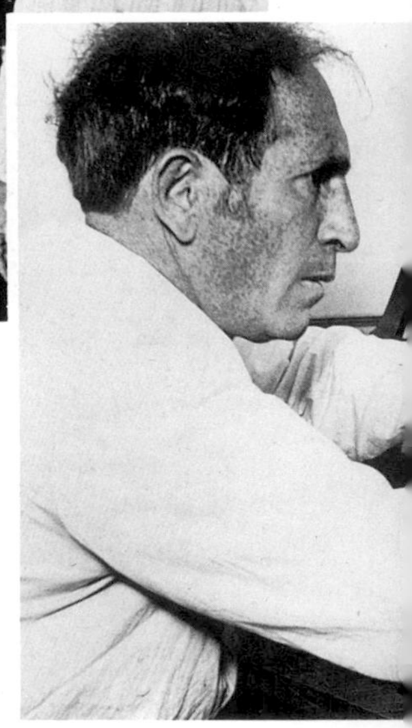

***Above:* The orchestra of the 'traditionalist' bandleader Juan de Dios Filiberto – double the size of the classic tango sextet. Filiberto is shown seated far right. *Inset right:* Filiberto composing at the piano.**

Filiberto was born in a *conventillo* in the *barrio* of La Boca. As a child he earned money as a shoeshine boy and street vendor before beginning work as a carpenter in the Mihanovich Shipyard. He was taught the rudiments of music by a fellow carpenter and later studied with several musicians. His attempts to master the piano were hampered by the fact that his hands had been deformed by carpentry.

Filiberto composed his first tango songs in 1915. One of his most famous tangos is 'Malevaje' (Underworld). He and his orchestra made numerous recordings.

The 'evolutionary' bands held to the classic tango sextet of two bandoneons, two violins, double-bass and piano, whereas the 'traditionalists' added three or four bandoneons and three or four violins. Other instruments introduced into the ensembles by traditionalist bandleaders included clarinet, drum, trumpet and *cornet-à-piston*.

By this time the advent of the microphone had made its impact on tango bands. In the pre-microphone years, bands performing at carnival balls had to be enlarged in order for the sound to reach all the dancers. In 1917 and 1918, for example, the bands of Roberto Firpo (1884-1969) and Francisco Canaro (1884-1964) had performed jointly for carnival balls and Canaro's orchestra alone numbered thirteen musicians. For the 1921 carnival Canaro presented a huge ensemble, featuring 12 bandoneons, 12 violins, 2 cellos, 2 double-basses, 2 pianos, 1 flute and 1 clarinet. But by the early 1920s such large ensembles were highly unusual.

Additional encouragement was given to tango musicians at this period by the setting up of tango music contests, the most important being those that were sponsored by the Disco Nacional Odeón from 1924 to 1930. The finest composers and poets presented their work, which was then judged by the members of the audience. The prize-winning compositions were made into records and the entire contest proceedings were broadcast.

The very best tango musicians were greatly in demand as accompanists to the silent movies of the time. Initially the accompaniment consisted just of piano. Good tango pianists were few and far between and cinemas paid well to attract the best: even the most modest cinema had its pianist. Between 1925 and 1930 the *sextetos típicos* took over, with occasional trios and quartets. People often went to the cinema every day to listen to their favourite musicians. The advent of sound – the first sound film in Spanish, *La divina dama*, premiered at the Gran Splendid cinema in Buenos Aires on 12 June 1929 – was greatly to reduce employment opportunities for both tango orchestras and sextets.

Although most tango musicians were male, there were some notable exceptions. When Paquita Bernardo presented her sextet in 1921 on the balcony of the Domínguez bar in Corrientes Street, the crowd that gathered was so huge that traffic had to be diverted. Paquita was the first professional female bandoneon player – Carlos Gardel called her 'the only woman who has mastered the macho character of the bandoneon'.

Above: Orquesta típica La Porteñita, 1933. From 1920 to the early 1930s women's orchestras performed in _confiterías_, cafés and bars and also for weddings, parties and dances. Sadly, they were never recorded.

***Below:* The *orquesta típica* of Roberto Firpo at the Ambassadeurs cabaret, 1936. Firpo is shown *left*, conducting.**

CARLOS GARDEL ★AND THE TANGO SONG★

Charles Romuald Gardes, who was to become known as Carlos Gardel, the most famous and best-loved tango singer of the twentieth century, arrived in Buenos Aires on 9 March 1893 on board the ship *Dom Pedro*. He was two years old. Born in Toulouse, France, on 11 December 1890, he was the illegitimate son of Berthe Gardes, later known to Argentines as Doña Berta. His father, Paul Lasserre, was a married businessman.[3]

On their arrival in Buenos Aires, Gardel's mother rented a room and began work ironing clothes. Carlos, who was soon given his *porteño* nickname El Francesito, went from one school to another and spent his teenage years

Carlos Gardel was the tango's greatest folk hero. To many millions of Latin Americans he is one of the authentic superstars of the 20th century. Born poor and illegitimate in Toulouse, France, on 11 December 1890, he was brought to Buenos Aires by his mother at the age of two, and later became the most famous tango singer of all time. For *porteños*, he represents the ideal man, personifying the rise of the tango itself from its roots in the *arrabal* to the heights of fashionable society.

Blessed with a remarkably beautiful baritone voice, Gardel was already a famous singer in Argentina before he turned his attention to the tango song, but it was he who established the new form in the public taste. This photograph was taken in the 1930s.

working at a number of ephemeral jobs – assistant to a cardboard maker, watchmaker's apprentice and typographer. He also wandered far from home.

He was fascinated by theatre and went as often as he could – mainly to opera, which has always been popular in Buenos Aires. He was eventually employed by Luis Ghiglione, the most famous turn-of-the-century *claqueur*, as part of the *claque* (a hired party, paid to applaud), and possibly on stage in secondary roles. Getting to know opera singers certainly influenced Gardel's own singing. He confessed later: 'I often entertained my co-workers in the style of Caruso or Titta Ruffo.' Legend has it that Ruffo himself once overheard a Gardel imitation and left his dressing room to enquire the name of the singer.

Between 1914 and 1925 the Gardel-Razzano Duo (Gardel, *left*; Razzano, *right*) was one of the most popular acts on the Argentine variety stage. Specializing in folk songs or songs written in the folk tradition, the duo performed in theatres, cinemas, cabarets and on the radio. In all, they made more than 100 recordings. The duo broke up in 1925.

The other great influence on Gardel were the *payadores* – the itinerant folk-singers who improvised words to their own guitar accompaniment. He was friendly with many of them. He met José Bettinoti and Gabino Ezeiza when they were at the peak of their careers and also got to know Arturo de Nava, whose song 'El carretero' (The Driver) he would make hugely popular in Paris years later. Gardel was not himself an improviser but he became adept at singing the 'creole' repertoire of folk songs – helped by his remarkably expressive baritone voice. Gardel's appearances as a rising folk-singer in the more modest *barrios* of Buenos Aires won him the affectionate nickname of El Morocho (roughly translated as The Swarthy One). Sometime in 1911, El Morocho met José Razzano (1887-1960), otherwise known as El Oriental.[4] Two years later, after a period of singing together as part of both a trio and a quartet, the two were to form the Gardel-Razzano Duo and embark on what would prove to be an enormously successful career.

Their first big break came in December 1913. One night in the Avenida de Mayo, Razzano bumped into Francisco Taurel, a wealthy man-about-town, who invited him to sing for a late-night party. Razzano suggested that he bring Gardel along. At the time Gardel did not own a guitar (he was hard up and had probably pawned it) so he borrowed one from a friend. The party started at the elegant Confitería Perú and included a senator, the provincial chief of police and the Chilean author of the popular song 'Ay, ay, ay'. After a few drinks they moved on to Madame Jeanne's (a brothel run by one of Buenos Aires's most famous madams, who was married to a Corsican immigrant who made his living managing brothels). Dinner was served and after midnight the whole party adjourned to the newly fashionable Armenonville cabaret. This two-storey building, named after the famous cabaret in the Bois de Boulogne in Paris, had a small stage, a dance hall and tables on the first floor and rooms on the second floor. In one of these rooms Gardel and Razzano continued to entertain their select audience. Champagne flowed. Within minutes a crowd had gathered in the corridor to listen to the singing. Their response was so enthusiastic that the owners of the cabaret called Razzano down to their office and offered the duo a contract for 70 pesos. Razzano returned to tell Gardel. '70 pesos a month or every two weeks?' asked Gardel. Razzano went back down and returned with the answer: '70 pesos a night!' 'For that', said Gardel, 'we will also wash the dishes!'

The following year the duo performed in Buenos Aires theatres and in Córdoba and Rosario. In 1915 they premiered at Montevideo and then in Brazil with a touring theatre company. On board the ship that took them to Brazil they met Enrico Caruso, who was returning to Europe after very successful and profitable performances in Argentina and Uruguay. On their return to Buenos Aires Gardel was out of action for a month, suffering from a gunshot wound received after a quarrel in a dance hall. The bullet was never removed, but after a short period of convalescence, the duo began performing once again, now accompanied on the guitar by José Ricardo (El Negro Ricardo: he was African-Argentine).

Gardel's first recordings (of folk songs) had been made in 1912 or 1913. But the year 1917 was to prove crucial for both him and the tango song. Firstly, he and Razzano were given a contract by the Nacional recording company, an affiliate of Odeon (though the company soon came to prefer Gardel's voice to Razzano's, which they found harsh and high pitched). And secondly, it was the year in which Gardel first sang and then recorded Pascual Contursi's lyrics to the tango 'Lita', by Samuel Castriota, which Gardel renamed 'Mi noche triste' (My Sorrowful Night).

The 1920s and early 1930s brought Gardel one success after another. In August 1924, the Gardel-Razzano Duo sang at the magnificent Huetel estancia, in the province of Buenos Aires, in honour of the Prince of Wales and the Maharajah of Kapurthala – the prince accompanied the singers enthusiastically on his ukulele. A few weeks later Gardel discontinued his artistic association with Razzano, who suffered a throat condition, and began an independent career as a tango singer with guitar accompaniment. The great majority of his recordings (nine hundred or so songs) are in this form.

Gardel performed in Argentina, Uruguay, Spain and France. In Paris in 1929 he took part in the 'Bal des Petits Lits Blancs', the biggest charity gala in the Paris social calendar, and made an appearance, as stars traditionally did, on the Pont d'Argent, along with his compatriot, the bandleader Osvaldo Fresedo. In Nice in 1931 he met and spent time with Charlie Chaplin. He starred in seven films, all for Paramount – three in France and four in the USA. From 1932 on, both the lyrics of his songs and the scripts of his films were written by the talented lyricist Alfredo Le Pera. It was a partnership that created many classic songs. In April 1935 he began a tour of the Caribbean for Paramount and RCA Victor, travelling eventually to Puerto Rico, Caracas, Maracaibo, Barranquilla, Cartagena, Medellín and Bogotá. On 24 June the aeroplane taking him to Cali collided with another plane on the airfield at

***Tango Bar*, directed by John Reinhardt in 1935, was the last of Carlos Gardel's US-made movies. A lighthearted comedy, it tells the story of an impoverished Argentine who tries to make his fortune by opening a tango bar in Barcelona. The Soleil Cinema in Corrientes Avenue, Buenos Aires, showed the film in 1936 (*below*).**

Medellín, killing both him and Le Pera. Gardel's body eventually arrived in Buenos Aires by ship in February 1936. On the day of his funeral tens of thousands of fans thronged the streets of the city to follow his hearse to the cemetery.

Alongside his tomb stands a bronze statue, known as 'the bronze that smiles'. Day after day admirers and pilgrims gather round it. Between its fingers a cigarette is nearly always kept alight – rather in the same way as a lighted candle might be kept burning in front of a statue of the Virgin Mary. For there is unquestionably a quasi-religious dimension to the worship of Carlos Gardel. The fiftieth anniversary of his death (1985), and the centenary of his birth (1990) were extensively commemorated all around Latin America. In some Argentine homes – not to mention on taxis and buses – his picture is often displayed next to pictures of saints. For many Argentines their hero will never die; 'Gardel', they say, 'sings better every day.'

Above: **Carlos Gardel on his successful Caribbean tour. On 24 June 1935, the plane preparing to take him on the last lap of the tour collided with another plane at Medellín, killing both Gardel and his lyricist Alfredo Le Pera. Gardel's admirers were shocked and griefstricken – several committed suicide. On the day of his funeral, the streets of Buenos Aires overflowed with mourners following his hearse to Chacarita Cemetery.**

The lifesize statue erected to his memory in the cemetery – 'the bronze that smiles' – is lovingly cared for by his admirers (*opposite*). The plaques attached to the monument come from tango clubs all over the world. The Gardel myth is maintained by, among other things, a never-ending supply of pictures (*right*) and the cigarette often burning between the statue's fingers.

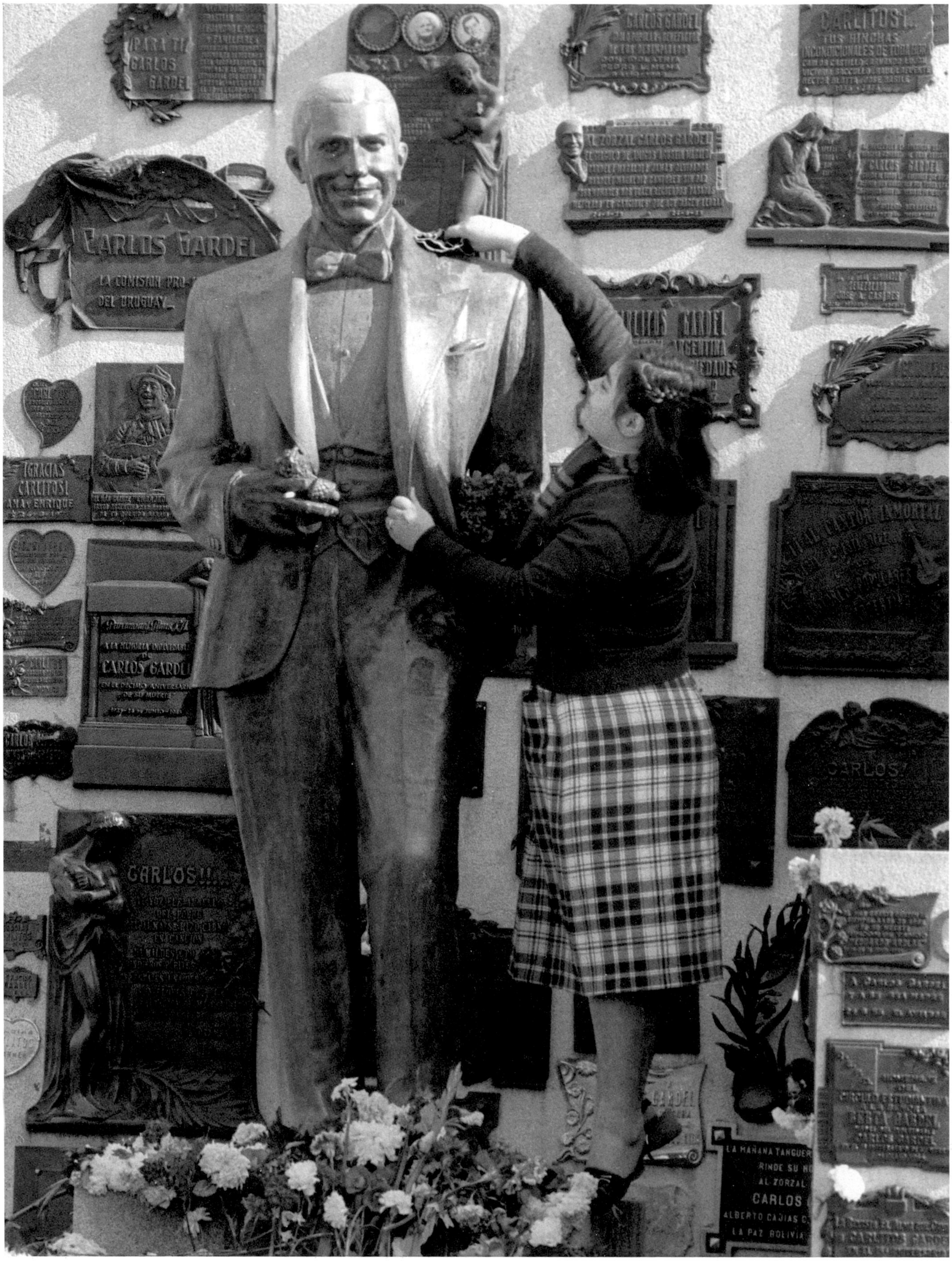
¡PARA TI CARLOS GARDEL
CARLOS GARDEL
CARLITOS!
TUS HINCHAS
AL ZORZAL CARLOS GARDEL
CARLOS GARDEL
LA COMISION PRO-
DEL URUGUAY
¡GRACIAS CARLITOS!
ANA Y ENRIQUE
CARLOS GARDEL
CARLOS!!!
CARLOS!
LA MAÑANA TANGUERA
RINDE SU
AL ZORZAL
CARLOS
LA PAZ BOLIVIA

The style of tango singing invented by Gardel has been followed by male and female singers ever since. In the 1920s, like most tango singers, Gardel sang to a guitar accompaniment rather than with an orchestra. This was also true of his only near-rivals among men singers, Ignacio Corsini and Agustín Magaldi. Singers who sang as part of a band – Roberto Díaz was taken on in 1924 by Francisco Canaro and, soon after, Roberto Ray began singing with Osvaldo Fresedo – were known as *estribillistas* or *chansonniers*. They played a very secondary role and sang only the refrain of the song.

By the early to mid-1930s, the practice of incorporating a singer was less common, and it was not until the late 1930s that the singer became a vital and essential component of tango orchestras. The bridge between the *estribillista* of the twenties and the *cantor de orquesta* of the forties was Francisco Fiorentino (1905-55), who joined the band of Aníbal Troilo in 1937 and remained with it until 1944. 'Fiore' had been *estribillista* for Juan Carlos Cobián but he moved easily from singing fragments of the song to singing the song in its entirety. With Troilo and Fiorentino the integration of band and singer was complete – theirs was a classic partnership.

In the 1940s the singer became the key to a band's success. *Tangueros* would follow bands if they admired the combination of bandleader and singer. At this time people danced to the sung tango; though if they liked the singer, they would often stop dancing to listen. Some singers in their turn respected the dancers – they would take account of the pauses in the dance and the tempo. Edmundo Rivero (1911-86), one of the few successful basses in the tradition, joined Troilo's band in 1947. He had previously been a guitarist, accompanying various singers, and his voice met with some resistance initially because the 1940s audience was more used to tenors. Like Gardel, Rivero was particular about his choice of songs – he favoured Enrique Santos Discépolo above other lyricists and specialized in singing tangos with a strong *lunfardo* content. Other notable combinations in the 1940s were Roberto Chanel and Osvaldo Pugliese, Alberto Marino and Aníbal Troilo, Floreal Ruiz and Aníbal Troilo, and Alberto Castillo and Ricardo Tanturi. Roberto Rufino began singing with Carlos Di Sarli in 1938 and joined the band of Francini-Pontier in 1947. He was particularly skilled at conveying the drama of the song and was admired by many younger singers.

Roberto Goyeneche (1926-94), who was of the generation after Rufino, made more than one hundred records over his forty-year career (he died in 1994) and recorded enduring hits such as 'La ultima curda' (The Last Binge), 'Garúa' (Mist) and 'María'. His fans called him El Polaco (The Pole) because of his fair skin and blond hair. From 1956 to 1964, he sang with Troilo's orchestra, a worthy successor to Rivero and Fiorentino. The most recent singer to attain stardom (from the late 1960s onwards) has been Susana Rinaldi, whose measured reading of classic songs is highly distinctive.

In the 1940s the singer contributed greatly to a band's success. One of the classic bandleader/singer partnerships was that of Ricardo Tanturi and Alberto Castillo. Castillo joined Tanturi's orchestra, Los Indios (The Indians), in 1939 and remained until 1944. Tanturi is shown *top centre* (conducting) and Castillo *centre left*. Castillo is still singing in the 1990s and is especially popular with *porteños*.

CARLOS GARDEL · VICENTE PADULA · TRINI RAMOS
DEPOSITO LEGAL M. 5566-1959
tango en Broadway

Carlos Gardel's films further increased his legendary fame in the Spanish-speaking world. They were immensely popular in the 1930s, so much so that audiences sometimes insisted on having the reels rewound in order to hear the songs for a second time. *Tango Bar* (*above left*) was Gardel's last movie. It was not released until after his death in 1935. A song from the film, 'Por una cabeza' (By a Head), *left*, became an immediate hit.

Opposite: Tango en Broadway, 1934.

Above: El día que me quieras, 1935.

'La cumparsita' (The Little Carnival Procession) is the most famous tango of all time. It is to the tango what the 'Blue Danube' is to the waltz. Written around 1917 by the Uruguayan Gerardo Hernán Matos Rodríguez as a marching tune for the student federation to which he belonged, it was turned into a tango by the bandleader Roberto Firpo. In 1924 lyrics by Pascual Contursi and Enrique Pedro Maroni were added and the song was recorded by Carlos Gardel, with guitar accompaniment.

There are approximately 200 versions of 'La cumparsita'. This edition (*right*) was published in Milan in 1927.

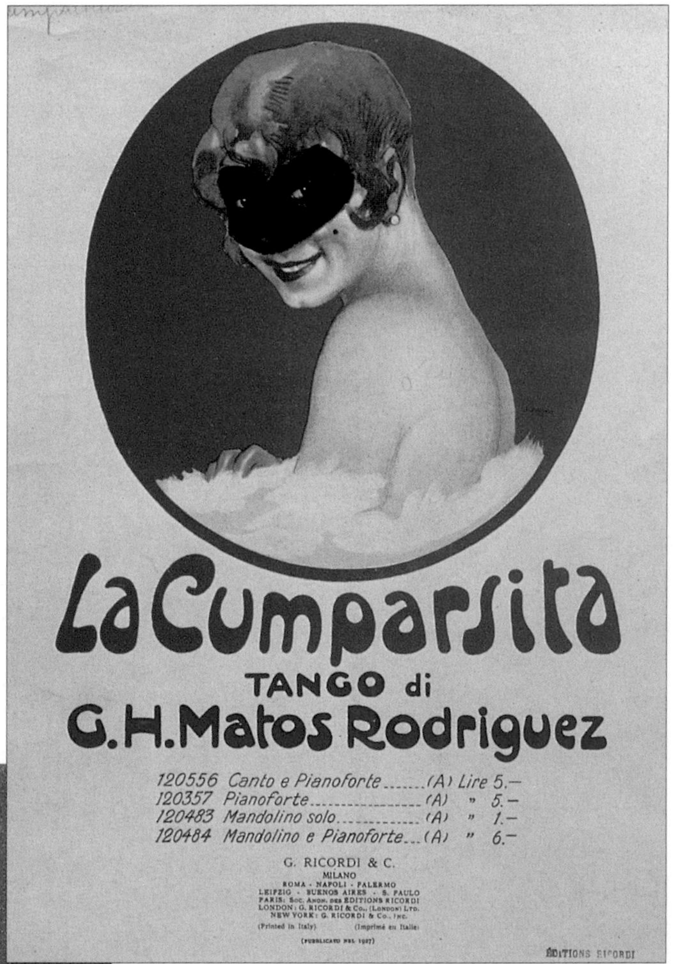

The song 'Mal de amor' (Lovesickness) (*left*), by the Spanish pianist and composer José Sentis, was very popular in Europe in the 1920s. Sentis had played the piano – often tangos – in Paris salons in the 1910s and had met many visiting Argentines, including the writer and playboy Ricardo Güiraldes. He also gave lessons in tango dancing. Sentis wrote some of Carlos Gardel's songs in the movie *Melodía de arrabal* and met Gardel in France during the shooting of the film.

Opposite above: 'Vida perdida' (Lost Life), music by J. Nirvassed, Paris, 1931.

'El gringo' (*right*) was a very early tango for piano, written by René Lyaz around 1900. In the Argentine context, 'gringo' means a foreigner, a European immigrant – mainly Italian. The early 'creole' tango was transformed by gringos, though the result, the *tango agringado*, was initially resisted by large sections of the Buenos Aires population.

Four of the tango's greatest stars are assembled *below*. The date is 16 February 1944; the occasion is the testing of the first Argentine-made bandoneon at the headquarters of the Argentine Society of Composers and Performers. Far left is Luis Mariani, the bandoneon manufacturer; then, left to right: José Razzano, of the legendary Gardel-Razzano duo; Aníbal Troilo ('The Fat Man'), the finest bandoneon player of all time; Enrique Santos Discépolo, the supreme tango lyricist; and the notable bandleader Francisco Canaro. The bandoneon, which is believed to have been brought to Buenos Aires by German sailors, has always been the chief instrument of the tango. Whereas the guitar is associated with the countryside, the bandoneon has entirely urban associations.

The illustration *opposite below* is by the poet Oliveiro Girondo and appears in his 1922 collection, *Veinte poemas para ser leídos en el tranvía* (Twenty Poems to be Read on the Tram).

In general, the world of the tango lyric is a hostile one, in which illusions are shattered and the prevailing emotions are necessarily pessimistic. Borges disliked this aspect of the tango: he preferred the very early lyrics, which he described as 'bold and gay'. He criticized the later tangos for 'indulging in loud self-pity while shamelessly rejoicing in the misfortunes of others'.[6]

Whether this is true or not – and Borges' opinions on the tango grew wayward in his later years – throughout much of the twentieth century, and particularly in the early decades, the tango provided a common platform for the many nationalities which found themselves in the melting pot of Buenos Aires. Even today many Argentines maintain that tango lyrics have helped them crystallize, understand and cope with feelings of loss and helplessness. And the songs themselves have become fully established as part of the modern culture of Latin America.

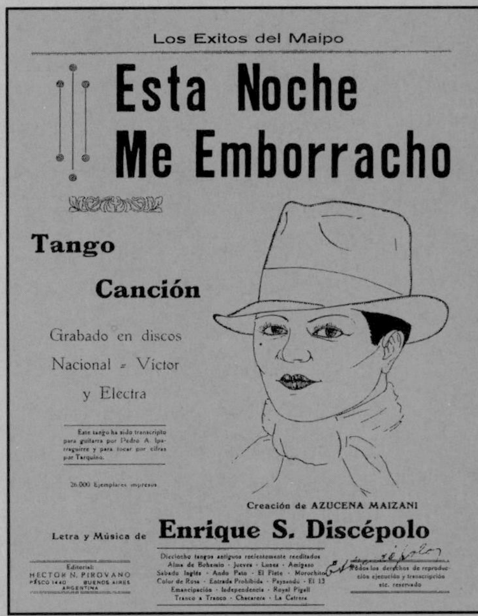

Discépolo, the finest tango lyricist of his generation, wrote both 'Malevaje' (*opposite above*) and 'Esta noche me emborracho' (*above*) in 1928. Shortly after, 'Esta noche...' (Tonight I'm Getting Drunk) was banned on the radio – a fate that was to befall many of Discépolo's bitter lyrics.

'Malevaje' (Underworld) is somewhat more lighthearted. Its hoodlum hero protests that he is forfeiting his reputation in the underworld because he has been softened by love for a woman: 'Not a trace is left', he complains, 'of my wild and wicked ways.' 'Malevaje' was sung for the first time by Azucena Maizani on the balcony of Juan de Dios Filiberto's house in La Boca on 21 September 1929, with Filiberto, the tango's composer, accompanying on the piano.

★ WOMEN SINGERS ★

Women singers have made a major contribution to the tango song. Mercedes Simone (1904-90), one of the best-known *cancionistas*, is shown *below* performing for Radio Splendid in Buenos Aires, around 1928. One of the accompanists is her husband Pablo Rodríguez, *left*. The child is her son, who died soon after the photograph was taken. Simone was a versatile singer, able to convey a range of tango moods. She had an enormously successful career, touring Latin America extensively and appearing in films and plays.

It is reported that around 1910 the Uruguayan singer Lola Candales asked the musician Enrique Saborido: 'Please write a tango that may be sung in the presence of women without making them blush.'[7] Saborido passed the request on to Angel Villoldo, who came up with 'La morocha'. Soon other male lyricists were also writing tangos especially for women.

The maleness of the tango is well known. Most tango lyrics have been written by men, and the 'ego' – the implicit singer – is almost always male. Many tango singers have been women, but when a woman sings the tango, she usually sings lyrics written by a man with a male singer in mind, and expresses lyrically the emotions of a male protagonist and a male's world-view. When Manolita Poli, for example, sang 'Mi noche triste' in 1918, the audience paid no attention to the fact that the lyrics were more appropriate for a man than for a woman. Out of respect for the author and his verse, the gender of the words (and the subject matter of the lyrics) were usually left unchanged. To change the words would also have meant changing the rhyme and rhythm. There are some exceptions – women who have been brave enough to re-gender

the lyrics – but the woman tango singer more often than not inhabits the persona of a male subject. This includes some *cancionistas* who dressed as men, such as Azucena Maizani (1902-70), fondly nicknamed La Ñata Gaucha (The Snubnosed Gaucha) and Mercedes Simone. In the early days cross-dressed performance was not unusual. (It should be noted too that very occasionally men sang the part of women. Carlos Gardel sang 'La morocha', which had been written for Lola Candales, and it was not unknown for an actor to take the part of a woman in a film.)[8]

There are also exceptions to the rule that tango lyrics have been written by men. María Luisa Carnelli (1898-1987) was one of the first and most prolific tango lyricists but because of parental disapproval she wrote pseudonymously, signing her lyrics with male names such as Luis Mario or Mario Castro – so successfully that her gender was entirely hidden. In those days 'decent' families strongly opposed the involvement of their children with this still marginal genre. Carnelli was a writer, poet and journalist as well as a tango lyricist. She wrote *lunfardo* tangos such as 'Cuando llora la milonga' (When the Milonga Weeps); 'Se va la vida' ('Life Goes By', which Azucena Maizani made into a hit in Spain); 'El malevo' (The Hoodlum) and 'Linyera' (The Vagabond).

In the 1930s Maizani was the leading *cancionista*. Born in 1902, she came from a poor family and had worked as a dressmaker and shirt-maker. In the district of the Abasto, where she lived, she was able to hear the Gardel-Razzano Duo as well as the best tango bands of the time, such as Canaro's and Firpo's. In 1923 the tango musician Enrique Delfino asked her to premiere his tango 'Padre nuestro' (Our Father) at the Nacional theatre. The lyrics were just right for a woman: 'Why', asks the singer, 'didn't you remember to return?/You said "See you later" and gave me a kiss/but . . . you never came back.'

The audience liked this tango so much that they demanded five encores. It was a performance that marked a turning point for female singers. Rosita Quiroga found fame in the same year, and was followed later by Libertad Lamarque, Mercedes Simone, Tita Merello, Tania, Sofía Bozán and Ada Falcón. All made many recordings, and, in the 1930s, just like Gardel, they starred in movies, which brought them both fame and fortune.

Maizani's career blossomed from 1923 on. She was given a contract by the Nacional theatre and went on to work also for radio and to make films and records. She wrote the music for numerous tangos, including 'La canción de Buenos Aires' (Song of Buenos Aires); 'Pero yo sé' (But I Know); 'Dejáme

Azucena Maizani was perhaps the most popular of all *cancionistas*. She started her career in 1920 with Francisco Canaro's orchestra at the Pigall cabaret. It was on her first night there that Canaro gave her the nickname Azabache (Jet) because of her black hair.

In 1923, she met the composer and conductor Enrique Delfino, who chose her to sing his famous tango 'Padre nuestro' (Our Father) at the Nacional theatre – she recorded the song in 1924.

It was through Maizani that Enrique Santos Discépolo first achieved recognition. She premiered both 'Esta noche me emborracho' (Tonight I'm Getting Drunk) and 'Malevaje' (Underworld).

In 1935, Maizani was given a second nickname, by Mercedes Simone, La Ñata Gaucha (The Snubnosed Gaucha). She is shown here dressed in gaucho costume.

Maria de Buenos Aires
de Astor Piazzola y Horacio Ferrer
SALA PLANETA ~ SUIPACHA 927

Susana Rinaldi, shown *left* performing in a Buenos Aires theatre in 1978, is known as La Tana Rinaldi (Italian Rinaldi). She is one of the most popular tango singers of recent years and has won acclaim in Paris as well as in her native Buenos Aires. Her repertoire is vast, ranging from Gardel and Troilo to Pugliese and Piazzolla.

María de Buenos Aires is a 'little opera' written in 1968 as the first collaboration between the avant-garde tango composer Astor Piazzolla and the poet Horacio Ferrer. The score is inspired by the traditional music of Buenos Aires – tango, creole waltz and milonga – which is recreated using the resources of contemporary music. The libretto incorporates elements of popular speech, including *tangueros*' slang and *lunfardo*.

The poster *left* is from the 1968 Buenos Aires production; *on the right* is the programme of a revival of the *operita*, performed in Houston, Texas, in May 1991. The Houston production was choreographed by Miguel Angel Zotto and Milena Plebs, two dancers from *Tango Argentino*, who in 1988 had created the successful show *Tango X 2*.

Maria
de
Buenos Aires
HOUSTON GRAND OPERA WITH THE MITCHEL PAVILION

The great actress and singer Sofía Bozán (1904-58) is shown *above* (seated, centre) on the set of the film *Puerto nuevo* (New Port). The film's director, Luis César Amadori, is seated at right. Bozán was well known for both her theatrical and film work. She gave the premiere performance of both Discépolo's first tango, 'Bizcochito' (Little Biscuit), and his 1930 song 'Yira, yira' (It Turns, It Turns). Amadori also wrote tango lyrics, mostly for plays and films.

entrar, hermano' (Let Me Come In, Brother); 'Aguas tristes' (Sad Waters); 'En esta soledad' (In This Solitude); 'Volvé, negro' (Come Back, Negro); 'En tu olvido' (In Your Oblivion); and 'Pensando en tí' (Thinking of You). A great friend of Carlos Gardel, she enjoyed his strong support both personally and professionally.

Maizani sang very masculine tangos so that cross-dressing made sense in the context of her performances. For the film *¡Tango!* (1933) she dressed as a *compadre* to sing Homero Manzi's 'Milonga sentimental'. Discépolo found in her the ideal singer for his lyrics.

Unisex and cross-dressing were part of the negotiation process for gender identity and for a place in the tango and in society. Later on, when women were accepted as lyricists and singers, they no longer needed either to cross-dress or to change their names. And today many lyrics are arranged so that women can feel comfortable singing them.

★ THE 1930S AND 1940S ★

In the 1930s, the expression 'riche comme un Argentin' (rich as an Argentine), which had been commonly used in France, fell into disuse. During that decade, Argentina, like almost everywhere else, though somewhat less than the USA or Britain, was to suffer the effects of the Depression. The thirties was to an extent the decade of disillusion, of the *tango descreído* (unbelieving tango), so well reflected in Discépolo's lyrics. It was also a period when an enormous number of migrant labourers from the provinces began to flood into Buenos Aires. These mestizos, known locally as *cabecitas negras* (little black heads), were to form some of the support for Peronism in the 1940s.

A combination of the general economic crisis and the corruption and inefficiency of the government administration of President Hipólito Yrigoyen (1916-22 and 1928-30) precipitated a military coup on 6 September 1930: General José F. Uriburu assumed power as President. The latter called elections and General Agustín P. Justo took over as President in 1932. A new regime of 'managed democracy' lasted until a second military coup, in June 1943.

One indication of the political instability and nervousness of the late 1920s and early 1930s was the ban imposed at that time on playing Discépolo's *tangos de protesta* on the radio. Instituted in February 1929 by the Ministry of the Navy – the most conservative of the services – the ban continued under successive governments. Three tangos were banned: 'Chorra' (Thieving Woman), 'Qué vachaché?' (Go on with You) and 'Esta noche me emborracho' (Tonight I'm Getting Drunk). All three made reference to moral and material misery, and to inequality and social injustice. Discépolo commented: 'I didn't take the State into account when I wrote my songs.'

Nevertheless, despite political uncertainties and fraudulent elections, the 1930s was also a period of regeneration. Buenos Aires was extensively renovated. The new Diagonal Norte and Diagonal Sur avenues were opened – events which were celebrated with dances in the streets. Similar festivities took place in 1936 to commemorate the 400th anniversary of the foundation of Buenos Aires, an anniversary that was also marked by the building of the 72-metre high Obelisk – later a potent symbol of the city for the *porteños*. In the following year, on 12 October 1937, the wide and splendid Avenida 9 de Julio was opened to much fanfare and public jubilation. The transformation of the city was reflected in various tango lyrics. In 'Casas viejas' (Old Homes), the singer asks: 'Who lived in those houses of yesteryear?/Old houses that time has

Below: **Osvaldo Fresedo and his orchestra, 1962. Fresedo was known as 'El pibe de La Paternal' (The Boy from the Paternal) – he grew up in the La Paternal neighbourhood in Buenos Aires. He had a brilliant career as a bandoneonist, composer and conductor. Born into a middle-class family, he was a good friend of Ricardo Güiraldes and he and his band were familiar figures at the elegant parties given by *porteña* high society. Known as 'the aesthete of tango music', Fresedo was a bridge between Argentina and Europe, between the tango of the *barrio* and the tango of the upper classes.**

turned to bronze'. And, 'They're playing games with the streets along Diagonal,' exclaims the protagonist of Enrique Cadícamo's 'Anclao en Paris' (Stranded in Paris).

For the tango, the 1930s stand for a transition, leading into the beginning of the Golden Age's second great period. It was a decade which saw many changes in the composition of the bands. The typical sextet was to lose ground as tango bandleaders belonging to both schools – the 'evolutionary' and the 'traditional' – expanded their ensembles. By 1932 the orchestras of Osvaldo Fresedo and Julio De Caro had already increased their numbers: De Caro's band now featured fourteen musicians and he was to abandon the sextet entirely two years later. Symphonic instruments (strings, wind and percussion) had to be adapted to the new bands. Fresedo added the vibraphone, the viola, the violoncello, some percussion instruments and the harp in 1932 and De Caro incorporated wind instruments in 1936. Francisco Canaro – a traditionalist – persisted with the trumpet and the *cornet-à-piston*.[9] Tangos were arranged so as to be suitable for performance by these larger ensembles. The great exception was the memorable (but, alas, unrecorded) sextet of Elvino Vardaro (1933).

The band of Juan D'Arienzo (1934 onwards) – who was to become known as 'The King of Rhythm' – followed the traditional school, emphasizing rhythm over harmony and melody. D'Arienzo (1900-76) was the son of an Italian couple who had settled in Argentina. Unlike the majority of tango artists, he came from an upper-class background and became a musician against the wishes of his parents, who had hoped that he would follow a career in law. By 1934, in fact, the tango was recovering from the damage it had suffered from the introduction of sound movies and from the performance and broadcasting of foreign popular music, mainly jazz. D'Arienzo and his band were the real turning point. They changed tango listeners back into tango dancers. The lively rhythm and strict beat of two of D'Arienzo's pianists – Rodolfo Biagi and Juan Polito – was instrumental in moving the tango 'from café tables and cinema seats to the feet of the dancers'.[10] Another key figure of the time was Angel D'Agostino, a neighbour, friend and colleague of D'Arienzo, and one of the best pianists in the genre. His aim, also, was to produce tangos which could be danced, but he cared about the singer and wanted the music to be a clear vehicle for the lyrics. He took on the singer Angel Vargas in 1932, and since Vargas, too, respected the rhythm, they made an ideal partnership for tango dancers.

Juan D'Arienzo, shown *above* on the cover of the music for 'Carancho', was known as 'The King of Rhythm'. Born in 1900, he began taking violin lessons at the age of 12 and played in various orchestras, including a jazz band, before starting his own group in 1929.

D'Arienzo belonged to the traditional tango school, favouring rhythm over harmony and melody. He was still performing in the 1960s and died in 1976.

The composer, pianist and conductor Atilio Stampone has called the thirties a magnificent decade, the decade in which the modern tango was born – its birth directly linked with the first appearance in 1937 of Aníbal Troilo (1914-1975) and his orchestra. Troilo was known as Pichuco or El Gordo ('Fat Man' – his girth was always prodigious) and symbolized for many the *hombre porteño* from the *barrios* of Buenos Aires. He was to become an enormously admired figure, idolized by his fans, and greatly influential among his contemporaries and later tango artists. He was also simply the finest bandoneon player there has ever been or is ever likely to be.

Troilo played in many tango bands before premiering his own ensemble at the Marabú, a *porteño* cabaret. His 1937 group consisted of three bandoneons, three violins, piano and double-bass as well as the singer Francisco Fiorentino. Troilo was instinctive, romantic and tender, qualities that he conveyed in his music. The innovations that he made in 1938 – daring to arrange 'La cumparsita' (The Little Carnival Procession) and playing it with variations – were strongly criticized, but by the following year he was being given standing ovations. The tangos he composed himself included 'Responso' (Dressing

Aníbal Carmelo Troilo (1914-75) was known as 'Pichuco, el Gordo' (The Fat Man). His status in tango music is second only to Carlos Gardel's.

Born in the district of Almagro in Buenos Aires, Troilo began taking bandoneon lessons at the age of ten and dropped out of school six years later to become a full-time bandoneonist with the Vardaro-Pugliese sextet. He played with various bands from then on, before forming his own group in 1937. He performed at the Tibidabo cabaret for 16 years.

Troilo is considered to be the greatest bandoneonist of all time. He was adored by his fellow *porteños* and the entire city mourned his death in 1975.

The Buenos Aires restaurant Pichuco (*opposite*) is named after him and its walls are covered with pictures showing him at every stage of his career. At the Pichuco a pianist plays tangos every night.

The man with his back to the wall in the photograph is Ben Molar, who in 1977 established National Tango Day. This takes place on 11 December – the anniversary of the births of both Carlos Gardel and Julio De Caro. Troilo's birthday is commemorated every July 11, which is known as Bandoneon Day.

Down), 'La ultima curda' (The Last Binge), 'Milonguero triste' (Sad *Milonguero*), and 'Quejas de bandoneón' (A Bandoneon's Complaints). In 1939 the young bandoneonist Astor Piazzolla joined Troilo's ensemble and took on the task of arranger and in the same year the band moved from the Marabú to the Tibidabo cabaret, where it would perform on and off for sixteen years.

Also hugely admired in the late 1930s and afterwards was Carlos Di Sarli, known as El Mufa (The Bringer of Bad Luck) and El Innombrable (The

Unnameable).[11] This extraordinarily talented pianist, composer and conductor was born in 1900 of Italian immigrant parents. Although influenced by Osvaldo Fresedo's ensemble, Di Sarli drew an entirely different sound from his own superb band, emphasizing melody without sacrificing rhythm. In his orchestra the piano prevailed, and his own left hand was prominent.

In May 1945, a gala was held at the Tabarís cabaret to celebrate Victory in Europe (***below right***). The Tabarís was an enormously popular tango venue during the Golden Age. The original building was demolished in 1936 when Corrientes Street was enlarged to become Corrientes Avenue but was rebuilt soon after.

'In my club (late forties and fifties), one side of the dance floor was called "the capital", the other side was called "the provinces". The girls from the provinces were on one side, the girls from the capital were on the other. We, the *milongueros*, were in the centre of the floor. We observed the following ritual: the beginner – for example myself – had to dance with girl number 1, then girl number 2, and so on. The girls from the provinces were ranked from 1 to 50, the girls from the capital were ranked from 50 to 100. The girls from the capital were prettier; they all went accompanied by their mothers. The girls from the provinces went by themselves (they were somehow unprotected). But I had to dance with the number 1 first. The *milongueros* watched you and would either approve of you or not. This was an unwritten law. This was the university: I got my Ph.D. as *milonguero*.'

Juan Carlos Copes, dancer and choreographer

The dancers of the 1930s are recalled by Carlos Estévez (Petróleo), one of key dancers of the century:

> There was much competition to see who was the best. Contests were held and El Vasco Aín ['el vasco' = the Basque] won almost all of them. [José] Méndez came later on and then I arrived even later. Méndez was extraordinary, the best dancer of the 1930s. His legs were fast, tango *a toda velocidad*. He went at the speed of light. As for El Mocho [Bernardo Undarz], he did a quieter tango, he had his own tempo, he stretched it out. El Vasco was elegant

and accurate. He was a terrific dancer. When I saw him dancing, I was so moved that he gave me goose pimples.[14]

The 1940s – the third and final decade of the Golden Age – witnessed the tango at the peak of its popularity. It was the centrepiece of the cabarets, the dance salons, the *dancings*, the cafés, the *confiterías*, the social and sports clubs and the soccer clubs. Newspapers now reserved several pages for advertisements of tango activities. There were hundreds of tango ensembles, each with its own style. *Tangueros* often followed their favourite bands to more than one venue per evening and some tango bands did thirty sessions a month.

***Inset:* 'El rey del cabaret' (King of the Cabaret), 1922.**

**'King of the cabaret,
heartless king:
women lost you
by stupidly adoring you...
you live without love
and through your soul
there always passes
a shadow of pain...'**

Most people could afford the price of the admission ticket and Corrientes Avenue – 'the street that never sleeps' – was always thick with revellers at four in the morning every day of the week.

Each district now had its own *club social y deportivo*; some had as many as four or five. These small sports and social clubs were crucial to the life of the districts and to the lives of many lower-middle-class Argentine and European families. They served as meeting places for friends and for families. Many had *bailes con orquesta* and those that could not afford to pay for a tango band used records. Admission prices varied for women and men – the former paid less, a practice that continues to this day.

The newly prominent soccer clubs also opened every available space to tango dancers. Some soccer clubs made enough money out of the dances to build their stadiums. Tennis courts, basketball fields and soccer fields were also put to use for tango dances – with tables laid out to hold drinks. The enormous space of River Plate Athletic Club, for example, was often turned into a dance hall, and people also danced under the grandstands of the huge stadiums. On these occasions large bands were essential: they often featured four or five bandoneons, four or five violins, piano, double-bass and two singers. At carnival time, dances were also held at theatres and at the Luna Park sports arena. These were often so crowded that dancers were forced to take shorter and shorter steps.

Theatres in the Centre, such as Maipo, Politeama, Broadway, Smart and Avenida, competed with the clubs, removing seats and turning the auditorium into a dancing area where tango contests took place. The best tango orchestras were hired a year in advance and new tangos would be premiered on such occasions.

María Nieves, one of the stars of the 1980s show *Tango Argentino*, recalls the tango's final heyday:

> To me, *el baile* represents life, love, death, hate. It makes my hair stand on end. I am a tango dancer who was brought up with the tango. It was the time when there were all the *clubes de barrio*. I used to go on both Saturdays and Sundays. On Thursdays and Fridays we used to go every single time a *baile* was held – not in the Centre, always in the clubs in the *barrios*. A decent girl went to the club just to dance, and she would dance with a *roñoso* ['meanie'] and with a *groncho* [swarthy] and with a mummy's boy – mummy's boys were hardly ever good dancers. We would

The tango of the Centre, 1935. The man walks the tango, moving always counter-clockwise. He presses gently on the woman's back to indicate the figures and poses. The woman adds adornment through her footwork. It is all simple and elegant, a stylized tango, not the spirited and exuberant tango of the *barrios*.

> dance with everybody – with *negros* too. We were swept away by our love for the tango, we just loved to go dancing. We didn't go out looking for sex, none of the girls in our *barra* [gang] did; we didn't care what the man looked like. It was a nice, beautiful, pure group of girls, interested only in the tango.[15]

In the 1940s clubs were so crowded that orchestras had to be hired a year in advance. Everyone went dancing – newspapers reserved page after page of advertisements just for dances. The ball shown *above* was held at the Workers' Club of the City of Buenos Aires on 14 January 1940.

Men went every day to the cafés in Corrientes Avenue to drink coffee and listen to the latest tangos. The customers did not dance, they just sat and enjoyed the music. There were three shows: *matinée*, *vermouth* and evening. The working class attended the first two and society people the last. The cafés attracted many of the best singers and tango bands.

The most momentous political development of the 1940s, the rise of the charismatic and populist Juan Domingo Perón (president, 1946–55), had a somewhat diffuse impact on the tango story. With one possible exception, there are no 'Peronist tangos', as such. A number of tango artists openly supported him, most notably Discépolo, who did some memorable radio talks on his behalf, while the lyricist Homero Manzi was expelled from the Radical Party because of his undue enthusiasm for the General. By contrast, the singer-actress Libertad Lamarque, who had once famously quarrelled with Perón's all-powerful wife Evita, found it advisable to pursue *her* successful career in Mexico. Most musicians, in traditional showbusiness fashion, avoided taking unduly specific attitudes to the government. Some bandleaders were annoyed by the new rules on hiring and firing imposed by Perón's labour laws, but, by the same token, the economic bonanza induced by the government (and rapidly rising wages) undoubtedly contributed to the brilliant fortunes of the tango during its last classic decade. Perón himself, indisputably a popular figure, was well aware of the tango's popularity, and was more than happy to be photographed in the company of musicians and to attend the occasional tango festival. In March 1949, after receiving a delegation of leading tango figures, he lifted the absurd censorship of lyrics instituted by the military regime in 1943.

★ KEEPING THE FLAME ALIVE ★

The 1950s brought more difficult times for Argentina. Perón was ousted from government and the country found itself in a state of decay and impoverishment, with its resources severely depleted, while military intervention in politics (1955, 1962, 1966, 1976) became alarmingly recurrent. The Golden Age of the tango now drew to a close. Tango cafés closed, as did cabarets, *confiterías*, *salones de baile* and *dancings;* soccer and other sports clubs could no longer afford to stage the huge gatherings of the previous decade. Although in 1950 Perón decreed that 50 percent of all music played on the radio was henceforth to be Argentine in origin, and though this act of cultural protectionism might, in principle, have boosted tango music in the 1950s, in fact, its real beneficiaries were the new generation of folk-musicians now putting together the magnificent tradition of 'neo-folklore' – so soon to challenge the tango in public affections. Folk music was given more air time than the tango; tango bands recorded less and less and the market for the records that were made was greatly diminished.

A further and vital factor in the tango's decline was the virtual assimilation of the immigrant community into Argentine society, a process that greatly reduced the function of the tango as a means of bringing many disparate nationalities together.

The large orchestras of the 1940s were now gradually replaced by smaller ensembles of between three and nine members and the relationship between the orchestra and audience changed. Whereas in earlier decades the people themselves had been active participants in the tango, they now simply paid the admission price and sat and listened. The habit of going regularly to hear tango music declined – there were fewer and fewer habitués, and the musicians played to different audiences every night.

What eventually developed from these 'concert' tangos – which were the great innovation of the 1950s and 1960s – was the 'new tango' (*el nuevo tango*). This was a development from the 'evolutionary' trend of the 1920s (whose pioneers had been Julio De Caro, Juan Carlos Cobián and Enrique Delfino) with its interest in expanding the resources of the music. The 'new tango' ensembles performed what amounted to 'chamber tango', the essence of which was the joining together of two elements: the traditional tango repertoire and outstanding musicians.

Enrique Delfino (Delfy) was a pioneer of the 'evolutionary' school. Born in 1895 in Buenos Aires, he began his career playing the piano in a cinema in the Centre. He had started composing tangos by 1917 and has been called 'the father of the tango song' because his music was so suited to lyrics.

Delfino had a successful career, performing in the USA and across Europe. By the 1950s he had lost his sight, but continued to compose, dictating his music once a week to the classical musician Pompeyo Camps.

Some serious musicians became exceptional soloists in this area, including Roberto Grela on guitar and Horacio Salgán on piano. Salgán was to push the development of tango music even further ahead in his eagerness not simply to renew traditional tangos but to create new ones. In 1959 he started a duo with the guitarist Ubaldo De Lío and a year later brought together the talents of De Lío, Pedro Laurenz (bandoneon), Enrique Mario Francini (violin) and Rafael Ferro (double-bass), to form the Quinteto Real.

Other key figures of the sixties 'avant-garde' were Atilio Stampone and the bandoneonist Eduardo Rovira. But altogether the greatest tango musician of these years and of recent times was Astor Piazzolla (1921-92). Born in Mar del Plata, Piazzolla lived as a child in New York. He came to love the tango by listening to the collection of records by Carlos Gardel and Julio De Caro that his father had taken with him to New York. He also grew up with a strong interest in jazz. As a boy Piazzolla met Gardel and (for $25) played the part of a newspaper vendor in the film *El día que me quieras* (1935).

Piazzolla returned to his native town in 1937 and two years later moved to Buenos Aires, where he became a bandoneonist for several tango bands. He went every night to the Café Germinal to listen to Troilo. One night the older musician called to him and asked him to play something on the bandoneon, as he was looking for a replacement bandoneonist. Piazzolla chose to demonstrate his talents with Gershwin's *Rhapsody in Blue*. Piazzolla would remain as

Troilo's bandoneonist and arranger from 1939 until 1944. In 1946 he formed his own first band and in 1960 started his influential Quinteto Nuevo Tango, consisting of bandoneon, piano, violin, guitar and double-bass.

Piazzolla was an intensely dedicated and disciplined musician. In the years when he played with Troilo at the Tibidabo until four in the morning he would go on three hours later to rehearsals with the Orquesta Filarmónica at the Colón Opera House. He studied with Alberto Ginastera in Buenos Aires and with the now legendary Nadia Boulanger in Paris. It was Boulanger who finally convinced him to play the tango rather than classical music. He saw himself as a Buenos Aires musician, interpreting the popular music of his country, just as Bartók, Stravinsky and Villa Lobos interpreted theirs.

Troilo once said to Piazzolla of his music: 'No, pibe, eso no es tango' (No, my boy, that isn't tango), a comment which was to hurt the younger man so deeply that their friendship, though not actually broken, would never be quite the same. For some, each man stands as a symbol for what the tango should and should not be. Piazzolla played the bandoneon on his right leg, standing; Troilo would play sitting in the traditional manner. And whereas Troilo was 'the last Bohemian of Buenos Aires', addicted to the night-life of the city, Piazzolla strongly disliked the bohemian life.

Although Piazzolla retained the tango's essential spirit, he introduced dissonance, chromatic harmony and a wider range of rhythm, with the result that his music was strongly resisted by the purists and proved too complex for most *tangueros*. His concerts were filled with jazz and classical music lovers – he did not play the tango for dancers. There was also a difference in ticket price and as a consequence he was often insulted in the streets of Buenos Aires.

In 1967 Piazzolla began his collaboration with the talented poet Horacio Ferrer. Their first major work, an *operita* (little opera), was *María de Buenos Aires*, starring the singer Amelita Baltar. In 1969 they scored an amazing hit with the song 'Balada para un loco' (Ballad for a Madman), which was popular throughout Latin America. This had nothing in common with the traditional tango song – not in theme, style, rhyme or rhythm. Its surreal, witty and very contemporary lyrics tell the story, at unusual length for a tango song, of a bowler-hatted apparition who appears to the singer on a Buenos Aires street. Half-dancing, half-flying, the apparition sings: 'I know I'm crazy, crazy, crazy,/... that a crew of astronauts and children are dancing a waltz around me.' This was so far from the traditional model that it drew a line forever between the pre-Piazzolla and the post-Piazzolla tango. Even today, traditional *tangueros* dislike this song intensely, and when it was premiered at Luna Park, the audience threw coins disapprovingly at the singer. Four days later, however, 200,000 records had been sold. Piazzolla and Ferrer collaborated on several other modern classics.

Piazzolla was a prolific composer who wrote more than 750 works, including concertos and film and theatrical scores. In the 1970s and 1980s he won increasing popularity in continental Europe and the USA, and his records continue to appear in a copious flood – more than ever since his death in 1992.

While the tango is never likely to recapture the vigour of its Golden Age, it remains a form of music and dance with its own substantial following in

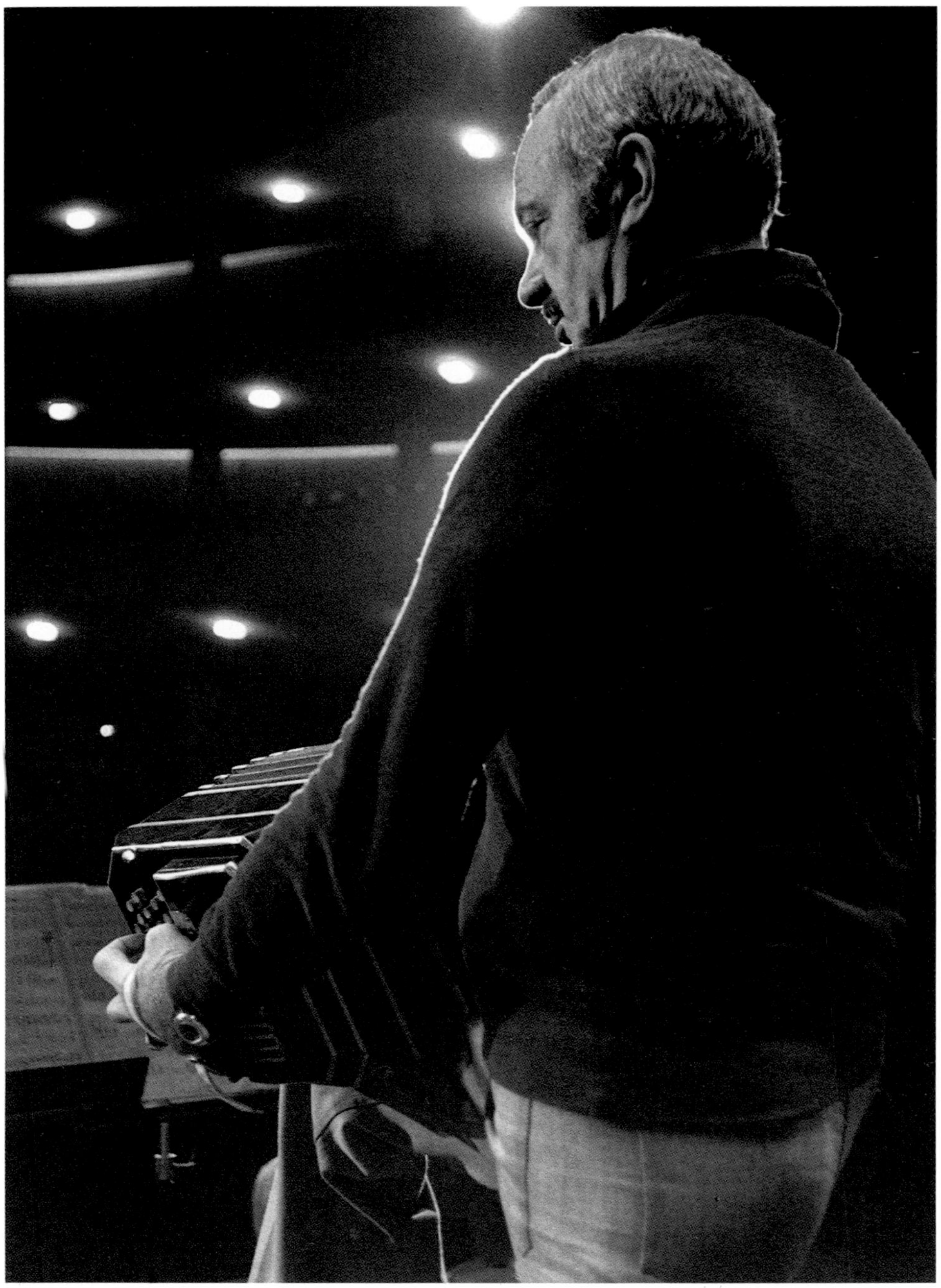

Astor Piazzolla, the controversial pioneer of the avant-garde tango, won international acclaim in the 1970s and 1980s. Born in 1921 in Mar del Plata, he joined Aníbal Troilo's band as bandoneonist and arranger in 1939.

In 1960 Piazzolla started his influential Quinteto Nuevo Tango. During the long period of his ascendancy in the avant-garde, his restless artistic temperament drove him to relax the orthodox conventions more drastically than anyone had done previously. But his roots lie firmly within the tradition and nobody has done more to renew tango music in recent times. Piazzolla was elected 'Distinguished Citizen of the City of Buenos Aires' in 1985. He is shown *left* on stage at the Teatro Regina in Buenos Aires in 1975.

The pianist Osvaldo Pugliese, shown here with his orchestra on the steps of the Faculty of Law, Buenos Aires University, in 1978, remained one of the major tango musicians right up to his death in 1995. He was greatly loved by *porteños*, who preferred dancing to his music than to any other. Pugliese's orchestra functioned as a kind of tango school, welcoming young musicians from both home and abroad. Many talented musicians served their apprenticeship with him.

Argentina, and throughout Latin America. In Buenos Aires itself, a tiny number of Golden Age bands survived into the 1970s and 1980s – and in the case of Osvaldo Pugliese's, a notable 'evolutionary' ensemble, into the mid-1990s, at which point the pianist-bandleader himself was in his late eighties, having formed his first orchestra in 1939. Other distinguished groups – the bands of Leopoldo Federico and Atilio Stampone, the Baffa-Berlingieri-Cabarcos Trio, the Sexteto Mayor, to name only a few – kept the flame alive in the 1970s and 1980s. During the latter decade, with Argentina's return to democracy after the harsh military regime of 1976-83, a municipally sponsored Orquesta del Tango de Buenos Aires joined the ranks of the front-running ensembles, and in the early 1990s there was an encouraging revival of interest in the *dance* by the younger generation. What the future holds we cannot be sure, but it is inconceivable that there will ever be a last tango in Buenos Aires.

★ **Pages 161–168: Whether in the sob of the bandoneon, the melancholy lyrics of a great singer like Beba Bidart (pages 162–163) or the hypnotic stare of the dancers themselves, the tango is always intense, passionate and sensual.**

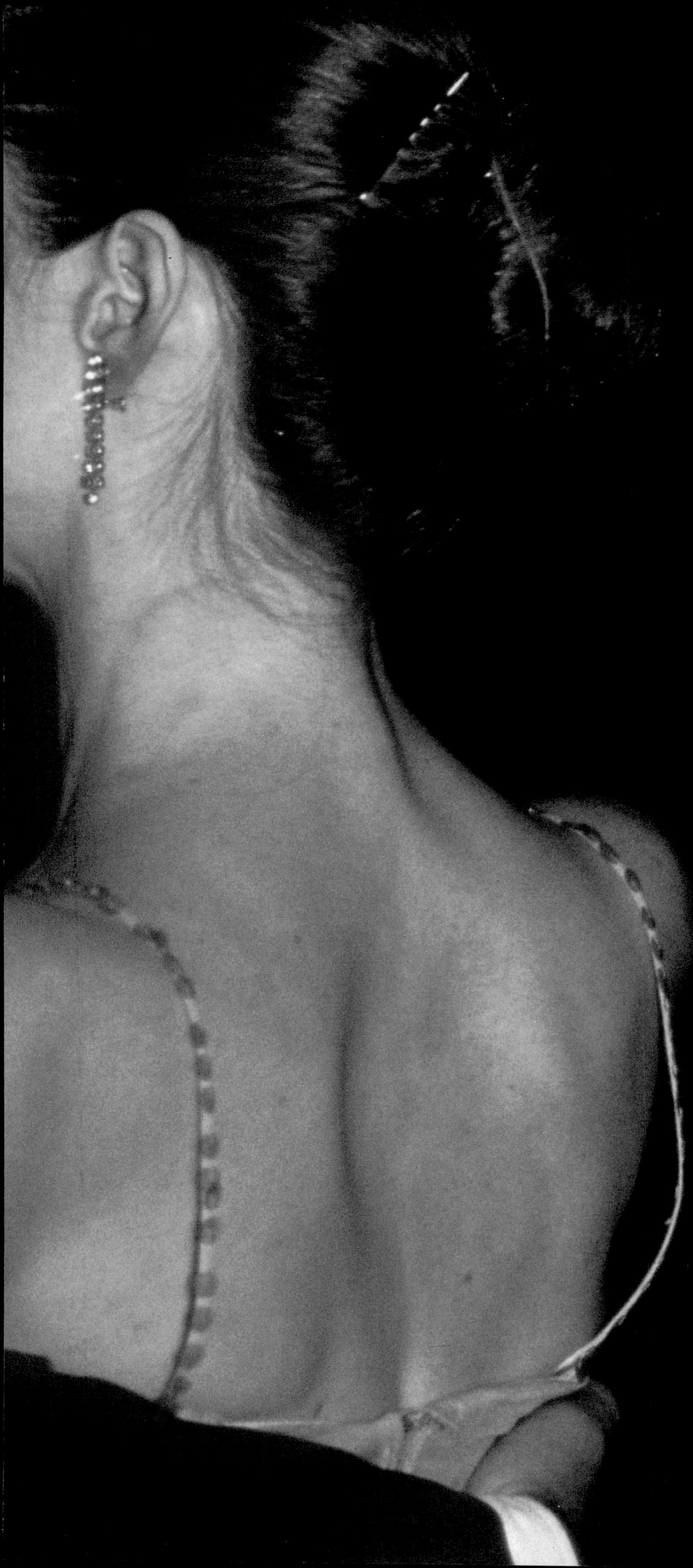

'The tango is man and woman in search of each other. It is the search for an embrace, a way to be together, when the man feels that he is a male and the woman feels that she is a female, without machismo. She likes to be led; he likes to lead. Disagreements may occur later or they may not. When that moment comes, it is important to have a positive and productive dialogue, fifty-fifty. The music arouses and torments, the dance is the coupling of two people defenceless against the world and powerless to change things. This is the best definition of the tango as a dance, I think.'

Juan Carlos Copes, choreographer and dancer

IV

RICHARD MARTIN

THE LASTING TANGO

> . . . the tango is rather like love in the afternoon. Naughty, but nice. Something for many (though by no means all!) to dream about, but not necessarily indulge in. For the fact is that the tango is not just a dance. In its purest form it's a sensual coupling, forged by raw emotion. The closest thing you'll find to a vertical expression of a horizontal desire . . .
>
> *Angela Rippon, 'Vertical Expression of a Horizontal Desire', 1993*

Sexy and syncopated; paired, promiscuous and predatory; the tango is both a dance and a modern secular symbol. As the twentieth century comes to its end, the tango remains a dominant metaphor of our age, a significant sign for a complex of ideas and possibilities. It conjures up images as diverse as ballroom and *barrio*, film seductions and spectacles, the poorer streets of Argentina and the sophisticated dance halls of France. Ineffably modern, the tango is the dance that, more than any other, declares our century.

Any dance can function as a sign, often giving us a sense of intangible time through familiar sounds, through intimations of social and sensual exchange, and through the intimacy of its isolations and couplings. Thus, we hear the waltz and we listen for the minuet in annals of time and in striving to understand the circumstance of their time and place. The patient protocol of the minuet, the jivey outburst of energy of the jitterbug, and the insistent tumult of the waltz inscribe themselves in our body language and in our historical memory. The tango, too, reveals its historical

Opposite: **Al Pacino and Gabrielle Anwar dancing to Carlos Gardel's tango 'Por una cabeza' in the film *Scent of a Woman*, 1992.**

Right: **Tango Lives! – an advertisement for a dance workshop in Berlin, 1993.**

moment, but it also flays the spirit of the dancers and becomes a metaphor of joined expression and suppression, power and enthrallment.

Dance can be merry and celebratory; it can be sinister and foreboding. Seldom have the light and dark aspects of dance been so thoroughly integrated as in the tango. The lindy cavorted; the charleston celebrated; the jitterbug rebelled; the twist lubricated; but only the tango has maintained its power to be evocative, to set off a mutual energy of music and dance that is more than mere sound and manoeuvre. It prevails as the most passionate portrayal of life's inherent feelings passing into a suite of prescribed motions.

No dance plays command against subjugation as supremely and concisely as the tango does. More than any other dance, it is gender-led. The tradition of the male as the leader who sets the protocol and the female as the subordinate, subject to a few extroverted flourishes to enhance the male's decorum, is a long-standing etiquette of gender relations. That the tango so alters that relationship sets it apart from all other dances in which we are assured of who leads and who follows. Similarly, leadership is both physical and emotional and the tango introduces the unprecedented gestures of male bravura and of female aggression. Dance's embrace and extension is largely an etiquette. In the tango, however, the slap of bodies in contact can appear almost violent and certainly naughty; danced with fervour, it can seem almost a ritual of abuse and mutual danger.

Key to the tango's salaciousness and physical challenge is the interlace of legs and balancing of bodies as they strike one another. Later dances have often attempted to introduce taboo gestures and coital simulations, but the tango remains the abiding dance of physical collision, the impact of which is ever that the dancers respond to one another as physical beings, if not only by the laws of physics, as they apply to colliding bodies, then by the principles of gender-dominated nature. The proponents of chastity who opposed the body contact of the tango were swimming against an ineluctable tide. The tango depends upon the friction of bodies. It cannot be danced or even viewed outside of the modern era's freedom to promiscuity.

Dance depends upon action and recoil. Of all ballroom dances, the tango shows most forcefully the body's responsiveness and energy in recoil. The supposedly licentious abutting of bodies at hips and torso and the supposedly salacious dovetailing of the dancers' legs makes the two figures mutually dependent and interactive throughout the dance. The tango's *corte* interlace of legs and flex of two bodies in unison demands a symmetry between the leading dancer and the responsive partner as if they were wholly united. The American writer Waldo Frank made this point clearly, and equally succumbed to the dance's compression of sexual desire and contact, in *America Hispana* (1917):

> The tango is a walk in which the vertical ecstasy of Spain is stratified to a horizontal pace . . . The man leads in low, lithe strides. His body is erect, it does not turn; the head is in profile to the body and flat against the profiled face of his partner . . . The effect is of rigorous sculpture. The world is a solid element that swirls, rises, falls: the world is the music. And the dancers are a continuous substance with it. But their deliberate pace – a natural effort turned delightedly to art like the effort of sexual love – transforms this world, makes it immobile, gives diapason to its flux. Within the chaste contours of the tango figures, rages the desire of sex. The bodies do not touch, yet they are joined. So intense is the current within the man and the woman, that it leaps in the air and copulates them. This blue current of sex is also in contact with the music that is the substance of life itself, for pampa and altar and forest are within it.[1]

The interlace of legs in the tango is recreated with wit and precision in the 1922 drawing *opposite* by the American poet e. e. cummings. It is shown in extreme form *above* in a tango number from the show *Tango X 2*. The dancers, Natalia Games and Gabriel Angió, are performing to the music of 'Libertango' by Astor Piazzolla.

Can the tango be so manifestly the enactment of desire and the fulfilment of orgasmic pleasure? Frank's resolution is another metaphor, this time of birth and the embryo:

> The tango is the plastic symbol of the way of the Porteño with and against his woman. In it is his will to hold her by all the primitive resource of the male; and also, through the prophecy of art, the revelation of their destiny and rebirth together. For the body of the tango is an *embryon*. That is why it stirs so larvally, why it repeats the ethnic stages of the past – Spanish, Indian, Negro – from which Argentina must emerge. That is why its dancers are enclosed by the embodying music, as the embryon by the womb; why it is a thing of stillness, conveying the sense of sleep, not waking. The man and woman must move will-less yet strict through the phylogeny that holds and moulds them. The body of the tango lives, yet is unborn.[2]

Faces matched in profile: the lady dances a tango with the 'Latin lover' in a 1970 performance of the 1931 ballet *Façade*, choreographed by Frederick Ashton, with music by William Walton.

Frank's passionate endorsement addresses many important issues. The degree of physical contact in the tango is critical to its understanding, not only as dance, but also as metaphor. The bodies are locked together with feet entwined, but the dancers are most notably dovetailed when they match their faces in profile. Traditional guidance in Western ballroom dance has always been to watch the partner's face, the assumption being that correct steps below will follow from the exchange of gaze. In the tango, this is not possible; the dance requires instead that the partners intuit the movements from the other's whole body. The tango is no mere matching of toes on the dance floor like an Andy Warhol dancing lesson of the early 1960s. The inexorable sensuality of the dance resides in the press of torso, face and mid-body which precipitates the further action, thus clearly simulating sexual action and coitus. The flattened body alignment of the two dancers suggests the elegant planarity of Art Deco sculpture, but it also realizes a melded unit of two bodies functioning in natural symmetry as if they were one.

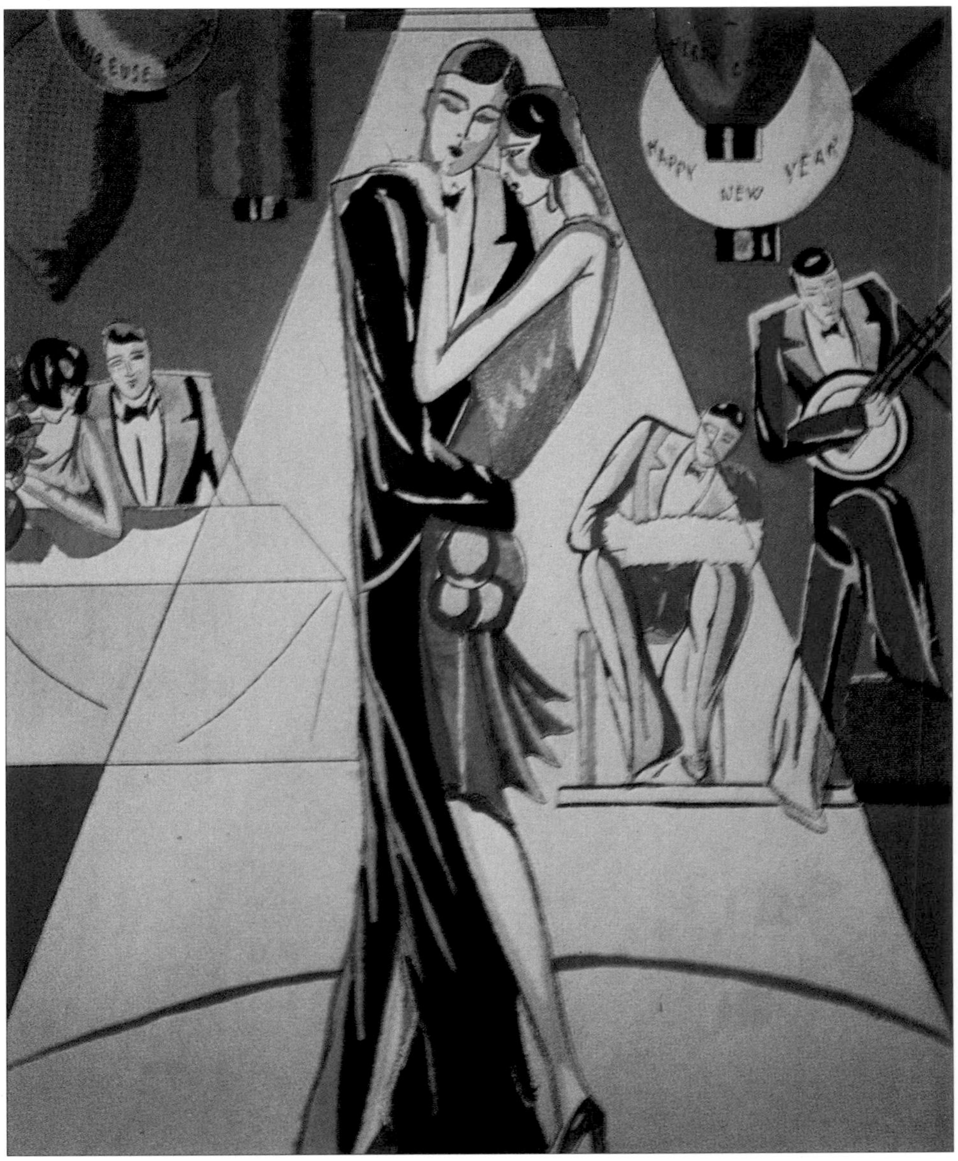

***Right:* New Year card by an anonymous artist, New York, 1925.**

Frank rightly observes that coordination between the partners in the tango is akin to sexual engagement. They move together as if in the magnetism of [illegible] d in sympathetic bodies and responsive needs. Deprived of the acc[illegible] ngo is always a dance of the blind, the *contre-danse* of raw [illegible] th only the body as guide. Dance always resembles or [illegible] he tango is, as Frank describes with apparent deli[illegible] e and desire, a passion of copulation. Further, one [illegible] rimal art was the fuel of European and Am[illegible] nd twenties, not only for Vernon and Irene Cas[illegible] ut also for culture at large, as it sought a mo[illegible] ore open society of aesthetic expansion. In [illegible] has admired in a raw state: the tango be[illegible] nitivistic' expropriations.

The [illegible] nsory contact is made explicit in Martin Brest's film *Scen*[illegible] 2), in which Al Pacino plays a blind former military officer, Frank S[illegible] erwise dysfunctional, Slade takes confidence in his assertion that there are 'no mistakes in tango . . . Not like life . . . If you get all tangled up, you just tango on.' The tango is the dance of uneducated, unseeing instinct: its nexus is lust; its animation is sexual.

For Waldo Frank, male dominance is unquestioned. Yet any observer of the dance might wonder whether the woman's role in the tango is not as

The tradition of male dancer as leader and female as follower is undercut by the tango, which more than any other dance questions the usual relationship of man to woman on the dancefloor. The gender parity of the tango is underlined by the frequency and general sanction of same-sex partners, as shown in *At the Cabaret* (*below*), a 1920s illustration by Lorenzi.

assertive as the man's. It is an expression of woman as much as of man. The embrace is an equal one: not a female subjugation but a hug of mutual force. Likewise, as the bodies unravel, the male is not dominant, but the mirror of the female. Male power is inevitably present in the dance, but female power is its partner. For every thrust of the male, there is female parry; for every loping gesture of the male, there is the parity of the female. The tango is a masculine noun in Spanish, but the dance has permeated Western culture precisely because it is of modern gender reading, more equal than most dance. What is most astonishing is that the woman is not called upon to perform any extraneous gesture unaccompanied by the male – gestures which do not necessarily typify female liberty (as some dance critics have averred) but are instead incidents of the male gaze directed to mandated performance imposed upon the female.

One reason why this dance was so immediately compelling to Parisians of the 1910s and 1920s was that it allowed the new woman of modernism the freedom that she demanded. Homosexuals, too, could dance together, in liberation and in mockery of machismo and its legion of gigolo dance-instructors. Women danced with women (as in Bertolucci's 1970 film *The Conformist*, set in the 1930s). Same-sex dancers simply offered a fascinating travesty to the intense equity of the tangoing man and woman.

Oddly, Argentina's machismo was blunted in the nation's most important aesthetic expression, at least in the translation of the tango elsewhere. Anthropologist Julie M. Taylor studied the tango in Argentina in the 1970s as an expression of gender that surpassed the cultural norm. Acknowledging that Argentine men practice and preserve the dance far more than women and consider that only they (often in training since boyhood) can teach women its rigours, Taylor devoted less interviewing to the female dancers. Arguably, we might have very different testimony had she concentrated on women who prize the tango, including perhaps the deposition that women are the better tango dancers and that men possess less skill.

Taylor found the attitudes of male tango dancers strangely ambivalent. The tango is an expression of power, yet, while dancing it, the male dancer sees himself, because of his sensitivity, great capacity to love, and fidelity to the true ideals of his childhood years, as basically vulnerable. 'When I dance the tango, I feel that I am myself. "The man who dances tango is more of a dreamer than others.'"[3] In particular, Taylor notes a phenomenon that might either be considered an element of machismo in the dance or might be regarded as its special, primal and most sophisticated melancholy. The male dancers spoke with particular intensity of their desire not to talk to the partner during the dance. The tango is a silent dance, its interaction being acutely limited to intense physical performance. This trait speaks to the dance's ritualistic certainty as well as perhaps to its surprising gender parity. Moreover, silent dance permits enhanced attention to the music and lyrics, the former strong in its implication of Argentine nationalism (a kind of collective *Marseillaise*), the latter explicit in tales of remorse, passionate love and grievous loss. In the dance's silent listening, the emotions of the lyrics prevail.

The ballroom of the West has civilized and burnished many folk dances to a protocol of courts or at the very least of rationalizing dance masters and proper ladies. The tango is the one dance to have entered the modern ballroom yet remained ungoverned, tainted and beloved of its peasant nature.

Again disrupting the usual reading of the tango as a dance of machismo and power: a tango danced by two transvestites in Paris in the 1910s (*opposite*) and a tango danced by the staid English bank clerk Henry Pulling and a male partner in Graham Greene's *Travels with My Aunt* at the Royal Dramatic Theatre, Stockholm, 1994 (*below*).

But if the tango is a dance of love, it is also a dance of death. Perhaps the most frequent image of it is that of a duel – open to love but susceptible to death – in which resolution is never achieved in the course of the dance. The first film ever devoted to the tango was called *El tango de la muerte* (1917), and even Bernardo Bertolucci's metaphor for loving and yielding to death in Paris was *Last Tango in Paris* (1972). The ever-present concept of a *danse macabre* fits well with the tango's ardour. It is seen by some as a near-religious ritual, in which fears – even of death – can be overcome.[4]

The traditional explanation of the tango is that it epitomizes male power in that the steps of the male and female partner are identical and there are no flourishes or caprices given solely to the woman. Taylor writes:

> The female shows no will of her own. Though they may be technically difficult for her, her steps must be performed to give the appearance that they are entirely due to her partner's masterful guidance. She is never allowed as in other dances to escape the man's embrace and must execute the most complex figures of the legs with her upper body immobile in a stylized, tense embrace, totally overpowered by the male.[5]

Yet the same facts can be given a completely opposite interpretation. The very equality of the steps is liberating for the woman. The intervention of the woman's legs into the man's stride (especially in any culture prizing phallic masculinity) is a bold departure from the pattern of male determinations of all mobility. The abutting of bodies and forward gesture of the woman's leg also constitute a significant intrusion into the male precinct. Even the man's upper-body strength and superior height can be compromised by the dance's glides and the parallelism of the male and female body. Does the female partner press voluntarily toward male vulnerability or does the man simply take over the dance? Taylor's certainty of male authority is vitiated by her acknowledgment of the lyrics. She argues:

> The sexual themes of the tango as a dance may seem to contradict those of tango as poetry. The man, active to the point of being physically aggressive, and the completely passive woman seem the opposites of the roles designated to the sexes in the tango lyrics. Although opposites on the surface, these two statements of relations between the sexes may both be forms of denying fear and timidity in the face of a threat of total failure. Perhaps a philosophy of bitterness, resentment, and pessimism may be oriented toward the same goal as that of a danced statement of *machismo*, confidence, and sexual optimism.[6]

Above: Drawing by Xavier Sager, 1920s.

The tango has long been a symbol of both passion and death. Bernardo Bertolucci's 1972 film _Last Tango in Paris_ (_below right_), starring Marlon Brando and Maria Schneider, is the story of a doomed love affair that ends in destruction.

The death-dealing aspect of dance has been expressed by many artists, including Edvard Munch (_opposite top_). The idea of the tango as a dance of sensuality and death is also exploited in both the music cover of 'Que chulo!' and the poster design for Patrice Leconte's 1993 film _Tango_ (_opposite_).

Whatever differences in attitude may be manifest between the poor, urban life of Argentina that created and has sustained the roots of the tango and its

international versions in brothels, ballrooms and the great display of twentieth-century life, we know that the tango came to be in its translated and transmitted form a dance that might bring more equity to the floor than almost any other. Perhaps it is the lyrics that have reinforced a sombre intensity and a dramatic intensity within the dance which transcends a more quotidian masculine aggression.

In the pivotal moves of the dance, those in which the dance partners exchange leadership, the power of the dance can be seen to alternate as quickly as that of sweat-slick wrestlers or fate-heavy duellists. Dominance is always fragile and unsure; subjugation is merely a quiescence in which to plot the regaining of the upper hand. Thus, energies of ego and control struggle in a *Psychomachia* in three dimensions on the dance floor. The dance of death as conceived by a succession of artists from the Middle Ages to Edvard Munch took no specific form but the clutch of the living

figure and the skeleton other. The metaphor is effective, though, because of dance's supposed gaiety and spontaneity combined with the slipping, switching dynamic of the dance, alternatively meshed and adversarial. Alfredo Le Pera's famous tango lyric, 'Volver', which claims that one always goes back to one's first love, echoes the dance's reactive return to the partner as a sympathetic accomplice, momentarily rejected, but never wholly forgotten.

It is reported that concentration camp orchestras favoured the tango, reifying this dance of death. The Nazis approved of it because it engendered no spirit of rebellion, unlike the African-American jazz that they so abhorred and interdicted. Rather it provided another spirit that broke into pieces and made individual the spirit of defiance; jazz was seen to encourage disobedience, to engender a collective delirium and feeling of abandon; the tango was seen to provide an escape, a willing preoccupation with the dance as an oblivion of the self rather than as an incentive to disobedience. Ironically, the historian Frederic Morton took the occasion of a Kristallnacht anniversary to tell the story of himself and his family as they escaped the Third Reich to America. Morton concludes his melancholy autobiography with the line that his parents are now taking tango lessons in Miami, forty years later. We know that the tango that they dance is their affirmation of life and love; they have evaded the concentration camps where the same dance betokened the sole freedom against an assumption of death.

The decorous Miami tango would be fundamentally different from the ultimate tango of defiance and

Left: **Catherine Deneuve and Linh Dan Pham dancing the tango in the film *Indochine*, 1992.**

Opposite: **A tango story in sculpture. François Faure, father of the artist Jean-Louis Faure, rented an apartment in Paris in 1945. He discovered a letter, hidden behind an eave, addressed to 'Monsieur Lucien, professor of tango at the St Didier skating rink'. The letter came from a married admirer of the professor and requested a secret rendezvous. It was dated 7 December 1913 – when tangomania was at its height in Paris.**

Jean-Louis Faure speculates that the professor, also married, hid the letter and was later killed in the trenches. The work *C'est fini, mon joli* (It's Over, My Lovely) shows a tango professor gliding smoothly across a polished floor, and being struck through the head and stomach by two explosions. Behind him the letter is displayed.

defense that one encounters, for example, in the two women dancing in Bertolucci's *The Conformist* (1970) or in the physically defiant Richard Gere tango in Francis Ford Coppola's *The Cotton Club* (1984). For Frederic Morton's parents, the tango lessons are both a small Latinism and a touch of old-style Europe, representing the very world before the Third Reich.

In a 1949 short story by the Bulgarian novelist Georgi S. Karaslavov, young communists are executed while the hero asks the heroine to listen to her favourite tango. The 1964 play *Tango*, by the Polish playwright W. Mrozek, concludes with a family/political murderer, after which a tango is danced slowly on the corpse. To these collusions of politics, dance and death, the tango plays an essential bonding role. If political action is composed of cooperation, seduction and abandonment, the tango promises nothing less. The apparent violence of rejection that is suggested in the dance combined with its essential contract for partnership lends itself to the concept of the political covenant. The tango dancer is the sublime renegade, even if opiated by the self-evident ego of the dance.

Significant among the characteristics of the tango is that it is an ageless dance and one that prizes the beauty of its motion above the beauty of the dancers. There have been times in the twentieth century when the tango seemed slightly fusty, given its great popularity at earlier times. Thus, the tango in the Billy Wilder film *Sunset Boulevard* (1950) and its musical version (1993) is a sign of the bygone, recalling Norma Desmond's heyday in the early days of film. But deliberate anachronism, as in Régis Warner's *Indochine* (1992), has also served to refresh the image of the dance. Not only is the dance timeless, but its dancers can be of almost any age and dimension. The

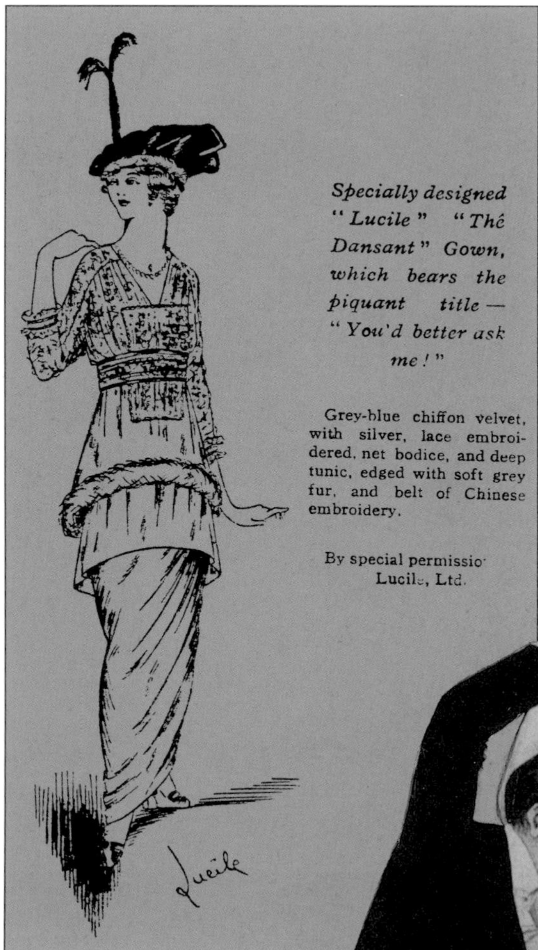

immensely popular 1980s production of *Tango Argentino* on Broadway, in London, and around the world featured an evening of nothing but tango. *Tango Argentino* is still the source of many local tango groups and a touchstone for contemporary tango. The production was notable for the diversity of the players, who were obviously chosen not out of a politically correct ideology, but because of their skill as dancers. Though the production included many dashing young couples, the Broadway audience gave its most passionate applause to the older tango stars Elvira Santamaría and Jorge Orcaizaguirre who took to the floor each evening with an abandon and a grace that the young, slender dancers could not equal, for all their youthful agility. To be sure, some of the more mature theatre-goers may have seen the older dancers as more likely role models, but it is nevertheless a reminder that the tango's appeal is not restricted to the young.

What are the visual associations of the tango? The forms of Art Deco, with which it grew up, seem effortlessly appropriate. It was also the age of Futurism, creative freedom and abstraction. But the more lasting association is with fashion, especially long dresses with slits or flounces which made easier the long strides and deep dips demanded by the dance, without revealing the movements of the dance itself. This was in contrast to other dances, especially the charleston, where short dresses were necessary to make knees visible in high steps and in patting the hands on the knees. A designer as otherwise demure as Jeanne Lanvin was well known for the versatility of her tango dresses. Male dancers initially wore the capacious gaucho pants which also swayed and shimmered in motion, with flat, broad-brimmed regional hats, but these were eventually largely supplanted by the black tie of formal ballroom wear.

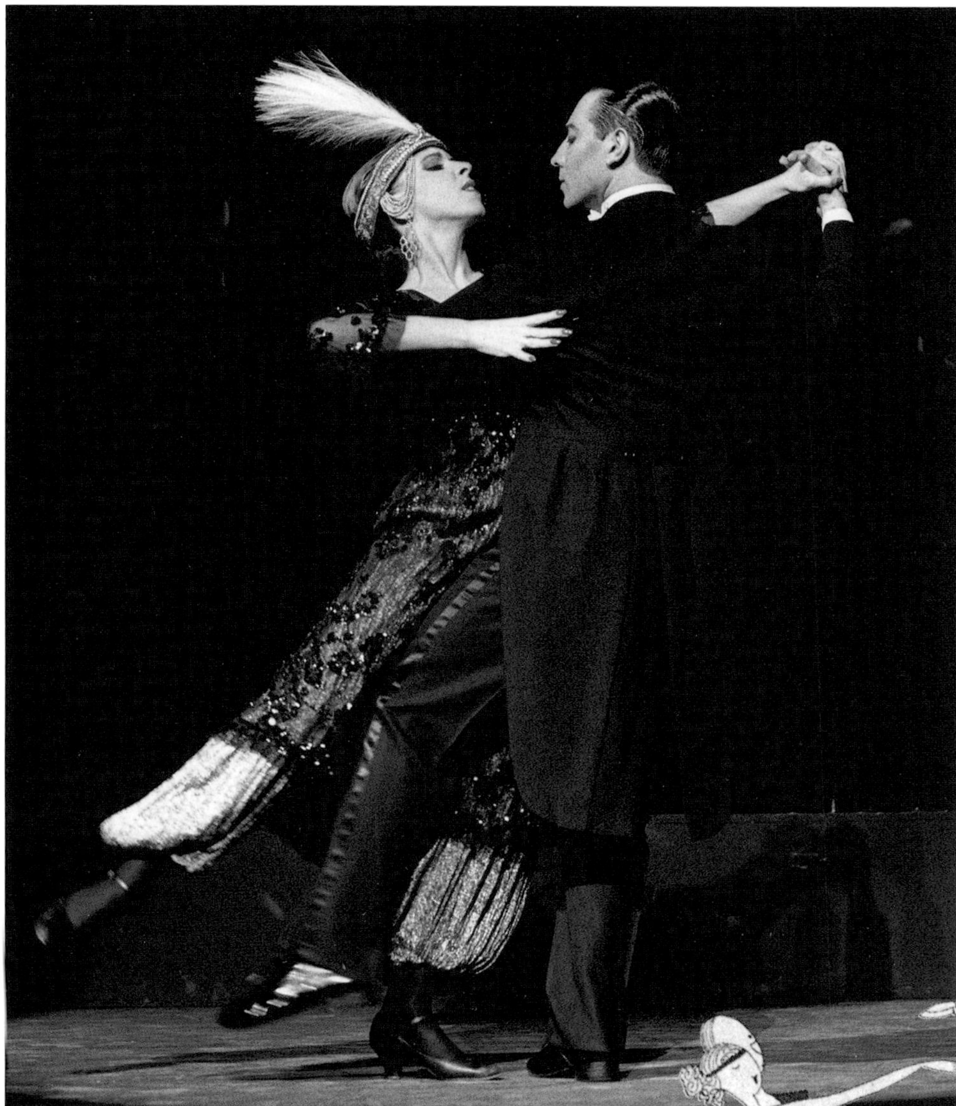

In 1913, Madame Lucile of Hanover Square, London, presented gowns designed especially for tango dancing (*opposite top*). The aigrette headdress, shown *opposite below*, became particularly associated with the dance. It is worn *left* by Milena Plebs in 'La cumparsita' from *Tango Argentino*. Plebs is partnered by Miguel Angel Zotto.

Secondly, the tango has long been the dance of fringe. The fashion doyenne Diana Vreeland, fondly remembering the 1920s in the fringe revival of the late 1960s, lamented the absence of fringe. Marking motion by its rhythms of sway, reverse, and sway again, the dashing lines of fringe were an important part of tango's visualization and allure. And the word tango was often insinuated into fashion advertising of the 1910s and 1920s as a means of proving that the garment was modern and functional for movement.

In the first era of the tango it was almost compulsory for dress and dance to be sanctioned by elements of primitivism and the folkloric. The West was under the spell of the Orient, and the Ballets Russes had established dance as a window through which the West could watch and eventually emulate an exotic

Tia Carrere and Arnold Schwarzenegger preparing to dance their sensuous and electrifying tango in the opening scene of the 1994 film *True Lies*.

***Below:* Fred Astaire and Ginger Rogers in *Flying Down to Rio*, 1933.**

and exuberant world, explicitly sensuous, and unrestrained by banal moral sanction. By the time of Fred Astaire's RKO film *Flying Down to Rio* (1933), his 'Orchids in the Moonlight' tango with Dolores del Rio was merely a part of a dance eclecticism that made all the world a dance floor for Astaire's terpsichorean talent. Furthermore, his partner did not have to be Latin to make the dance effective: in Warners' *Go into Your Dance* (1935), Ruby Keeler performed and proclaimed 'She's a Latin from Manhattan'; later, Betty Grable achieved stardom in the Fox film *Down Argentine Way* (1940). The tango added a frisson of the foreign and wondrous to the dance films of the 1930s and 1940s, but it was not alone. Many other dances competed or came to vie for an exotic place in the modern imagination, among them the cha-cha-cha, merengue, rumba and mambo. Lesser dance steps, too, were discovered or invented in the hope that they would enter into a standard ballroom vocabulary, but with little success. Even the mambo, with its Latin lineage and lusty sheen, is greatly eclipsed by the larger, more resonant, more complex image of the tango. In the 1994 film *True Lies*, the tango danced by Arnold Schwarzenegger testifies to the hero's sensuousness and grace at large scale.

Of the many dances to have entered the modern ballroom repertoire, the tango has been the most successful in preserving its sense of tempestuous ethnicity. In part because its Argentine origins suggest not only a cultural connection with Europe but also a political anarchy and social upheaval, the dance has come to represent a strong sense of difference and alienation.

From 1913 on the tango has been an inspiration to fashion designers, with splits, frills, flounces and fringes all making their appearance in both day and evening wear. The influence revived in the 1980s and 1990s with the international success of shows such as *Tango Argentino* and *Tango X-2*.

Here the tango theme is used to show to best advantage a silk flowered dress by Gianni Versace and a white wool suit by Lanvin *(left)*. The bandoneon-player below is wearing a printed and embroidered crepe dress by Hanza and hoop earrings and bangles by Alexsa, from the French magazine *Madame Figaro*, 17 April 1993.

Above: Cecilia Narova as Milonguita and Nelson [Avila] as El Rufián in *Tango Argentino.*

Tango Argentino, the most spectacular tango show ever produced, was the creation of the Buenos Aires designers Claudio Segovia and Héctor Orezzoli. It opened in Paris in 1983 as part of the Festival d'Automne. Although by the opening night only 200 or so advance tickets had been sold, the rave reviews that greeted the first performance ensured that the entire run would be a huge success. The show went on to conquer Broadway and also played to highly enthusiastic audiences elsewhere in the USA and across Europe and Japan.

Above: Nélida [Rodríguez] and Nelson [Avila] on the left and Gloria [Julia Barraud] and Eduardo [Arquimbaud] on the right dance to the music of 'Quejas de bandoneón' by Juan de Dios Filiberto in the finale of *Tango Argentino*.

Tango Argentino relates the history of the tango through a sequence of dances and songs. It includes all the great tango classics, from Villoldo to Troilo, Discépolo to Piazzolla, Filiberto to Pugliese, and explores the major tango themes.

Below: In the first dance number of *Tango Argentino*, two male couples – *compadritos* – perform the tango to the music of 'El apache argentino' by Manuel Aróztegui, written around 1910.

The dancers shown here, from the performance in Vienna on 28 April 1989, are: *back, left and right*, Carlos Bórquez and Luis Pereya; *front, left and right*, Miguel Angel Zotto and Nelson [Avila].

Opposite: Pablo Verón and Gisela Graf Merino dancing to 'Quejas de bandoneón' by Juan de Dios Filiberto in *Fous des Folies*, directed by Alfredo Arias, at the Folies-Bergère, Paris, 1993.

Above: **María Nieves and Juan Carlos Copes in *Tango, Tango*, at the Teatro Lola Membrines, Buenos Aires, 1988. This show was a homage to the tango, composed of a series of historical vignettes. Nieves and Copes are shown here dancing to the 1888 tango 'Dáme la lata'.**

Right: **Miguel Angel Zotto and Milena Plebs dance to the music of 'Inspiración' by Peregrino Paulos and Luis Rubinstein in *Tango Para Dos* (*Tango X 2*).**

Tango X 2, a tribute to Carlos Gardel, was conceived, choreographed and directed by Miguel Angel Zotto and Milena Plebs, who began their career together performing in *Tango Argentino.* Created in 1988, *Tango X 2* toured throughout Latin America, Eastern and Western Europe and the Far East. The London production, shown here, was called *Tango Para Dos.*

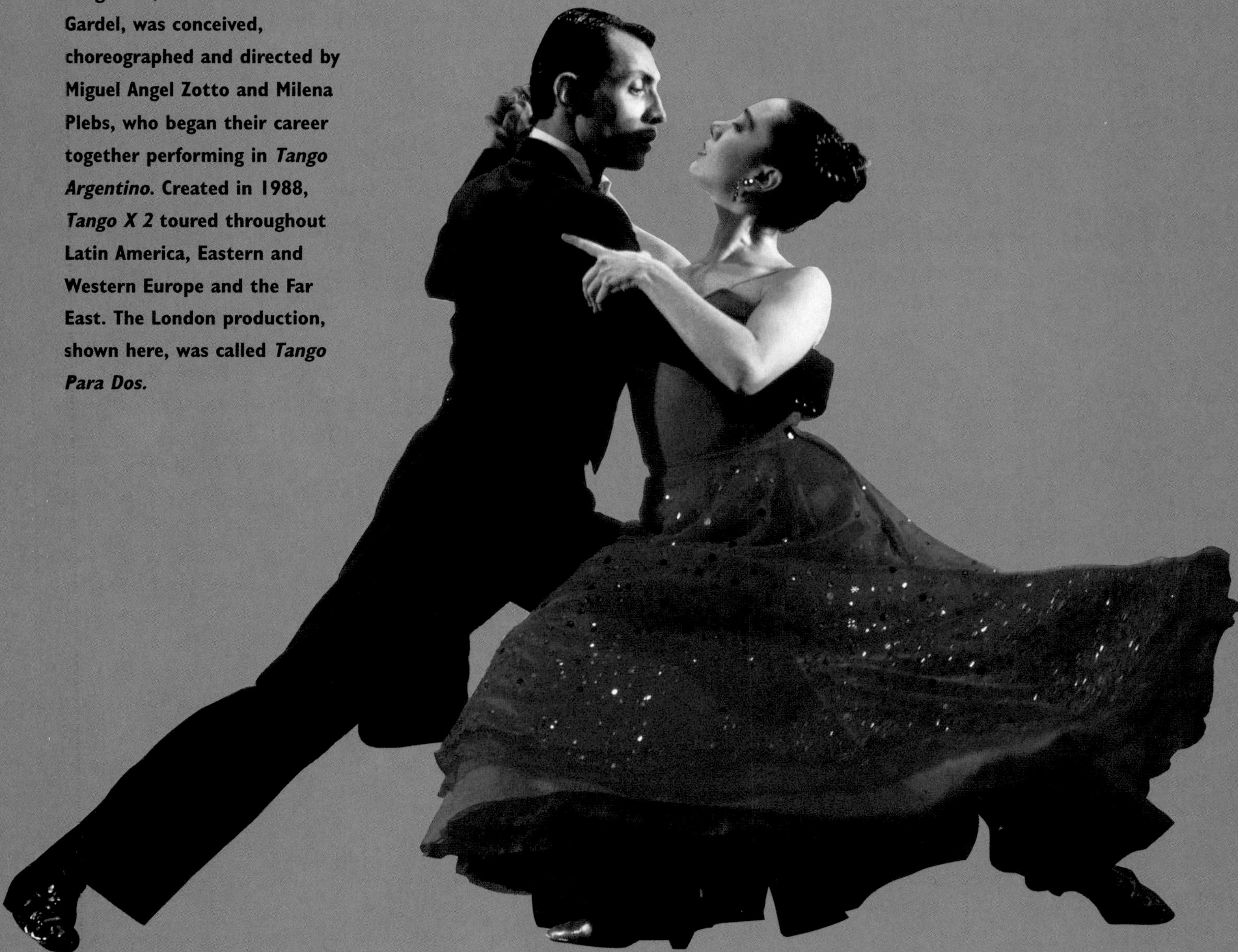

Above: Osvaldo Zotto and Mora dance 'Tango Americano' from *Tango Para Dos* (*Tango X 2*). This dance was inspired by the ballroom partners Vélez and Yolanda in the film *The Pride of the Bianchis*, 1941.

The tango arrived in Helsinki in 1913 and has since become the national dance of Finland, so much so that the Finns do not think of the tango as Argentine, but as Finnish. The Finnish tango is not an urban dance; it is typically danced in the summertime in country pavilions like the one *above*.

***Right:* A young couple dancing the tango in Rutan Park, Beijing.**

National Geographic reported in July 1991 that Chinese young people meeting in Beijing's Ditan Park in the mornings had forsaken the measured movements of *tai ji quan*, an ancient martial art, in favour of the tango, transmitted on portable stereos. Still associated in the Western mind with the political instabilities and romanticist desires of Argentina, topped up by the romanticism of Paris, the tango remains a dance of rebellious spirit even as it has been incorporated into the modern canon of ballroom dancing. In fact, contemporary Beijing is only one among many capital cities smitten over the years with the tango. Czech historians Eve Uchalova and Milena Zeminova have described its role in Prague just before the First World War:

> The metropolitan character of Prague was also underlined by a number of newly opened restaurants, cafés and also entertainment halls such as Montmartre in Retezova street, which was founded in 1911, or Tabarin and Alhambra, which were the first places in Prague where modern dance styles like 'Maxixe Brasilienne', 'Tao-tao', 'Two-step', and tango become common. Before the First World War, the tango predominated society life in Prague – there were even advertisements for corset 'tango' and dress 'tango', which had a purple-orange colour. Tango dance style was taught at dancing schools and the Vinohradské Theatre prepared an original operette of R. Piskacek, 'Madame Tango'.[7]

By the 1920s, the tango had become a dance form associated with the avant-garde, seldom to be detached from its spirit of insolence and insurgence. Later in the century, rock 'n' roll, with its most atomized dancing, would take on a similar sensibility, but for the middle third of the twentieth century the tango shared a place with all advanced art forms. Even as the political life of Argentina passed from expression to repression and back to expression again, the tango enthralled the avant-garde in the arts through to the legendary beatniks of the 1950s. María Susana Azzi has captured the convolution of the tango's social message and therapy in arguing for its indivisible wholeness:

> Tango is a whole system of concepts, images, words, and practices, some of them ritual ones. One cannot possibly understand a part of the whole, if isolated from the remaining parts of that whole. In the context of tango, dancing makes sense along with music, the *bandoneón* along with the nostalgia evoked, memories from the past together with a given way of visualizing

One of the tango's strongest bases over the past few decades has been Japan. The pioneer of the tango in Japan was an aristocrat, Baron Megata, who learned the dance in Paris in the 1920s. He took some French recordings back home and started giving lessons himself. A number of Japanese tango bands were formed in the 1930s and by the 1950s at least two dozen were working. The most celebrated ensemble, the Orquesta Típica Tokio, led by Shimpei Hayakawa, was established in 1947. In 1954 Juan Canaro and his band became the first Argentines to play in Japan. Juan's more famous brother, Francisco, followed in 1961. Since then many Argentine bands have toured Japan. In 1987, when *Tango Argentino* was shown on Japanese television, the magazine *Asahi Graph* devoted an entire issue to the show (*above*).

The 1921 box-office hit *The Four Horsemen of the Apocalypse* made Rudolph Valentino a star. In the film Valentino played the archetypal 'Latin lover' and danced the tango in both 'Hollywood gaucho' and Parisian style.

The 1977 film *Valentino*, by the British director Ken Russell, tells the story of the actor's life from his early days to his years as an international screen idol.

Valentino arrived in New York from Italy in 1913 – the year of the tango. He took a series of menial jobs before eventually becoming a dancer in nightclubs and dance halls. He is shown *above*, played by Rudolf Nureyev, teaching the tango to the ballet dancer Vaslav Nijinsky, played by Anthony Dowell.

> the world, which is characteristic of the true tango lover. Tango is a complex social phenomenon.[8]

In the same years of Prague's infatuation with the dance and Buenos Aires's great international reputation, Paris had been enthralled for similar reasons. The second and third decades of the twentieth century were notable for the infusion of foreign and exotic influences into Western culture, assimilating Poiret's overt exoticism of dress, allowing for the influences of Africa to emerge triumphant in the arts and popular entertainment of North America and Europe, jazz's jubilant rise from African-Caribbean cultures into a high aesthetic of music, and the tango, with its history of South American exoticism, its link with black culture, and its unrepentant, smouldering sensuality. The tango was not unaccompanied then or now as a powerful agent of cultural change. The intervention of another cultural model meant that each of these possibilities arrived whole and internally coherent, not subject to the parsing of dominant Western culture, but as the 'whole' culture of the tango as postulated by Azzi. By the 1920s, the détente in high art in the West was being offset by the ideas of foreign or forgotten cultures that offered an actuality or cultural conviction largely vitiated in the West. Jazz's power is indicative: first embraced more as fad than as musical canon by the dominant culture, jazz proved its place in mainstream Western culture where it could be regarded as more powerful because of its black and innocent roots. Similarly, the tango earned its integration into Western culture after a first advent at the invitation of fad. Arriving in mainstream Western culture, the tango as a dance was accompanied by its own music of memory and melancholy and its volatile world of passionate love and expressive lovers.

In the United States, the vision of the tango was especially linked in the popular mind to the 'Latin lover', the romantic leading man embodied in the 1920s films of Rudolph Valentino. Tangos figure in the Valentino films *The Four Horsemen of the Apocalypse* (1921) and *Blood and Sand* (1922), as well as in the Ken Russell film *Valentino* (1977). Like the ostensible machismo of the dance, the actual personifications of the Latin lover that Hollywood created were probably more sexually complex than the overt image, but the dance was associated with a particular male icon, one that reinforced even in the movies the exoticism of the tango. In like manner, the recent revivals of the tango in Japan and Finland suggest the considerable reach of the tango and its continuing ability to perform as a dance of the exotic in far-flung parts of the globe. Ironically, dance has often become a cultural symbol either in terms of high-art dance or ballet or, at the other extreme, folk dance. Ballroom dancing, from which the tango propagated its worldwide fascination, has seldom taken on the supposed value of its more sophisticated cousins in performance or its lesser relations in peasant and ritual dance. The tango began in brothels and bars; its social codification and even its uneasy role in the ballrooms of the world were possible only in the century that exalts in a *nostalgie de la boue* and is capable of engendering art from the most squalid and commonplace of emotions and circumstance.

The renewed upsurge of interest in the tango since the 1980s has led to a proliferation of tango clubs and classes throughout Europe (*below*) as well as in Japan and other areas of the Far East.

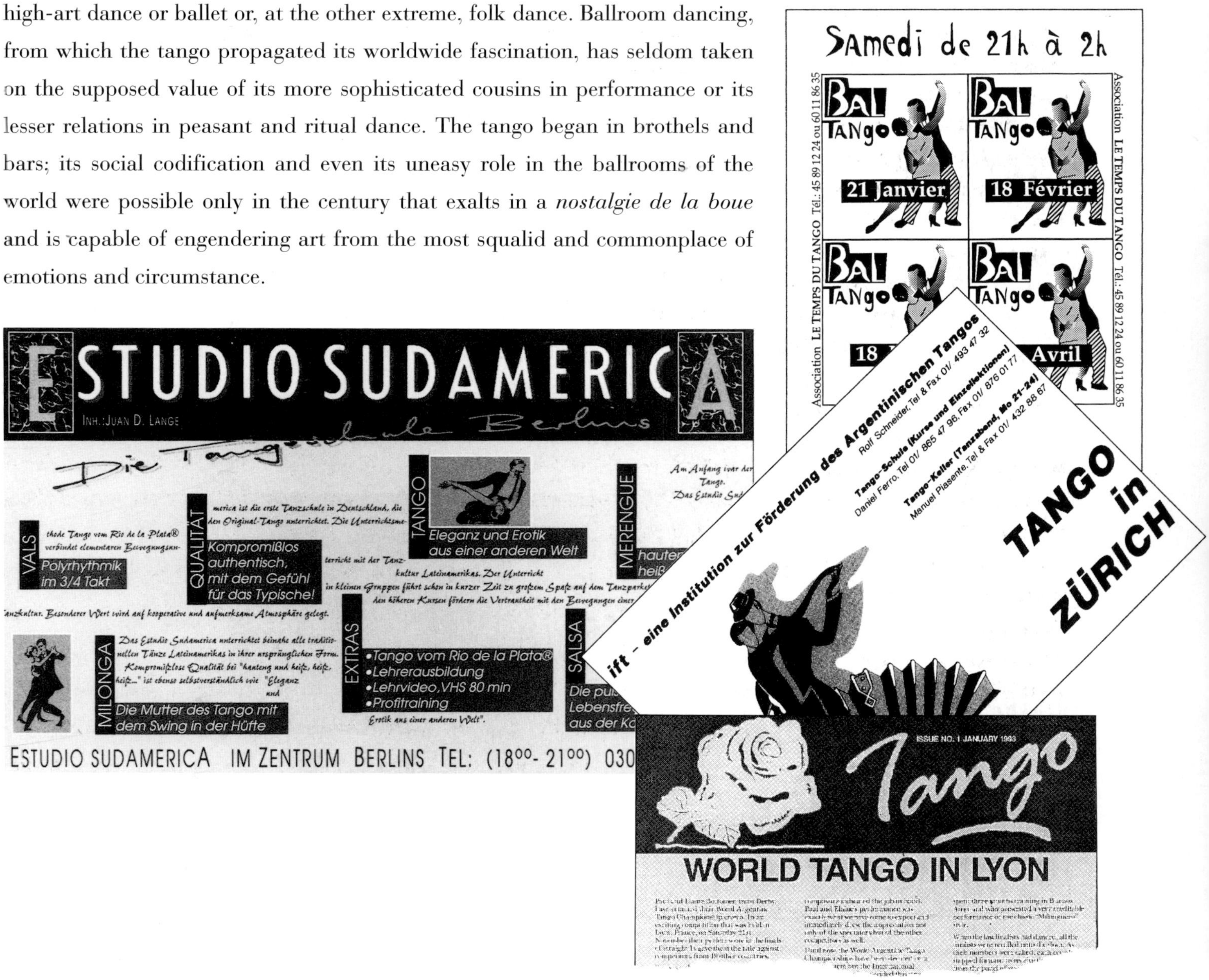

The tango thrives in clubs and dance halls across the world (*below*). It is kept alive by the skill and enthusiasm of dancers like Paul and Elaine Bottomer,

shown *above right* performing the final movement of the tango. The Bottomers are four times undefeated Supreme World and European Argentine Tango Champions and World Cup Winners.

To describe the tango in twentieth-century culture is not to perceive a dance alone, but to realize concepts of gender, sexuality, physicality and sensual desire in pre-Millennial times. Like other phenomena of significance to the century, the tango's principles are not wholly fixed. One can still dispute the exact equilibrium between male and female, violence and control, but the continuing uncertainty regarding its meaning is another warrant for its cultural importance. Further, the tango seemed to come from an illicit and deprived culture, with elements of destitution and coarseness. The century's special privilege is given only to that which still carries overtones of lust and earth. The tango arrived as a tawdry seduction like the ladies of Picasso's *Les Demoiselles d'Avignon*, similarly to become an avatar of the modern spirit, a distilled emotion of the senses brought to the culturally prismatic mirror of the modern.

The tango's passionate dance has become a compelling metaphor of the modern. Hence, there will never be a last tango: the tango is the ceaseless dance that we may choose to call death, that we affirm as sensual expression, that we gauge as political or individual liberty, that we see as life, and that we cannot stop.

FURTHER INFORMATION

Chart of the History of the Tango................ 198

Tango Music on Compact Disc.............. 199

International Tango Centres..............201

Notes.............................203

Bibliography.................. 204

Sources of Illustrations................205

Sources of Quotations................. 206

Acknowledgments........... 206

Index.............................207

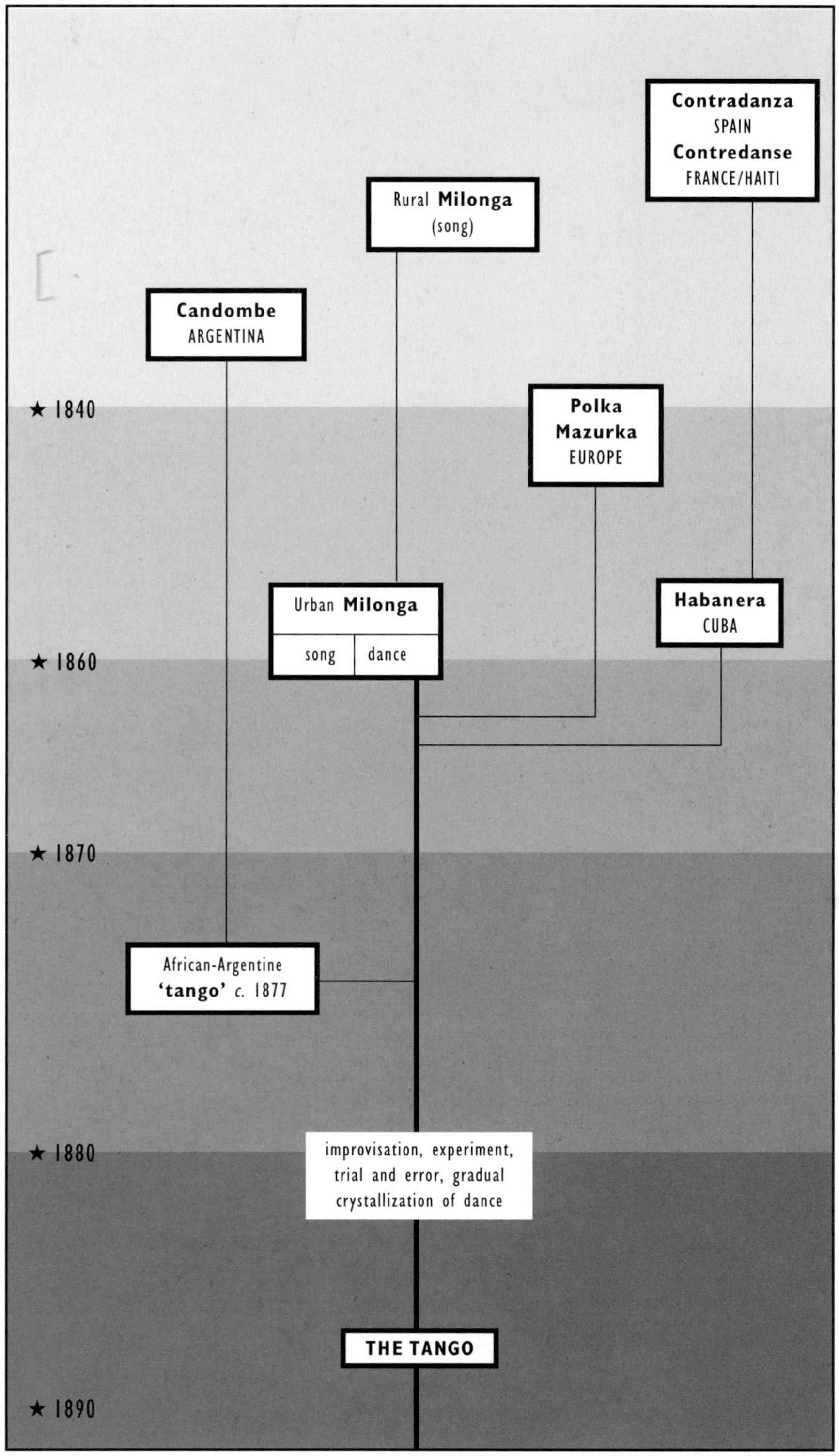

Dates approximate

THE TANGO'S FAMILY TREE

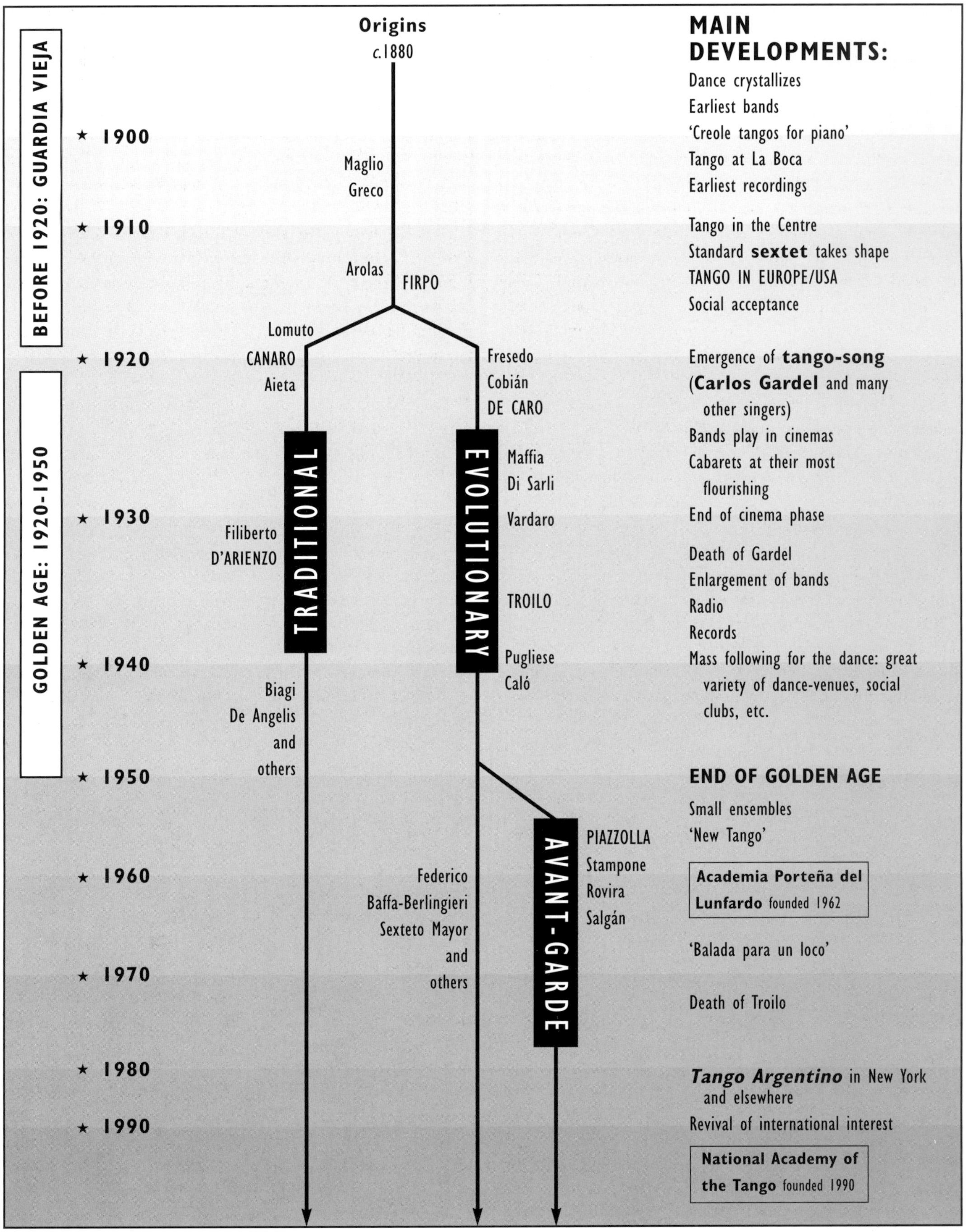
BEFORE 1920: GUARDIA VIEJA
GOLDEN AGE: 1920-1950
Origins
c.1880
MAIN DEVELOPMENTS:
Dance crystallizes
Earliest bands
'Creole tangos for piano'
Tango at La Boca
Earliest recordings
★ 1900
Maglio
Greco
★ 1910
Tango in the Centre
Standard sextet takes shape
TANGO IN EUROPE/USA
Social acceptance
Arolas
FIRPO
Lomuto
★ 1920
CANARO
Aieta
Fresedo
Cobián
DE CARO
Emergence of tango-song (Carlos Gardel and many other singers)
Bands play in cinemas
Cabarets at their most flourishing
End of cinema phase
TRADITIONAL
EVOLUTIONARY
Maffia
Di Sarli
★ 1930
Vardaro
Filiberto
D'ARIENZO
Death of Gardel
Enlargement of bands
Radio
Records
TROILO
★ 1940
Pugliese
Caló
Mass following for the dance: great variety of dance-venues, social clubs, etc.
Biagi
De Angelis
and
others
★ 1950
END OF GOLDEN AGE
Small ensembles
'New Tango'
AVANT-GARDE
PIAZZOLLA
Stampone
Rovira
Salgán
★ 1960
Federico
Baffa-Berlingieri
Sexteto Mayor
and
others
Academia Porteña del Lunfardo founded 1962
'Balada para un loco'
★ 1970
Death of Troilo
★ 1980
Tango Argentino in New York and elsewhere
★ 1990
Revival of international interest
National Academy of the Tango founded 1990

CHART OF THE HISTORY OF THE TANGO

★ ★ ★ ★ ★ ★ ★ ★ TANGO MUSIC ON COMPACT DISC ★ ★ ★ ★ ★ ★ ★ ★

Tango music, first recorded in 1902, is successfully surviving the transition from the eras of the classic 78 rpm record and the 33 rpm LP to the age of the compact disc. New albums are constantly being released, not only by the various national affiliates of the multinational record companies (especially EMI, Polygram and BMG) but also by an apparently growing number of independent labels doing valuable work in reissuing historic recordings. (Some of the most promising such labels are those releasing the albums suggested below.) No complete tango 'discography' can possibly hope to remain up-to-date for very long. As for availability, the position varies according to country and, indeed, city. For obvious reasons, the largest selection of tango CDs is always to be found in Buenos Aires. In record stores in Britain and the USA, tango records should be looked for in the trays marked **World Music** (a category invented in London in 1987), and usually in the **Argentina** sections. Carlos Gardel sometimes has a section to himself, as does Astor Piazzolla (who is now also occasionally found under 'P' in the **Classical** trays).

The eighty or so titles listed below represent only a selection of the good-quality tango CDs available in the mid-1990s. For convenience, a country of release is shown for each title (after the *label* and *number*), though this does not, of course, mean that the CD has not been released elsewhere or that distribution is restricted to the country named.

THE GOLDEN AGE

There is now a good (and growing) choice of albums by both 'traditional' and 'evolutionary' bands: **Julio de Caro y Su Sexteto Típico 1926-1928** (El Bandoneón EBCD 6 /Spain); **Francisco Lomuto, Vol. 1, 1927-1930** (A.V.Alma CTA-731 /Japan); **Juan Maglio (Pacho), 1929-1930** (A.V.Alma CTA-721 /Japan); **Tangos: Francisco Canaro** (EPM Musique 995322 /France); **Francisco Canaro: 20 Grandes Exitos** (EMI 7 978782 /Argentina); **Francisco Canaro: la Melodía de Nuestro Adiós, 1932-1938** (El Bandoneón EBCD 30 /Spain); **Quinteto Pirincho (Dir. Francisco Canaro) en FM Tango** [the quintet formed by Canaro in 1937] (EMI 8 28541-2 /Argentina); **Orquesta Típica Víctor, 1925-1934** [legendary 'house band' of the Victor label] (El Bandoneón EBCD 41 /Spain); **Orquesta Típica Select 1920** [an interesting precursor band] (Harlequin HQ CD 47 /UK); **Edgardo Donato, Vol. I, 1932-1941** (A.V.Alma CTA-241 /Japan); **Ciriaco Ortiz, Vol. I, 1933-1952** [one of the greatest bandoneonists] (A.V.Alma CTA-251 /Japan); **Miguel Caló y Su Orquesta Típica en FM Tango** (EMI 8 285422 /Argentina); **Yo Soy El Tango: Miguel Caló y Su Orquesta Típica** (El Bandoneón EBCD 34 /Spain); **Carlos Di Sarli: Milonguero Viejo** (Music Hall 10.018-2 /Argentina); **Todo Carlos Di Sarli de FM Tango Para Usted** (RCA/BMG 74321-16108-2 /Argentina); **Osvaldo Fresedo: Vida Mía** (RCA/BMG 74321-18711-2 /Argentina); **Osvaldo Fresedo, 1927-1928** (A.V.Alma CTA-741 /Japan); **Roberto Firpo, Vol. I, 1927-1929** (A.V.Alma CTA-711 /Japan); **Alma de Bohemio: Roberto Firpo y Su Cuarteto** (El Bandoneón EBCD 8 /Spain); **Trío Argentino** [the celebrated Irusta-Fugazot-Demare Trio] (Pentagrama PCD 214 /Mexico); **Juan D'Arienzo For Export** (RCA/BMG ECD 1004 /Argentina); **Todo D'Agostino-Vargas de FM Tango Para Usted, Vol. I** (RCA/BMG ECD 50617 /Argentina); **Alberto Castillo y Su Orquesta Típica: 50 Años de Su Primera Grabación 1943-1993 en FM Tango** (EMI 8 27832-2 /Argentina); **Todo Tanturi-Castillo de FM Tango Para Usted** (RCA/BMG ECD 50642 /Argentina); **Osvaldo Pugliese y Su Orquesta, 1949** (El Bandoneón EBCD 5 /Spain).

Useful Golden Age anthologies include **Instrumental Tangos of the Golden Age** (Harlequin HQ CD 45 /UK) [period tracks from the bands of Julio De Caro, Pedro Laurenz, Juan de Dios Filiberto, Roberto Firpo, Carlos Di Sarli, Francisco Canaro, Aníbal Troilo]; and **La Cumparsita: 20 Veces Inmortal** (EMI 7 97519-2 /Argentina) [Firpo, Canaro, De Caro, Rodolfo Biagi, Troilo, D'Arienzo, Pugliese, Alfredo de Angelis and others].

Among welcome compilations of *ANIBAL TROILO*'s recordings are: **Aníbal Troilo: Quejas de Bandoneón** (Music Hall 10.016-2 /Argentina); and **Aníbal Troilo, el Inmortal Pichuco, 1941** (El Bandoneón EBCD 1 /Spain); and his successive collaborations with vocalists are available on **Todo Aníbal Troilo-Fiorentino de FM Tango Para Usted, Vol. I** [Francisco Fiorentino] (RCA/BMG ECD 50628 /Argentina); **Todo Troilo-Marino de FM Tango Para Usted** [Alberto Marino] (RCA/BMG ECD 74321 16109-2 /Argentina); **Todo Aníbal Troilo-Floreal Ruiz de FM Tango Para Usted** (RCA/BMG ECD 74321 16110-2 /Argentina); and **¿Te Acordás, Polaco?** [Roberto Goyeneche] (RCA ECD 1002 /Argentina).

Important *MEN SINGERS* of the time are also anthologized on **El Tango Canción: Gardel, Corsini, Magaldi...** (EPM Musique 995222 /France). Albums of individual singers include: **Ignacio Corsini, El Caballero Cantor, 1935-1945** (El Bandoneón EBCD 37 /Spain); **Agustín Magaldi, La Voz Sentimental de Buenos Aires** (RCA/BMG 74321 20758-2 /Argentina); **Los 20 Super Exitos de Floreal Ruiz** (Sony/Microfon 2-30110 /Argentina); **Angel Vargas, El Ruiseñor de las Calles Porteñas** (RCA/BMG ECD 74321 19955-2 /Argentina); (Microfon C-83 /USA); **Edmundo Rivero, 'Mano a Mano'**

Con Celedonio Flores (Philips 510512-2 /Argentina); **Edmundo Rivero Canta a Discépolo en FM Tango** (Philips 512649-2 /Argentina). Two rich anthologies of the great *WOMEN SINGERS* of the Golden Age (including Ada Falcón, Rosita Quiroga, Azucena Maizani, Mercedes Simone and Libertad Lamarque) are **Tango Ladies** (Harlequin HQ CD 34 /UK) and **Se Va La Vida** (Harlequin HQ CD 52 /UK).

CARLOS GARDEL

The fullest collection so far available (nearly 300 songs, grouped thematically, with subtitles for each record) is a seventeen-CD set, **Carlos Gardel, Su Obra Integral** (El Bandoneón EBCD 11-26 and EBCD 50 /Spain). A number of anthologies have also appeared, e.g., **Las 60 Mejores Canciones de Carlos Gardel**, 2 CDs (Planet P 6006-07CD/ USA), **Carlos Gardel Está Siempre Vivo** (Music Memoria 30829 /France), **Su Majestad El Tango: Carlos Gardel** (RCA 6290-2-RL /USA), or **20 Exitos Originales de Carlos Gardel** (EMI 6387-2RL /Mexico). Gardel's handful of recordings with Francisco Canaro's band have been usefully reissued on **Gardel-Canaro: 20 Grandes Exitos** (EMI 766663-2 /Argentina). Whether Gardel's complete recordings become available on CD (as they were on LP and cassette) remains to be seen.

AFTER THE GOLDEN AGE

Any selection of recommendable albums has to include: **Leopoldo Federico and His Orchestra: Buenos Aires Today** (Music Hall, 10.008-2 /Argentina); **Tango Vol. 1** [Horacio Salgán, piano, Ubaldo de Lío, guitar] (Mandala 4830 /France); **Gran Quinteto Real** (Philips 832 798-2 /Netherlands); **Horacio Salgán en FM Tango** (Philips 518037-2 /Argentina); **Horacio Salgán-Horacio Ferrer: Oratorio Carlos Gardel** (Melopea CDMPV 1070 /Argentina); **Atilio Stampone: Imágenes** (Microfon C-97 /USA); **Osvaldo Berlingieri: Identificación** (Music Hall MH 10.105-2 /Argentina); **Ernesto Baffa** [bandoneon] (Polydor 511409-2 /Argentina); **Mederos Quinteto** [avant-garde] (M&M TK(35)17034 /Argentina); **Sexteto Mayor: 20 Años con Exito en FM Tango** (EMI 8 27776-2 /Argentina); **La Orquesta del Tango de Buenos Aires, Vol. I** (Milan Sur CD CH 702 /Argentina). Some classic 'chamber tango' recordings can be heard on **Aníbal Troilo-Roberto Grela y Su Cuarteto Típico** (RCA/BMG ECD 74321 24418-2 /Argentina). Women singers of the more recent period are represented on **FM Tango Susana Rinaldi** (Philips 518550-2 /Argentina) and **Rosanna Falasca: Los Tangos de Mi Ciudad y Mi Gente** (Diapasón MH 10091-2 /Argentina).

Available recordings by *ASTOR PIAZZOLLA* are abundant, and we make no attempt to be comprehensive. Two thoroughly good collections are **Astor Piazzolla: Tangamente, 1968-1973**, 3 CDs (Just A Memory JAM 9107-9 2 /USA) and **Piazzollissimo: Astor Piazzolla 1974-1983**, 3 CDs (Just A Memory JAM 9013-5 2 /USA). His final, intensively creative years are well displayed in **Astor Piazzolla: the Late Masterpieces**, 3 CDs (American Clavé AMCL 1022 /USA). The Piazzolla-Ferrer 'little opera' is available on **María de Buenos Aires** (Milan 73138 35602-2 /USA). Live recordings of several of his concerts in the 1980s have been released as albums: **Astor Piazzolla y Su Quinteto Nuevo Tango: The Vienna Concert** [October 1983] (Messidor 15922-2 /Germany); **Astor Piazzolla: The Central Park Concert** [September 1987] (Chesky Records JD107 /USA); **Astor Piazzolla: The Lausanne Concert** [November 1989] (Milan 73138 35649-2 /USA).

THE TANGO IN PARIS AND ELSEWHERE

Le Tango à Paris, 1907-1941, 2 CDs (Frémeaux FA012 /France) is a rich collection of recordings by the leading Paris-based tango bands of the 1920s and 1930s, including those of Manuel Pizarro, Eduardo Bianco, Rafael Canaro and Salvador Pizarro. **Original Tangos: Bianco Bachicha y Su Orchestra** [*sic*] (EPM 995302 /France) is an album of recordings from the celebrated band led by Eduardo Bianco and Juan Deambroggio ('Bachicha'). Bianco was the only major tango musician to play before both Hitler and Mussolini. Genaro Espósito's Paris band (tracks from 1924 to 1935) can be heard on **Tango Genaro** (Music Memoria 0777 7 88314 2 6 /France). **Tangos Argentinos: Carlos Gardel** (Music Memoria 30803 /France) is a splendid mish-mash of Paris recordings (including Manuel Pizarro, and six by Gardel; hence the slightly misleading title).

The music from the show that took New York by storm in the mid-1980s is preserved on **Tango Argentino** (Atlantic 7 81636-2 /USA). A praiseworthy album by New York musicians (though with an accordion used in place of the bandoneon) is **The Tango Project** (Elektra/Nonesuch 9 79030-2 /USA). The tradition of tango music in Finland can be sampled on **Tangokuninkaat** (Fazer Finnlevy MCD 29 /Germany) and **Eino Grön: Parhaat** (Fazer Finnlevy 420122 /Austria).

Some of the above-listed albums are also available on cassette.

FM Tango, which forms part of thirteen of the titles shown above, is an all-tango radio station in Buenos Aires (95.9 on the FM dial) collaborating in the production of the CDs mentioned.

★ ★ ★ ★ ★ ★ ★ ★ INTERNATIONAL TANGO CENTRES ★ ★ ★ ★ ★ ★ ★ ★

Many tango centres are long-established. Some appear for a few years and then disappear, to be replaced by others. Up-to-date information on new centres can often be obtained by contacting national ballroom dancing organizations or by telephoning the relevant Argentine embassy.

ARGENTINA (country code: 54)

BAHÍA BLANCA
Academia del Tango de Bahía Blanca, Mitre 259 p. 7'B', CP 8000. Tel.: (91) 25136

BUENOS AIRES (dance salons)
Buenos Aires Hoy, Bulnes 1598. Tel.: (1) 825 3740
Club Akarense, Donado 1355. Tel.: (1) 552 1561
Club Almagro, Pedro A. Medrano 522. Tel.: (1) 744 7454
Club Social Rivadavia, Av. Rivadavia 6465. Tel.: (1) 632 8684
Club Sunderland, Lugones 3161. Tel.: (1) 541 9776
Ideal, Suipacha 384 p.1. Tel.: (1) 553 2466
La Argentina, Rodríguez Peña 361. Tel.: (1) 413 7239
La Galería, Boedo 724. Tel.: (1) 93 7527/957 1829
La Trastienda, Balcarce 460. Tel.: (1) 342 7650
Parakultural, Chacabuco 1072. Tel.: (1) 362 2408
Regin, Riobamba 416
Salón Canning, R. Scalabrini Ortiz 1331. (1) 831 2662/856 4798
Sin Rumbo, José P. Tamborini 6157. Tel.: (1) 571 9577

CÓRDOBA
Academia del Tango de Córdoba, Cleto Peña 1860/62 - Barrio Maipú 2da Sección CP 5000. Tel.: (51) 55 0493

LA PLATA
Asociación Amigos del Tango, Calle 2 no.711, CP 1900

LOMAS DE ZAMORA
Academia del Tango de Lomas de Zamora, Cerrito 1559, CP 1834. Tel.: 243 6444

MAR DEL PLATA
Academia de Tango de Mar del Plata, Av. Colón 1835 p. 1 'B', CP 7600. Tel.: (23) 20699

QUILMES
Academia del Tango de Quilmes, Jujuy 268, CP 1878. Tel.: 252 7394 Fax: 259 0389

SANTIAGO DEL ESTERO
Asociación Barrio de Tango, Calle 53 no 74, CP 4200. Tel.: (85) 31 1718

AUSTRIA (country code: 43)

VIENNA
Toledo Tango Club (dance salon), Andino, Münzwardeingasse 2/1 Stock. Tel.: (1) 402 2922 / 403 1815
Tango im La Colombie (dance salon), Laudongasse 57. Tel.: (1) 408 3045

BELGIUM (country code: 32)

ANTWERP
Danscentrum Polariteit (school), ISO, Rembrandtstr. 22. Tel.: (3) 238 2630

BORGERHOUT
Doble 'T (school, dance salon), Nieuwe Ringtheater, Pastorijstr. 23. Tel.: (3) 232 6720/281 0684

BRUGES
Polariteit (school), St. Jansstr. 11 (zij ingang). Tel.: (50) 38 2686

BRUSSELS
Buenos Aires Tango Club. Tel.: (2) 512 9143
Canal Tango (school, dance salon), Au Tropical, 43 Chaussée de Waterloo, 1060
Christiane & Pedro, Jazzcenter Monetta Loza (school), 11 Rue de la Concorde; 39a Rue du Pont Neuf (dance salon)
Christina & Adriaan (school), Académie de musique et de la dance. Tel.: (2) 736 0577

GHENT
Danscentrum Polariteit, Verkortingsstraat 55, 9040 Gent/St Amandsberg (school).Tel.: (91) 238 2630. *And* Kunstcentrum Voruit, St Pieternieuwstr. 23 (dance salon)

LOUVAIN
Christiane y Pedro (school), De Smet-Camby Dance School, Mechelsesteenweg 732, 3020 Herent

CANADA (country code: 1)

MONTREAL
Denis Beauchamp, 5420 Rue St. Denis. Tel.: (514) 279-6139

TORONTO
Grupo de Tango de Buenos Aires (school, dance salon). Tel.: (416) 638 1285

CHILE (country code: 56)

SANTIAGO
Agustín Magaldi (school, dance salon), Nataniel 1220. Tel.: (2) 556 6761
Argentino Ledesma (school, dance salon), Portugal 1288. Tel.: (2) 556 1786
Buenos Aires (school, dance salon), Recoleta 1267. Tel.: (2) 777 9226
Enrique S. Discépolo (school, dance salon), San Francisco 668. Tel.: (2) 639 9407
Taller de Tango (school), Lano Subercaseaux 3597. Tel.: (2) 555 2262

CUBA (country code: 53)

HAVANA
Academia del Tango de Cuba, Justiz, 21 Bajos

DENMARK (country code: 45)

COPENHAGEN
Tangoskolen (school), Kronprinsessegade 43, 3.tv. Tel.: (1) 3314 1489

FINLAND (country code: 358)

SEINÄJOKI
Tangomusiikin Edistämisyhdistys Ry, (The Association of Promoting Tango Music), Chair, Reijo Pitkäkoski, Kauppakatu 15C, 60100 Seinäjoki. Tel.: (9) 64 414 7205. Fax: (9) 64 414 2350
Kansainvälinen Tangokeskus (International Tango Centre), Kauppakatu 15C, 60100 Seinäjoki. Tel.: (9) 64 414 7204. Fax: (9) 64 414 2350

The following are chiefly dancing pavilions, where the tango, the jenkka and the humppa are danced.

HELSINKI AREA
Helsinki Pavi, Honkanumment 6, Vantaa. Tel.: (90) 875 2595
Korpilampi, Korpilammentie, Espoo. Tel.: (90) 86721
Männistön Lava, Kellokoski. Tel.: (949) 800 453
Mäntsälän Lava, Mäntsälä. Tel.: (90) 871 524
Nupurinkartano, Nupurinkalliont, 3, Espoo. Tel.: (90) 86701

OTHER LOCATIONS *(listed alphabetically by location)*
Hämeen Lääni, Katuman lava, Haukipolku 2, Harvialan kylä, Hämeenlinna. Tel.: (917) 6196981
Lapin Lääni, Perävaaran Huvikeskus, Kemijärvi. Tel.: (949) 693775
Kymen Lääni, Tykkimäen Tanssipalatsi, Tykkimäen huvipuisto, Kouvola. Tel.: (951) 3724777
Keski-Suomen Lääni, Kuikan lava, Kuikka. Tel.: (941) 752616
Kuopion Lääni, Ilveskasino, Pellesmäki, Kuopio. Tel.: (971) 3623523
Vaasan Lääni, Hakosaaren huvikeskus, Lappajärvi. Tel.: (966) 66015
Pohjois-Karjalan Lääni, Liperin lava, Liperi. Tel.: (973) 651351
Mikkelin Lääni, Tommolan suurlava, Tommolansalmi, Mäntyharju. Tel.: (956) 31155
Oulun Lääni, Hietasaaren tanssipaviljonki, Hietasaarent, Oulu. Tel.: (981) 5541931
Turun-Ja Porinlääni, Uittamo-paviljonki, Turku 10. Tel.: (921) 2356153

FRANCE (country code: 33)

ARRAS
Dance Club Arrageois (school), 175 av. John Kennedy, 6200. Tel.: 21 71 53 37

BORDEAUX
Association Cruz del Sur, 15 rue du Port, 33800. Tel.: 56 31 47 13
Ecole de danse espace forme (dance salon), 136 bd. Pierre Dignac, 33470. Tel.: 56 66 00 25

MARSEILLE
Tango Argentin Les Trottoirs de Marseille, 18 rue Lodi, 13006. Tel.: 91 48 09 29

MONTPELIER
Tango Théâtres, 16 rue René Cassin, 34000. Tel.: 67 42 32 04

NICE
Les Amis du Tango, c/o Mme Claudine Cousin, 31 rue Delille, 06000. Tel.: 93 62 15 99

PARIS
Le Bistro Latin (school, dance salon), 20 rue du Temple 75004. Tel.: (1) 42 77 21 11
Centre d'Animation Point du Jour (school, dance salon), 1 rue du Général Malleterre, 75016. Tel.: (1) 45 25 14 19
Gymnase Club Lafayette, 10 rue Victoire, 75009. Tel.: (1) 48 74 58 49
La Maison Verte (dance salon), ANS, 13 rue Meilhac, 75015. Tel.: (1) 43 06 02 82
Smoking et Brillantine (school, dance salon, show), 13 rue Guyton-de-Morveau, 75013. Tel.: (1) 45 65 92 29

GERMANY (country code: 49)

BERLIN
La Caminada (school), Böckstr. 21-Kreuzberg. Tel.: (30) 216 3643
Stephan Wiesner & Ulrike Schladerbach (school), Friedrichstr. 217. Tel.: (30) 251 9197
!Tango Vivo! (school), Gneisenaustr. 109/110, 3e Aufgang, 2e Stock *Inf.*:Krummestr. 6 PLZ 12203. Tel.: (30) 833-3166
Tanzart (dance salon), Hasenheide 54 PLZ 10967, 3e Aufg. 3e St. Tel.: (30) 693 6019
Irmel Weber (school), Querhaus, Moskauerstr. 24. Tel.: (30) 251 9197

BREMEN
Amira & Michael (workshop, show), Staderstr. 35 PLZ 28205. Tel.: (421) 44 2284
Tanguero (dance salon), Sielwall 44
Tango-Tanz-Tee (dance salon), Karree-Raum für Kulturarbeit, Hollerstr. 6

COLOGNE
Estudio Tango Argentino (school), Basement Herwardthstr. under the church. *Inf*: Alpenerplatz 2 PLZ 50825. Tel.: (221) 34 1234

CONSTANCE
Tango-Argentina Club. Tel.: (7531) 65 684
Tango-Tanzcafé 'Café Muse' (dance salon), Benediktinerplatz 2

DARMSTADT
Tango (dance salon), Restaurante Barcelona, Erbacherstr. 18. Tel.: (6151) 29 6499

DORTMUND
Piano-Theater-Bar (dance salon), Lütgendortmunderstr. 43
Tango vom Rio de la Plata (school). Tel.: (231) 49 8505

ERKRATH HOCHDAHL
Tango-Treff, Studio Leiendecker, Hauptstr. 1. Tel.: (2103) 69368

FRANKFURT
Tango Café (school, dance salon), Kasselerstr. 1a in Öko-Haus. Tel.: (69) 77 8055

FREIBURG
Tango (dance salon), Tap Dance Company, Wallstr. 14
Los Tangueros del Puente Azul (dance salon), Habsburgerstr. 9

FÜRTH
Tango Bar (dance salon), Café Fürst, Ludwig-Erhard Str. 2

GÖTTINGEN
Academia de Tango Argentino (dance salon), Komm. and Arktionszentrum, Hospitalstr. Tel.: (551) 57 883

HAMBURG
Tango Azul (dance salon), Beim Grünen Jäger 6A. Tel.: (40) 430 6168/742 4635
Tangogotan (school), Leverkusenstr. 25 PLZ 22761. Tel.: (40) 494097

HANOVER
Tango im Loft (dance salon), Georg Str. 50b
Tango in Milieu (dance salon), Wilhelm-Bluhm Str. 12

KARLSRUHE
Patio de Tango (dance salon), Café Havanna, Hardtstr. 37A

KASSEL
Tango Zero (school, dance salon), Sandershäuser Str. 77. Tel.: (561) 28 1209

MARBURG
Tango Los Malditos, Lahngarten, Wehrdaerstr. 102
Tangoschwof (dance salon),

Hansenhaus 'Rechts'
Sonnenblickallee 9

MUNICH
I.B.P. (school), SchleissheimerStr. 22-24 PLZ 80333. Tel.: (89) 52-9970
Tango Feroz (dance salon), Innere Wienerstr. 19
Tango Forum (dance salon), Lothringer Str. 10
Tango Tanz Momente (dance salon), Teamtheater Tankstelle, Am Einlass 2a
Que Tango!, Lothringer Str. 9 PLZ 81667 (school). Tel.: (89) 448 8266
Lothringer Bierhalle, Lothringer Str. 10 (dance salon)

MUNSTER
Tango-Abend (dance salon), Aegidistr. 46

REGENSBURG
Tango-Werkstatt Regensburg (school), *Inf:* Christiane Kroniger, Tannenstr. 10, D-93152 Undorf. Tel.: (941) 2176

SCHAFFHAUSEN
Tango-Tanzabend (dance salon), Safrangasse 8, im Kellergewölbe. Tel.: (53) 33 4665

STUTTGART
Tango Vorstadt (school, dance salon), Friedhofstrasse 71, PLZ 70191. Tel.: (711) 640 2039

WIESBADEN
Tango Treff (dance salon), Hachbarschafthaus, Rathausstr. 10 (Biebrich)

WILLICH
Tango im Zollhaus (dance salon), Franzen Zollhaus, Hardt 29

WUPPERTAL
Tango Bar (dance salon), Haus der Jugend Barmen, Geschwister-Scholl-Platz 4-6

GREAT BRITAIN (country code: 44)

LONDON
Christine Denniston (general information for London). Tel.: (171) 385 6011
'Gavito' Tango Salon (school, dance salon), 117 Brad Street, SE1. Tel.: (171) 928 3485.
The London Welsh Centre (school, dance salon), 157 Grays Inn Rd, WC1. Tel.: (171) 720 7608
El Once Club de Tango (school, dance salon), El Cafetin Porteño, Loughborough Hotel, 39 Loughborough Rd, SW9. Tel.: (171) 582 0910. *Or* The School of Pharmacy, 29/39 Brunswick Sq., WC1
Miguel Gonzalez & Nubia Merchan (school), Las Estrellas, 2/3 Inverness Mews, W2. Tel.: (171) 221 8170. *Or* The 1a Centre, 1a Roseberry Avenue, EC1. Tel.: (181) 346 4024
Rincon del Tango (dance salon), Tropical Las Palmas, 10-12 Westmoreland Rd, off Walworth Rd, SE17. Tel.: (171) 701 6184
The Salon (school, dance salon), Central Club Hotel, 16 Great Russell St, WC1. Tel.: (171) 385 6011

OXFORD
South Oxford Community Centre (school), Lake Street. Tel.: (1865) 71 4163

ITALY (country code: 39)

BOLOGNA
Bert Tobias (school), Fernesina Club, Via de Gessi 1B. Tel.: (51) 368 118/636 8559

VENICE
Mirachiara Micheli (school), Castello 5007. Tel.: (41) 522 6913

JAPAN (country code: 81)

KANAGAWA
Shingo & Asuka (school), Showachiku Plaza, Showachiku SC, Mitsukoshi 2F, 1, Ohfuna-6, Kamakura-shi
Yuko Harada (school), Subaru Building 3-4-32 Isoga, Isoko-ku, Yokohama 235

SAITAMA
Shigeru Ida, 1-11-2, Tsukakoshi, Warabi-shi, 335

TOKYO
Nostalgias (show, dance salon), Tango Academia, Shimizu Building 5F 3-1409, Akasaka Minato-ku, 107. Tel.: (3) 3334 4828
Shingo & Asuka (school), 5-45-10-201 Nakano, Nakano-ku. Tel.: (3) 3319 9130
Tango Argentina Club, Sumida-ku Jamesawa 4-15-3-601. Tel.: (3) 3624 6680
T. Kobayashi (school), Tokyo Music, Culture Centre, 11th Mori Building Trononom
Toshiko & Kozo Miura (school), TOI Kenpo Kaikan, 4 Minamimoto machi, Shinjuku-ku,160. Tel.: (3) 3920 7245

MEXICO (country code: 52)

Academia Mexicana del Tango, Carril 52, 5ta, Ursula Xitla, 1442 Mexico DF. *Inf:* Jorge Bartalucci. Tel.: (5) 683 4714

NETHERLANDS (country code: 31)

AMSTERDAM
Academia de Tango Akhnaton (school, dance salon), Korte Leidsedwarsstraat 12. Tel.: (20) 691 3619
Café Boulevard (dance salon), Cruquisweg 3. Tel.: (20) 663 2156
De Witte (school), De Wittestraat 100. Tel.: (20) 682 9410
Open Space, Korte Prinsengracht 14. Tel.: (20) 420 0958
Tango Palace Dansstudio (school), Westergasfabriek. Tel.: (20) 626-0257
Tangoschool Amsterdam (school, dance salon), Willemstraat 24A. Tel.: (20) 6256 4420

ARNHEM
Flor de Tango (school), Dijkstraat 65. Tel.: (85) 421 321

BREDA
Tango Guapo (school), Dansinstitut Oremans, Ginnekenweg 133. Tel.: 76 22 7883

DEVENTER
Ovi-Art (school), Hallenstraat 8, 7411 CZ. Tel.: (5700) 19 576

DORDRECHT
Pablo's salon (dance salon), Houttuinen 32. Tel.: (78) 14 2126

EINDHOVEN
Tango Tarro (school), Hoogstraat 297A. Tel.: (40) 65 400

GRONINGEN
Ocho de Mayo (school, dance salon), Hoekstraat 297A. Tel.: (50) 137 668

THE HAGUE
Het Syndicaat (school), Nieuwe Molstraat 10. Tel.: (70) 360 0053

S'HERTOGENBOSCH
Tango Guapo (school), Kardinaal van Rossumplein 15. Tel.: (73) 227 883

MAASTRICHT
Tangoschool Maastricht (school), Prins Bisschopsingel 27. Tel.: (43) 25 0763

NIJMEGEN
El Corte (school, dance salon), Graafseweg 108B. Tel.: (80) 23 9104
Ma Joie (school), Groesbeeksedwarsstraat 233. Tel.: (80) 23 9104

ROTTERDAM
Quartito Azul (school), Teatro Popular, Westkruiskade 26. Tel.: (10) 411 6443

TILBURG
La tarde de Tango Duco (dance salon), Café du Commerce, Stadhuisplein 36B
Tango Guapo (school), De Koninklijke Harmonie, Stationsstraat 26. Tel.: (13) 22 7883

UTRECHT
El Gancho (school), Van Meurstraat 9, 3532 CH. Tel.: (30) 93 3608

SPAIN (country code: 34)

BARCELONA
Barcelona Tango Club. Tel.: (3) 487 4754/226 1841
Aurora Mestre (school), 'Rosita Segovia', Gelabert 42044. Tel.: (3) 330 6299
Bolero (dance salon), Diagonal 405. Tel.: (3) 416 1450
Jimmy Ray (school), Gimnasio Los Altenas, Mèxecio 13. Tel.: (3) 426 4334
Norma Depaola (dance salon), c/Gran Gracia no 194 bis 120. Tel.: (3) 217 5024
Patio de Tango (school), Plaza Regomir 3 pral 1. Tel.: (3) 420 9556
Toni Lopez & Anna Castelblanque (school), Centro Asturiano, Paseo de Gracia 78. Tel.: (3) 373 4355

MADRID
Marcelo & Marcela (show, school), Sala San Pol, Plaza San Pol. Tel.: (1) 547 6903
Mauro Barreras (school, dance salon), Casa de Granada en Madrid, Doctor Cortezo 17 piso 5. Tel.: (1) 530 1987/429 6007

SWEDEN (country code: 46)

STOCKHOLM
El Tabano, Bondegatan 1. Tel.: (8) 641 14700

SWITZERLAND (country code: 41)

BASLE
Danzaria (dance salon), Sommercasino, Münchensteinerstr. 1

BERNE
Tobias Bäumlin (dance salon), Länggasstreff *and* Treffpunkt Untermatt, Looslistr. 15. Tel.: (31) 302 0347

LAUSANNE
Tangofoolies (school), Ch. de Centre 43, CH-1025 St. Sulpice. Tel.: (21) 691 8655

LUCERNE
Tango im Restaurant Karibia (dance salon), Pilatusplatz. Tel.: (41) 36 6920

ZURICH
Club Silbando (school), Geroldstr. 5. *Inf:* D. Ferro, Schügistr. 76. Tel.: (1) 321 2772
Theatersaal Rigiblick (dance salon), Germaniastr. 99. Tel.: (1) 363 5479

USA (country code: 1)

CALIFORNIA
Los Angeles area:
Alberto Toledano & Loreen Arbus (school). *Inf:* Tanguero Productions, 5351 Corteen Place, North Hollywood, CA 91607. Tel.: (818) 506 0780
Paul Palmintere. Tel.: (909) 885 7606 *and*
Linda Valentino (dance salon). Tel.: (213) 650 0509
Michael Walker & Luren Bellucci (school, dance salon). Tel.: (310) 377 9695

San Francisco area:
Bay Area Argentine Tango Association. *Inf:* Barbara Garvey, 524 San Anselmo, # 104, San Anselmo, CA 94960. Tel.: (415) 453 7009
Chez Louis (dance salon), 4170 El Camino Real, Palo Alto. Tel.: (415) 326 1060
Nora Dinzelbacher (school, dance salon), The Jewish Community Centre, 1414 Walnut Ave, Berkeley. Tel.: (415) 482 2524
La Milonguita (dance salon), 4170 El Camino Real, Palo Alto
Becky Oler (school). Tel.: (415) 368 3144. *Inf.:* Alberto Paz, 1111 W. El Camino Real, # 109, Sunnyvale, CA. 94087. Tel.: (408) 720 9506
Ruvano's Dance Studio (dance salon), 1290 Sutter St., San Francisco
Spectrum (dance salon), 1707 South Bascom Ave. Tel.: (408) 720 9506
La Tangueria (dance salon), Fairfax Women's Club, 46 Park Rd, Fairfax, CA 94930. Tel.: (415) 456 4373

ILLINOIS
Chicago
Chicago Tango Club. *Inf:* Charlotte Vikstrom, 5844 S. Stony Island Avenue, Chicago, ILL 60637-2022. Tel.: (312) 493 0666

MASSACHUSETTS
Rug Cutters Dance Studio, Malden, MA 02148. *Inf:* Ron Gursky. Tel.: (617) 397 6362

NEW YORK
Amigos del Tango en Nueva York. *Inf:* Josephine Malvestiti, 99-40 64th Road, Rego Park, NY 11374. Tel.: (718) 699 4319
Bailamos Tango (school), Dorothy's Dance Centre, 156 Mt. Vernon Ave, Mt. Vernon. Tel.: (718) 325 6579
Dance Manhattan (dance salon), Trenner's Tango Salon, 119 East 15th St. Tel.: (212) 228 0844
Danel & Maria (school), 939 Eighth Ave. *Or* 156 Mt. Vernon Avenue, Mount Vernon
Mostly Tango (dance salon). *Inf:* A. Rimalovski, 11 Elmshirst Drive, Old Westbury, NY 11568. Tel.: (516) 626 1822
Sandra Cameron Dance Center, (school), 439 Lafayette Street, NY 10003. Tel.: (212) 674 0505
Thiasos (dance salon), 59 West 21 St. Tel.: (212) 727 7775

OHIO
Cincinnati Tango Society. Tel.: (606) 341 3573

WASHINGTON
Seattle
Club Tango, Art Hemenway, 2019 Fairview Avenue East, Houseboat D, Seattle WA 98102. Tel.: (206) 323 2143

NOTES

PART I

1. R. B. Cunninghame-Graham to his mother, *c.* 1914/1915, quoted in A. F. Tschiffely, *Don Roberto, being the Account of the Life and Works of R. B. Cunninghame-Graham*, London, 1937, p. 362.
2. Donna J. Guy, *Sex and Danger in Buenos Aires. Prostitution, Family and Nation in Argentina*, Lincoln, Nebraska, 1991, pp. 5-77.
3. The term *bonaerenses* is applied to the inhabitants of the *province* of Buenos Aires, not the city.
4. *La historia del tango*, 19 vols., Buenos Aires, 1976-87, I, pp. 57-58.
5. George Reid Andrews, *The Afro-Argentines of Buenos Aires, 1800-1900*, Madison, Wisconsin, 1980, p. 161 and p. 164.
6. Ventura Lynch, *La provincia de Buenos Aires hasta la definición de la cuestión Capital de la República*, Buenos Aires, 1883, 2nd ed. 1925, quoted in José Gobello, *Crónica general del tango*, Buenos Aires, 1980, p. 16. Lynch's choice of title was odd. It translates as 'The province of Buenos Aires prior to the solution of the Capital of the Republic question,' [i.e., 1880]. It is as if someone had written an account of the rise of British rock music in the 1960s and called it: 'England prior to the Conservative election victory of 1970.' When the book was reissued in 1925 it was given the more appropriate title *Cancionero bonaerense* ('Buenos Aires Province book of airs').
7. Francisco Canaro, *Mis bodas de oro con el tango y mis memorias*, Buenos Aires, 1957, pp. 63-65.
8. Borges, 'El tango' [1964], in *Obras completas de Jorge Luis Borges*, Buenos Aires, 1974, p. 889.
9. Canaro (note 7), pp. 105-106.

PART II

1. Gabriel Louis Pringué, *Trente Ans de dîners en ville*, Paris, 1948, p. 12.
2. *Ibid.*, p. 13.
3. Maurice Rostand, *Confession d'un demi-siècle*, Paris, 1948, p. 167.
4. Jean Cocteau, *Portraits-souvenir, 1900-1914*, Paris, 1935, p. 239.
5. Quoted in Charles Spencer, *The World of Serge Diaghilev*, London, 1967, p. 51.
6. Troy and Margaret Kinney, *The Dance, Its Place in Art and Life*, London, 1914, p. 270.
7. Ricardo Güiraldes, *Obras completas*, Buenos Aires, 1962, p. 63.
8. Pringué (note 1), p. 47.
9. Adry de Carbuccia, *Du Tango à Lilly Marlene*, Paris, 1987, p. 41.
10. *Ibid.*
11. Elisabeth de Gramont (Duchesse de Clermont-Tonnerre), *Mémoires, Les Marronniers en fleurs*, Paris, 1929, p. 276.
12. *Ibid.*
13. *Ibid.*, p. 277.
14. Cocteau (note 4), p. 241.
15. *New York Times*, 15 March 1914.
16. *The Dancing Times*, August 1913.
17. *Ibid.*
18. *The Daily Graphic*, 21 May 1913.
19. Kinney (note 6), p. 292.
20. *The Sketch*, 12 November 1913, p. 159.
21. *See* pp. 75-77, 85-87.
22. Irene Castle, *Castles in the Air*, New York, 1980, p. 81.
23. Harold Acton, *Memoirs of an Aesthete*, London, 1948, pp. 37-39.
24. Quoted in Fernando Assunçao, *El Tango y sus circunstancias*, Buenos Aires, 1984, p. 244.
25. *Mercure de France*, 16 February 1914.
26. *Ibid.*
27. *The Times*, 10 January 1914.
28. *The New York Times*, 15 February 1914.
29. *The New York Times*, 4 January 1914.
30. *Ibid.*
31. *The New York Times*, 5 January 1914.
32. *The New York Times*, 4 January 1914.
33. *The New York Times*, 2 January 1914.
34. *The New York Times*, 5 January 1914.
35. *Ibid.*
36. *The New York Times*, 11 January 1914.
37. Marcel Fouquier, *Jours heureux d'autrefois*, Paris, 1960, p. 146.
38. Jorge Luis Borges, *La historia del tango in Evaristo Carriego, Obras completas*, Buenos Aires, 1974, p. 239.
39. *Mercure de France*, 16 February 1914.
40. Donald Castro, *The Argentine Tango as Social History, 1890-1955*, New York, 1991, p. 93.
41. Alfonso Reyes, *Obras completas*, Mexico City, 1958, Vol. VIII, p. 64.
42. Quoted in Fernando Assunçao (note 24), p. 250.
43. Quoted in Claude Fléouter, *Le Tango de Buenos Aires*, Paris, 1960, p. 46.
44. Quoted in Fernando Assunçao (note 24), p. 242.
45. *Ibid.*
46. *Ibid.*
47. Quoted in Fernando Assunçao (note 24), p. 245.
48. Ricardo Güiraldes (note 7), p. 362.

PART III

1. Combined quote from Tania [Discépolo] (transcriber: Jorge Miguel Couselo), *Discepolín y yo*, Buenos Aires, 1973, p. 32-33, and personal communication to author, 2 June 1994.
2. Donna J. Guy, *Sex and Danger in Buenos Aires. Prostitution, Family and Nation in Argentina*, Lincoln, Nebraska, 1991, p. 103.
3. For information on Gardel, I am greatly indebted to Simon Collier and to his *The Life, Music and Times of Carlos Gardel* (1986).
4. Razzano's nickname is explained by the fact that he came from Uruguay. Uruguayans are *orientales*, easterners; the full name of their country is República Oriental del Uruguay, The Eastern Republic of the Uruguay [River]. Uruguayans sometimes give their addresses as in 'R. O. del Uruguay'.
5. Jorge Luis Borges, *Evaristo Corriego*, New York, 1984, pp. 143-148.
6. *Ibid.*
7. Estela Dos Santos, 'Mujeres en el Tango', in *Primer encuentro de estudios y debates sobre Carlos Gardel*, Buenos Aires, 1986, p. 121.
8. 'Carlos Gardel sang "La morocha" and "Padre nuestra" and Agustín Magaldi played the role of the woman in *La muchacha del círco*,' Estela Dos Santos, 'Mujeres en el tango', in *Primer encuentro de estudios y debates sobre Carlos Gardel*, Buenos Aires, 1986, p. 129.
9. On this, see especially Luis Adolfo Sierra, *Historia de la orquesta típica*, Buenos Aires, 1976, pp. 89-90.
10. *Ibid.*, p. 92.
11. There was a superstition among tango musicians never to name Di Sarli openly: he had been accidentally shot in the eye as a child and always wore dark glasses.
12. María Susana Azzi, *Antropología del tango: Los protagonistas*, Buenos Aires, 1991, p. 87.
13. *Ibid.*, pp. 86-87.
14. *Ibid.*, pp. 41-42.
15. *Ibid.*, pp. 48-49.

PART IV

1. Waldo Frank, *America España* [1917], New York, 1931, pp. 115-16.
2. *Ibid.*, p. 118.
3. Julie M. Taylor, 'Tango: Themes of Class and Nation', in *Ethnomusicology* 10 (1976): 289.
4. María Susana Azzi, *Buenos Aires Herald*, 9 December 1991. Azzi writes: 'Men and women facing critical moments in life, especially death, ever-present in tango, release tensions through their fears and anxiety, and overcome despair by means of some nearly religious rituals: the *milonga* could be one of them.'
5. Taylor (note 3), p. 282.
6. *Ibid.*
7. Eva Uchalova and Milena Zeminova, *Fashion in Bohemia, 1870-1914: From the Waltz to the Tango* (exhibition catalogue, Museum of Decorative Arts, Prague), 1994, p.15.
8. Azzi (note 4).

BIBLIOGRAPHY

GENERAL

Albuquerque, M.A. (ed.), *Antología de tangos*, Mexico, 1956.

Assunçao, Fernando, *El tango y sus circunstancias*, Buenos Aires, 1984.

Bates, Hector and Luis, *La historia del tango (Vol. I)*, Buenos Aires, 1936.(Vol. II was never published)

Carella, Tulio, *El tango, mito y esencias*, Buenos Aires, 1956.

Cerdan, Francis (ed.), *Le Tango, Hommage à Carlos Gardel*, Toulouse, 1985.

Collier, Simon, *The Life, Music and Times of Carlos Gardel*, Pittsburgh, Pennsylvania, 1986.

—, 'The Popular Roots of the Argentine Tango', in *History Workshop* 34 (Autumn 1992): 92-100.

De Caro, Julio, *El tango en mis recuerdos*, Buenos Aires, 1964.

Del Priore, Oscar, *El tango de Villoldo a Piazzolla*, Buenos Aires, 1975.

Ferrer, Horacio, *El tango: su historia y evolución*, Buenos Aires, 1960.

—, *El libro del tango, crónica y diccionario 1850-1977*, Buenos Aires, 1980.

Fléouter, Claude, *Le Tango de Buenos Aires*, Paris, 1960.

Franco-Lao, Nery, *Tempo di Tango*, Milan, 1975.

García Jiménez, Francisco, *Así nacieron los tangos*, Buenos Aires, 1965.

Gobello, José, *Crónica general del tango*, Buenos Aires, 1980.

—, *Nuevo diccionario lunfardo*, Buenos Aires, 1990.

Guy, Donna J., *Sex and Danger in Buenos Aires. Prostitution, Family and Nation in Argentina*, Lincoln, Nebraska, 1991.

Historia del tango, La (19 vols.), Buenos Aires, 1976-87.

Jakubs, Deborah L., 'From Bawdyhouse to Cabaret: The Evolution of the Tango as an Expression of Argentine Popular Culture', in *Journal of Popular Culture* 18 (No.1, 1984): 133-45.

Lara, Tomás de, *El tema del tango en la literatura argentina*, Buenos Aires, 1982.

Martini Real, Carlos, *La historia del tango*, Buenos Aires, 1976.

Rodríguez, Adolfo Enrique, *Lexicon de 16,500 voces y locuciones lunfardas, populares, jergales y extranjeras*, Buenos Aires, 1991.

Romano, Eduardo (ed.), *Las letras del tango. Antología cronológica 1900-1980*, 3rd ed., Rosario, 1991.

Romero, José Luis (ed.), *Guía Atlántida de Buenos Aires*, Buenos Aires, 1978.

Salas, Horacio, *El tango*, Buenos Aires, 1986.

Sareli, Jorge, *El libro mayor del tango*, Mexico City, 1974.

Stilman, Eduardo, *Historia del tango*, Buenos Aires, 1965.

Ulla, Noemí, *Tango, rebelion y nostalgia*, Buenos Aires, 1982.

PART I

Canaro, Francisco, *Mis bodas de oro con el tango y mis memorias*, Buenos Aires, 1957.

Carretero, Andrés, *El compadrito y el tango*, Buenos Aires, 1964.

Casadevall, Domingo F., *Buenos Aires. Arrabal, sainete, tango*, Buenos Aires, 1968.

Collier, Simon, *The Life, Music and Times of Carlos Gardel*, Pittsburgh, Pennsylvania, 1986.

Guy, Donna J., *Sex and Danger in Buenos Aires. Prostitution, Family and Nation in Argentina*, Lincoln, Nebraska, 1991.

Lafuente, Raúl F., 'Juan Maglio "Pacho", una vida para el tango,' *Club de tango* 5 (Buenos Aires, May-June 1993): 16-20.

Puccia, Enrique H., *El Buenos Aires de Angel C. Villoldo*, Buenos Aires,1976.

Reid Andrews, George, *The Afro-Argentines of Buenos Aires, 1800-1900*, Madison, Wisconsin, 1980.

Romero, José Luis, and Romero, Luis Alberto (eds), *Buenos Aires. Historia de cuatro siglos*, 2 vols., Buenos Aires, 1983.

Scobie, James R., *Buenos Aires. Plaza to Suburb, 1870-1910*, New York, 1974.

Sierra, Luis Adolfo, *Historia de la orquesta típica*, Buenos Aires, 1966.

Sosa Cordero, Osvaldo, *Historia de los varietés en Buenos Aires, 1900-1925*, Buenos Aires, 1978.

Tallón, José, *El tango en su etapa de música prohibida*, Buenos Aires, 1964.

'Viejo Tanguero', *El tango, su evolución y su historia*, Buenos Aires, 1987.

PART II

Baez, Martha, *Los heredos del exilio*, Buenos Aires, 1990.

Battistessa, Angel, *Ricardo Güiraldes*, Buenos Aires, 1987.

Blasi, Alberto, *Güiraldes y Larbaud. Una amistad creadora*, Buenos Aires, 1970.

Borges, Jorge Luis, *La historia del tango in Evaristo Carriego, Obras completas*, Buenos Aires, 1974.

Cadícamo, Enrique, *Gardel en París*, Buenos Aires, 1984.

—, *Mis Memorías*, Buenos Aires, 1989.

Carbuccia, Adry de, *Du Tango à Lilly Marlene*, Paris, 1987.

Castro, Donald, *The Argentine Tango as Social History, 1890-1955*, New York, 1991.

Cocteau, Jean, *Portraits-Souvenir, 1900-1914*, Paris, 1935.

Collier, Simon, '"Hullo Tango!" The English Tango Craze and Its After Echoes', in Alistair Hennessy and John King (eds), *The Land that England Lost. Argentina and Britain, A Special Relationship*, London, 1992.

Colombo, Ismael, *Ricardo Guïraldes*, Buenos Aires, 1952.

Cowles, Virginia, *1913: The Defiant Swan Song*, London, 1967.

De Caro, Julio, *Paginas de oro para la historia del tango*, Buenos Aires, 1955.

Eichelbaum, Edmundo, *L'Age d'or du tango: Carlos Gardel*, Paris, 1984.

Fouquier, Marcel, *Jours heureux d'autrefois*, Paris, 1941.

García Jimenez, Francisco, *Historia de medio siglo, 1880-1930*, Buenos Aires, 1964.

Gramont, Elisabeth de (Duchesse de Clermont-Tonnerre), *Mémoires, les marronniers en fleurs*, Paris, 1929.

Güiraldes, Ricardo, *Obras completas*, Buenos Aires, 1962.

Kinney, Troy and Margaret, *The Dance, Its Place in Art and Life*, London, 1914.

Orgambide, Pedro, *Gardel y la patría del mito*, Buenos Aires, 1985.

Patout, Paulette, *Alfonso Reyes et la France*, Paris, 1978.

— (ed.), *Valery Larbaud - Alfonso Reyes. Correspondence*, Paris, 1972.

Pringué, Gabriel-Louis, *Trente Ans de dîners en ville*, Paris, 1948.

Reinoso, Pablo, *Tango*, Paris, 1982.

Richepin, Jean, *A propos du Tango*, Paris, 1913.

Rostand, Maurice, *Confession d'un demi-siècle*, Paris, 1948.

Spencer, Charles, *The World of Sergei Diaghilev*, London, 1967.

Teisseire, Luis, *El tango, un poco de historia*, Buenos Aires, 1933.

MAGAZINES:
The Dancing Times
Elegancias
Illustration
Revue sud américaine
La Vie heureuse
A Revista de América

NEWSPAPERS:
Mercure de France
The Times

PART III

Allen, Don (ed.), The World of *Film and Filmmakers*, New York, 1979.

Alsogaray, J.L, *Trilogía de la trata de blancas, rufianes y policías*, Buenos Aires, 1933.

Appadurai, Arjun, 'Global Ethnoscapes', in *Recapturing Anthropology*, Richard G. Fox (ed.), School of American Research, Santa Fe, New Mexico, 1991.

Azzi, María Susana, *Antropología del tango. Los protagonistas*, Buenos Aires, 1991.

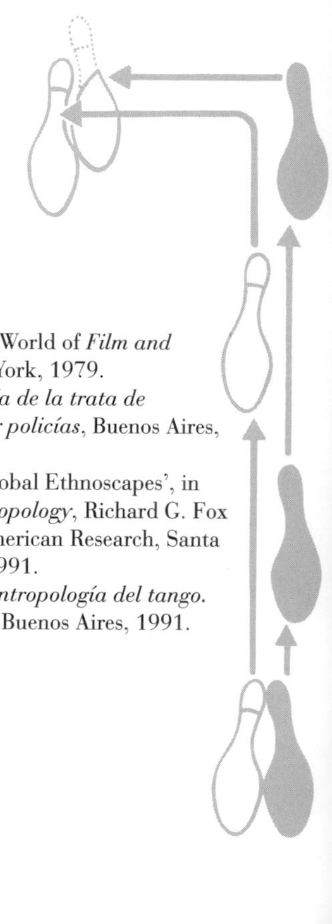

Azzi, María Susana, and Fernández, Felipe, 'El duende de tu son', in *Temas y fotos* 21 (June 1991): 77-82.
Azzi, María Susana, *Sobre minas, percantas, milongueras y flores de tango*, Olavarría, *El Popular*, January and February 1992.
Bateson, Gregory, *Naven*, Stanford, California, 1958.
Berger, Peter, *The Sacred Canopy*, New York, 1990.
Berger, Peter, and Luckmann, Thomas, *La construcción social de la realidad*, Buenos Aires, 1984.
Borges, Jorge Luis, *El tamaño de mi esperanza* [1926], Buenos Aires, 1993.
Collier, Simon, 'Carlos Gardel et l'âge d'or du tango', *Revue des deux mondes*, Paris (December 1990): 119-32.
Del Greco, Orlando, *Carlos Gardel y los autores de sus canciones*, Buenos Aires, 1990.
Discépolo, Enrique Santos, *Mordisquito, la mí no me la vas a contar!*, Buenos Aires, 1986.
Dos Santos, Estela, 'Mujeres en el tango', in *Primer encuentro de estudios y debates sobre Carlos Gardel*, Buenos Aires, 1986.
Douglas, Mary, *Pureza y peligro. Un análisis de los conceptos de contaminación y tabú*, Madrid, 1973.
Ferrer, Horacio, *El libro del tango*, Antonio Tersol (ed.), Buenos Aires, 1980.
Gambini, Hugo, *La verdadera historia de la marcha peronista*, Buenos Aires, *La Nación*, 17 October 1992.
Gobello, José (ed.), *Communicaciones de la Academia Porteña del Lunfardo*, Buenos Aires, 1966 to the present.
Gorín, Natalio (ed.), *Astor Piazzolla, a manera de memorias*, Buenos Aires, 1990.
Guy, Donna J., *Sex and Danger in Buenos Aires. Prostitution, Family and Nation in Argentina*, Lincoln, Nebraska, 1991.
Houghton, Walter E., *The Victorian Frame of Mind, 1830-1870*, New Haven and London, 1985.
Irigoin, Alfredo M., *La evolucíon industrial en la Argentina (1870-1940)*, in *Libertas*, Buenos Aires, 1984.
Korn, Francis, *Buenos Aires, Los huéspedes del 20*, Buenos Aires,1989.
López Ruzi, Oscar, *Piazzolla loco loco loco*, Buenos Aires, 1994.
Morena, Miguel Angel, *Historia artística de Carlos Gardel*, 3rd ed., Buenos Aires, 1990.
Piazzolla, Diana, *Astor*, Buenos Aires, 1987.
Pujol, Sergio, *Valentino in Buenos Aires. Los años veinte y el espectáculo*, Buenos Aires, 1994.
Rock, David, *Argentina 1516-1987*, London, 1987.
Rodríguez, Tino, *Primer diccionario de sinónimos del lunfardo (La palabra en movimiento)*, Buenos Aires, 1987.
Romano, Eduardo, *Las letras del tango. Antología cronológica: 1900-1980*, Rosario, 1991.
Rosselli, John, 'The Opera Business and the Italian Immigrant Community in Latin America 1820-1930: The Example of Buenos Aires', in *Past & Present, A Journal of Historical Studies* 127 (May 1990): 155-82.
Sanguinetti, Horacio, 'Caruso y Buenos Aires', in *Todo es historia* 49 (Buenos Aires, May 1971): 40.
Tania (Ana Luciano Divis/Discépolo), and Couselo, Jorge Miguel (transcriber), *Discepolín y yo*, Buenos Aires, 1973.
Turner, Victor, *The Ritual Process, Structure and Anti-Structure*, Ithaca, New York, 1985.

Cancioneros, Buenos Aires:
'Cadícamo, Enrique', 1985.
'Carriego, Evaristo', 1977.
'Castillo, José González y Cátulo', 1985.
'Centeya, Julián', 1979.
'Contursi, Pascual y José María', 1981.
'Discépolo, Enrique Santos', 1990.
'Ferrer, Horacio', 1980.
'Flores, Celedonio', 1987.
'García Jiménez, Francisco', 1990.
'Le Pera, Alfredo', 1985.
'Manzi, Homero', 1985.
'Romero, Manuel', 1982.

MAGAZINES:
Caras y caretas, Buenos Aires, 1913-14
Fray mocho, 1913, Buenos Aires, 1913-14
El alma que canta, Buenos Aires, 1916-1961
Temas y fotos, Buenos Aires, 1991-92
La maga, Buenos Aires, August 1994, no. 4

NEWSPAPERS:
Buenos Aires Herald
La Nacion, Buenos Aires
Clarin, Buenos Aires
El Popular, Olavarría

PART IV

Azzi, María Susana, *Buenos Aires Herald*, 9 December 1991.
Frank, Waldo, *America Hispana*, New York, 1931.
Rippon, Angela, 'Vertical Expression of a Horizontal Desire', in programme for 'Tango Para Dos, A Homage to Carlos Gardel', Sadler's Wells, London, 22 June – 10 July 1993.
Taylor, Julie M., 'Tango: Themes of Class and Nation', in *Ethnomusicology* 10 (1976): 289.
Uchalova, Eva, and Zeminova, Milena, *Fashion in Bohemia, 1870-1914: From the Waltz to the Tango* (exhibition catalogue, Museum of Decorative Arts, Prague), 1994, p. 15.

★ ★ ★ ★ ★ ★ ★ ★ ★ SOURCES OF ILLUSTRATIONS ★ ★ ★ ★ ★ ★ ★ ★ ★

Numbers refer to pages.
Abbreviations: AGN = Archivo General de la Nación, Buenos Aires; BMT = Bibliothèque Municipal, Toulouse; **t** = top, **b** = bottom, **l** = left, **r** = right, **c** = centre, f = front.

5,6-7 Photos: Dee Conway. **9-11** Illustrations from G.B. Crozier, *The Tango and How to Dance It*, London, 1913. **12**, **17** Photos: Ken Haas. **18** AGN. **19** BMT. **20t** Title-page vignette from *Martin Fierro*, 1874, Buenos Aires. **20-21**, **20b** Wagons on Plaza, 11 September, Buenos Aires, *c.* 1865; photo: B. Panunzi; Haffenberg Collection, Biblioteca Nacional, Caracas. **20-21c** Lithograph by Carlos Morel, 1841; British Museum. **21t** Photo: S. Boote, *c.* 1880; Haffenberg Collection, Biblioteca Nacional, Caracas. **22**,**23** AGN. **24** From the *General Census of the City of B.A.*, London, Paris, 1910. **33** AGN. **34t** Illustration to Manuel Galvez, *Historia de Arrabal*. **34b**,**35** AGN. **36b** 'The Welcome'. Illustration from *Fray Mocho* by A. Alvarez, 1906; AGN. **36t**,**37** AGN. **38t** From *Caras y caretas*, 1905. **38l** From *Caras y caretas*, 1913. **38r** Drawing by Luciano Payet. **39** AGN. **40** *Martin Fierro*, 1897 edition, Buenos Aires. **42** Drawing by Pedro Figari, 1922; by courtesy of Alfredo Halegua, Monumental Publishing, Washington D.C. **43** Drawing by Pedro Figari, *c.* 1922; by courtesy of Alfredo Halegua, Monumental Publishing, Washington D.C. **44** 'El Tango' popular print, Buenos Aires, *c.* 1880 (published in *La Illustratión Argentin*, Nov. 1882). **45** Drawing by Pedro Figari, 1920s; by courtesy of Alfredo Halegua, Monumental Publishing, Washington D.C. **46** BMT. **47** From *Caras y caretas*, 1909. **48** German press advertisement for a bandoneon. **49t** Detail from the painting *The Tango* by Pedro Figari, *c.* 1930; Collection of Ricardo Deambrosio, New York. By permission of Ediciones de Arte Gaglianone, Buenos Aires. **49b** *Candombe*, painting by Pedro Figari; Collection of Ricardo Deambrosio, New York. By permission of Ediciones de Arte Gaglianone, Buenos Aires. **50** BMT. **51** *Historia del Tango* by Rodríguez Peña, Corregidor, Buenos Aires, 1976/79. **52t**,**52b**,**53** Private Collections. **53r** Detail from music cover 'El Cachafaz' by Manuel Aroztegui, tango criollo; BMT. **54-55** AGN. **54-55** Dancing couple from the tango 'El Maco', published in *Caras y caretas*, 1903, BMT.**55br** AGN. **56t**,**56b**,**57t**, **57b**,**58t**,**58b**,**59t** Private Collections. **59b** *Historia del Tango* by Rodríguez Peña, Corregidor, Buenos Aires, 1976/79. **60t** AGN. **61** Private Collection. **62t**,**62b** *Historia del Tango* by Rodríguez Peña, Corregidor, Buenos Aires, 1976/79. **63t** Private Collection. **63b** 1910; *Historia del Tango* by Rodríguez Peña, Corregidor, Buenos Aires, 1976/79.**65** Photo: Ken Haas. **66** *Tango*, colour print by Edouard Malouze, Paris, 1919. **67** Detail from a design by 'Fish', *c.* 1925. **68t** From *La Vie heureuse*, Paris,

1913; J.L. Charmet. **69** J.L. Charmet. **70,71** Collection Eduard Pecourt. **73** Illustration from the 1954 edition of Ricardo Güiraldes *Raucho* [1917]. **74b** Deutsche Bücherei, Leipzig. **75tl** Private Collection. **75tr** Collection Eduard Pecourt. **75b** From *Jugend*, Munich, 1913. **77** Collection Eduard Pecourt. **78t** 'Tout au Tango', illustration for the play *Le Tango* by M. and Mme. Richepin; from *La Vie heureuse*, Paris 1914; J. L. Charmet. **78r** Collection Eduard Pecourt. **79t,79b,80,81t, 81bl,81br** Illustrations from 'Les Modes de Tango' in the special number on Richepin's play from *La Vie heureuse*, 1914; photos J. L. Charmet. **82t** 'Faut il danser le Tango?', from *La Vie heureuse*, 1913; photo J. L. Charmet. **82b-83b** Cover and illustrations from G. B. Crozier, *The Tango and How to Dance It*, London, 1913. **83br** Advertisement from *The Dancing Times*, 1913. **84** Mansell Collection. **85** Mander & Mitcheson Collection. **86t** Advertisement for a tango manual, Berlin, 1913; Deutsche Bücherei, Leipzig. **87t** From the periodical *Argos*, St Petersburg, 1913. **87b** From *Jugend*, Munich, 1920. **88** From *La Vie heureuse*, 1913; photo J. L. Charmet. **89** From *La Vie heureuse*, 1914; photo J. L. Charmet. **90** From *L'Illustration*, 1914; J. L. Charmet. **9lm** Headline from the *New York Times*, January 1914. **91,92** Irene and Vernon Castle dancing the tango. From Irene and Vernon Castle, *Modern Dancing*, New York, 1914. **93** Drawing by Elie Nadelman. Metropolitan Museum of Art, N.Y. Gift of Lincoln Kirstein. **94,95** Bibliothèque National, Paris. **96** BMT. **97t** Woodcut by Adolfo Bellocq, 1922. **97b** Private Collection. **98t** Part of poem by Vladimir Mayakovsky, published in the Russian Futurist journal, 1914. **98tr** *Tango Rausch*, Artist's Album published by the Berlin satirical weekly *Lustige Blätter*, 1913. Deutsche Bücherei, Leipzig. **98f,99t,99b** J. L. Charmet. **100** Turner Entertainment Co. **101** Advertisement from *The Dancing Times*, 1925. **102-103** Collection Eduard Pecourt. **102** J. L. Charmet. **103t** Private Collection. **103b** AISA Barcelona. **104** Collection Eduard Pecourt. **113** Photo: Ken Haas. **114** AGN. **115** Private Collection. **116-117** AGN. **117t,117m,117b** BMT. **118,119,120t,120-121,121t** AGN. **122** Private Collection. **123** BMT. **124** Photo: Horacio Coppola. **125t** Photo: O. J. Obando, Medellin. **125b** Photo: Luis Martin. **126** Photo: Mario Gallo. **129** AGN. **130** *El tango en Broadway*, film poster, Paramount, 1934; Collection Eduard Pecourt. **131lt** *Tango Bar*, film poster, Paramount, 1935; Collection Eduard Pecourt. **131lb** 'Por una cabeza', song from the film *Tango Bar*, Private Collection. **131** *El día que me quieras*, film poster, Paramount, 1935; Collection Eduard Pecourt. **132** AGN. **132b,133** Private Collections. **134** J. L. Charmet. **134b** Private Collection. **135** J. L. Charmet. **135b** BMT. **136** Private Collection. **137t** AGN. **137b** Drawing by Julia Peyrou. **138t** Private Collection. **138b** AGN. **139t** Private Collection. **139b** Illustration by Oliviero Girondo from his *Veinte poemas para ser leidos en el tranvia*, Buenos Aires, 1922. **140,141** AGN. **142** Collection Horacio Ferrer. **143t** Photo: Alicia D'Amico. **143b** Collection Horacio Ferrer. **144,146,147** AGN. **148,149** Photos: Alicia D'Amico. **151,152-153,153inset, 154,155,157** AGN. **159** Photo: Alicia D'Amico. **160** Photo: Osvaldo Salzamendi. **169** Photo: Ken Haas. **170** The Ronald Grant Archive. **171** Advertisement for dance workshop, Berlin, 1993. **172** 'Dancers', drawing by e. e. cummings, 1922; Bequest of Scofield Thayer, Metropolitan Museum of Art, New York **173** Photo: Dee Conway. **174t** Photo: Dominic. **174b** Private Collection. **175** J. L. Charmet. **176** Roger-Viollet. **177** Photo: Bengt Wangelius, Royal Dramatic Theatre, Stockholm. **178t** Roger-Viollet. **178b** The Ronald Grant Archive. **179t** *The Dance of Life*, painting by Edvard Munch, 1910; National Gallery Oslo. **179bl** Design by Lionel Koechlin for the poster of the film *Tango* by Patrice Leconte, 1993; Poster by TBWA, Paris. **179cr** J. L. Charmet. **180** *It's Over, My Handsome*; figure by the surrealist artist Jean-Louis Faure in wood, enamel, copper and resin, 1991; By courtesy of the artist and Galerie Arlagos, Nantes; photo: Raymond de Seynes. **181** The Ronald Grant Archive. **182t** From G. B. Crozier, *The Tango and How to Dance It*, London, 1913. **182b** Collection Eduard Pecourt. **183t** Photo: Tristan Vales/Agence Enguerand. **183b** Detail from a design by 'Fish', *c.* 1925, London. **184t** By courtesy of CIC Video/Universal. **184b** The Ronald Grant Archive. **185** *Madame Figaro*, April, 1993, Paris; Photos: Pascal Chevallier. **186,186-187,188** *Tango Argentino*, Vienna, 1989; Photos: Tristan Vales/Agence Enguerand. **189t,189b** *Fous de Folies* directed by M. and Alfredo Arias at the Folies-Bergère, 1993; Photo: Marc Enguerand. **190** Photo: Pilar Bustelo. **190-191,191** Photos: Dee Conway. **192** 1988; Photo: M. Jämsä, Helsinki. **192b** Photo: Jeffrey Aronson/Network Aspen. **193** *Tango Argentino*: cover of *Asáhi Graph* magazine, 1987. **194** The Ronald Grant Archive. **195b clockwise** French, Swiss, English and German advertisements for tango schools and events. **196tr** Courtesy Paul and Elaine Bottomer. **196tl**, **196bl** Tango advertisements.

The publishers would like to thank the following: María Susana Azzi for her involvement with all the pictures and for information from Buenos Aires; Eugenio Rom, the Director, and the staff of the Archivo General de la Nación, Buenos Aires; Gabriela Hanna and Juan Carlos Copes, Buenos Aires, for photographs; M.T. Hirschkoff, Paris, for her search for tango ephemera.

SOURCES OF QUOTATIONS

12 From 'Streetcorner Man' from *THE ALEPH AND OTHER STORIES* by Jorge Luis Borges, translated by Norman Thomas di Giovanni. Translation copyright © 1968, 1969, 1970 by Emece Editores, S.A. and Norman Thomas di Giovanni. Used by permission of Dutton Signet, a division of Penguin Books USA Inc.
113 Rodolfo Mederos, quoted in María Susana Azzi, *Antropología del tango. Los protagonistas*, Buenos Aires, 1991, pp. 76-77. Susana Ratcliff, quoted in Azzi, *Antropología del tango*, Buenos Aires, 1991, pp. 82-83. **152** Juan Carlos Copes, quoted in Azzi, *Antropología del tango*, Buenos Aires, 1991, pp. 30-31. **153** Extract from 'El rey del cabaret', music by Enrique Delfino, words by M. Romero, 1922. **169** Juan Carlos Copes, quoted in Azzi, *Antropología del tango*, Buenos Aires, 1991, p. 23.

ACKNOWLEDGMENTS

PART I: SIMON COLLIER
I would like to thank Mrs Sally Miller (Vanderbilt University History Department).

PART II: MARÍA SUSANA AZZI
A scholar's work always benefits from the advice and ideas of others. I am indebted for their insight and encouragement to the late María Angélica Correa, to Dr Ezequiel Gallo and to Dr Pedro Herscovici.

Dr Simon Collier offered valuable advice and suggestions, in particular with reference to structure.

My contribution to this book was significantly enriched by the help of the following: Amelita Baltar, Bruno Cespi, Juan Carlos Copes, Tania [Discépolo], Horacio Ferrer, Eino Grön, Agustín Larreta, Pablo Larreta, Héctor Lucci, Ben Molar, María Nieves, the late Sebastián Piana, Milena Plebs, Susana Rinaldi, Horacio Salgán, Claudio Segovia, Atilio Stampone, Pablo Ziegler and Miguel Angel Zotto. I am grateful to them all for their valuable information.

Thanks to Ricardo and Nicole for their tango guides and to Pirjo Kukkonen at the University of Helsinki for information on Finnish tango centres.

Thanks to Nélida Y Nelson [Nélida Rodríguez and Nelson Avila], Jorge L. Manganelli, and Helio Torres, for their precious help.

My greatest debt of all is to the people of the tango (more than 500 informants), particularly those of Buenos Aires, for their friendship and trust. Their thoughts contributed enormously to my work.

THE PUBLISHERS WOULD LIKE TO THANK THE FOLLOWING:
Simon Collier for the charts on pp.197-198.

Simon Collier and María Susana Azzi for 'Tango Music on Compact Disc'.

Ricardo and Nicole for permission to use in 'International Tango Centres' material from 'la Milonguita' world-wide Tangoguide and 'el Compadrito' Tangoguide for Buenos Aires by RICARDO Y NICOLE, Buenos Aires.

Simon Collier and Lara Speicher for their invaluable translations of the lyrics of the songs.

The dancers Horacio Fernandez and Nancy Beatriz Andrada for kindly allowing a photograph showing them performing at the Taconeando Club, Buenos Aires, to be used on the front of the jacket.

María Susana Azzi for her very generous help with research in the preparation of this book.

INDEX

Numbers in *italic* refer to illustrations.
Song, film and show titles are entered under **SONGS**, **FILMS** and **SHOWS**

Academia Porteña del Lunfardo 44
academias 47, 57
Acton, Harold
  Memoirs of an Aesthete 87
African-Argentines, influence on tango 42-6, 47; *42, 43, 44*
aigrettes 78; *78, 79, 81, 82, 83*
Aieta, Anselmo 119
Aín, Casimiro 80
Albéniz, Isaac
  'Tangos for Piano' 42
Alfonso XIII, King of Spain 87
Alippi, Elías 59
Alvear, President Marcelo T. de 119
Amadori, Luis César *144*
Angió, Gabriel *5, 173*
Anwar, Gabrielle *170*
Apollinaire, Guillaume
  The Tango 79
Aragón, Prudencio (El Johnny) 51
Argentina 19, 20-1, 36, 40
  economic growth 20-1, 115;
  depression 145, 156
  immigration 21, 35, 36, 115; *36*
Armenonville cabaret *see* Buenos Aires
Arolas, Eduardo 56, 59, 101; *59*
Arquimbaud, Eduardo *187*
Aróztegui, Manuel *188*
arrabales 34, 35, 37, 38, 39, 47; *105-12*
arrangers, in tango orchestras 150-1
Art Deco, association with tango 174, 182
Astaire, Fred 184; *184*
avant-garde, association with tango 193
Avellaneda, Pepita 63; 63
Avila, Nelson (Nelson) *186, 188*
Azabache *see* Maizani, Azucena
Azzi, María Susana 193-4

Baffa-Berlingieri-Cabarcos Trio 160
Bakst, Léon 69
Ballets Russes 69, 70, 183
ballroom dancing, tango and 51, 184, 195
bals persans 69
Baltar, Amelita 158
bandoneon 47, 57, 113, 121; *48, 113, 138*
Bandoneon Day 148
bands 60, 119-20, 146 *see also* orchestras, *orquestas típicas*
Barraud, Julia (Gloria) *187*
barrios 33, 35, 37, 38, 39, 47, 50, 51, 136; *34, 37*
Barthe, Carlos 133
Battistella, Mario 48, 136
Beaumont, Comte Etienne de 79
Beijing, China 193; *192*
Bernado, Paquita 121
Bernstein, Arturo Hermán ('the German') 58
Biagi, Rodolfo 147
Bianquet, José Ovidio *see* El Cachafaz
Bidart, Beba *162-3*
Bizet, Georges
  Carmen 40
Blasco, Armando *119*
blouse-tango 78
Borbón, Princess Isabel de 68, 72
Borges, Jorge Luis 59, 96, 132, 139; *12*
Bórquez, Carlos *188*
Boston, the 70, 83, 88
Bottallo, Professor 68; *68*
Bottomer, Paul and Elaine *196*
Boulanger, Nadia 158
Bozán, Sofía 141; *144*
Bradley, Josephine 101
Britain 81-5, 101; *84*
Broglie, Princess Jacques de 69
brothels *see* prostitution
Buenos Aires 19, 20-4, 33-9, 42, 47, 145; *20, 22, 23, 24, 34, 35, 36, 37, 105-12*
  Armenonville cabaret 61, 101, 123-4; *61*
  Avenida de Mayo 23; *22*
  Barrio Norte 33, 62
  Café Royal 58
  Centro, el 24, 33, 34, 61
  Corrales Viejo 34, 44
  Corrientes St (Avenue) 61, 115, 152, 154, 155; *54-5, 112*
  Florida Street *23*
  La Boca 57-8; *118*
  'La Marina' café 58
  La Vasca's 48
  Laura's 48-50, 51
  Madame Jeanne's 123
  Marabú cabaret 147
  Nacional café 115
  Pabellón de las Rosas (Rose Pavilion) *18*
  Pichuco restaurant *149*
  San Martín dance salon 55
  Scudo de Italia 50
  Soleil Cinema *125*
  Stella de Italia 50
  Tabarís cabaret 116; *152-3*
  Tibidabo cabaret 148, 158

cabarets 115-6, 153, 156 *see also* Buenos Aires, Paris
Cacha *see* El Cachafaz
Cadícamo, Enrique 137, 146
cafés 57, 153, 155 *see also* Buenos Aires
Calderón, Carmencita *151*
Calderón, José García 101
Canaro, Francisco 33, *57*, 57-8, 59, 62, 101, 119, 120, 128, 146, 150; *138*
Canaro, Juan 193
cancionistas see women singers
Candales, Lola 140
candombe 43, 44; *43, 49*
cantor de orquesta 128
Caras y caretas 36, 96
Carbuccia, Adry de 77
Carnelli, María Luisa 141
Caro, Julio de *119*
Caruso, Enrico 124
Casimiro *see* El Negro Casimiro
Castillo, Alberto 128; *129*
Castillo, Cátulo 136
Castle, Irene and Vernon 86, 99; *92*
Castriota, Samuel 58
  'Mi noche triste' ('Lita') 64, 124; *56*
Catholic church, disapproval of tango 90-1, 92-3
cha-cha-cha 184
Chanel, Roberto 128
chansonniers 128
Chaplin, Charlie 125
charleston 182
Ciancio, Guillermo del 133
cinema *see* films
cinemas, tango musicians in 120-1
clandestinos 38, 48
Clermont-Tonnerre, Comtesse Blanche de 69, 79-80
Clifford Barney, Natalie 79
Cobián, Juan Carlos 119, 128, 157
cocoliche 36
Cocteau, Jean 69, 80
Columbia records 60, 68; *60*
compadres 37, 38, 45; *46*
compadritos 38, 40, 44, 45, 46, 50, 55, 132, 133; *38, 39, 47, 137*
confiterías 153, 156
contests, dance 152, 154; music 120
contradanza 40
controversy, tango and 87-97
Contursi, Pascual 56, 63-4, 132, 134
  'Mi noche triste' ('Lita') 124, 133-6; *56*
conventillos 35, 55, 117; *35*
Copes, Juan Carlos 152, 169; *190*
cornet-à-piston 120, 146
Corrientes St *see* Buenos Aires
Corsini, Ignacio 128, 150
cortes 46, 50
costume *see* fashion
'couleur tango' 77
country dance 40, 88
'creole' Argentines 36, 37
'creole tangos for piano' 51, 54, 59; *52*
Crozier, Gladys Beattie
  The Tango and How to Dance It 9-11, 82-3
Cunninghame-Graham, R. B. 24, 87

D'Agostino, Angel 147
dance halls, salons and *dancings* 115-16, 153, 156
dance of death 177, 179-80; *179*
Dancing Times, The 81, 83; *83*
dancewear *see* fashion
Dare, Phyllis 82, 87
Darío, Ruben 95
D'Arienzo, Juan 147, 150; *147*
De Caro, Julio 119, 146, 157; *119*
De Lío, Ubaldo 157
Deauville 76, 77
Delfino, Enrique 141, 157; *157*
Denmark, Queen of 92
Desmond, Norma 181
Devis, Ana Luciana *see* Tania
Di Sarli, Carlos 128, 148-9
Díaz, Roberto 128
Discépolo, Enrique Santos 117, 128, 136-7, 141, 144, 145, 156; *137, 138, 139*
Dodworth, T. George 94
Domínguez, Beatrice *100*
Donato, Edgardo 119
Dubois, Lucile 88

Eduardo *see* Arquimbaud, Eduardo
El Cachafaz 59, 150; *53, 151*
El Gordo *see* Troilo, Aníbal
El Indio *see* Simara, Bernabé
El Innombrable *see* Di Sarli, Carlos
El Johnny *see* Aragón, Prudencio
El Mocho 152
El Morocho *see* Gardel, Carlos
El Mufa *see* Di Sarli, Carlos
El Mulato Sinforoso 47
El Negro Casimiro 47
El Negro Ricardo *see* Ricardo, José
El Oriental *see* Razzano, José
El Pardo *see* Ramos Mejía, Sebastián
El Polaco *see* Goyeneche, Roberto
El Rengo Cotongo 151
El Vasco Aín 152
Elegancias 95, 96, 100
Espósito, Genaro 58, 59
Estévez, Carlos 152-3
estilos 115
estribillistas 128
Eulalia, Infanta of Spain 80
'evolutionary' school of tango musicians 119-20, 146

Falcón, Ada 141, 150
fandango 87
Farley, Cardinal 92-3
fashion, tango and 69, 77-9, 95, 104, 182-3; *79, 80, 81, 182, 183, 185*
Federico, Leopoldo 160
Ferrer, Horacio 143, 158, 159
Ferro, Rafael 157
Figari, Pedro *43, 45, 49*
Filiberti, Juan (Mascarilla) *118*
Filiberto, Juan de Dios 33, 119, 139, 150; *120*
FILMS featuring the tango 101, 150
  Blood and Sand 195
  Conformist, The 176, 181
  Cotton Club, The 181
  Dancing 150
  Día que me quieras, El 157; *131*
  Divina Dama, La 121
  Down Argentine Way 184
  Flor de Durazno 101
  Flying Down to Rio 184; *184*
  Four Horsemen of the Apocalypse, The 101, 194, 195; *100*
  Go into Your Dance 184
  Idolos de la radio (Radio Idols) 150
  Indochine 181; *181*
  Last Tango in Paris 177; *178*
  Melodía de arrabal 134
  Nobleza gaucha 101
  Pride of the Bianchis, The 191
  Puerto nuevo (New Port) 144
  Scent of a Woman 175; *170*
  Sunset Boulevard 181
  ¡Tango! 144, 150
  Tango Bar 125, 131
  Tango de la muerte, El 101, 177
  Tango en Broadway 130
  Tres Berretines, Los (The Three Strong Desires) 150
  True Lies 184, *184*
  Valentino 195; *194*
Finland 195; *192*
Fiorentino, Francisco 128, 147
Firpo, Roberto 52, 58, 59, 62, 63, 119, 120, 134; *62, 121*
Flores, Celedonio Esteban 137
Francini, Enrique Mario 157
Frank, Waldo 173-5
  America Hispana 173
Fresedo, Osvaldo 101, 119, 125, 128, 146, 150; *146*
furlana 91

Gálvez, Manuel 97
  Historia de Arrabal 97
Games, Natalia *5, 173*
Garbo, Greta 104
Gardel, Carlos 56, 64, 101, 122-8, 134, 136, 141, 148, 157; *110-11, 122, 123, 126, 127, 130, 131*
  films by 150
Gardes, Charles Romauld *see* Gardel, Carlos
gauchos 19-20, 37; *20, 21, 45*
gender and the tango 140, 172, 175-7, 177-9
Germany, tango in 86, 104
Ghiglione, Luis 123
Ginastera, Alberto 158
Gloria *see* Barraud, Julia
Gobbi, Alfredo 67
Gobbi, Flora Rodríguez de *see* Rodríguez de Gobbi, Flora
Gobello, José 44, 45
Goyeneche, Roberto 128-9, 133
Grable, Betty 184
Graf Merino, Gisela *189*
Greco, Vicente 55, 58, 59, 60, 62
Grela, Roberto 157
Grossmith, George 82, 84
Guardia Vieja tango musicians 57
Gueté, Yvette 72
Guillaume, Albert
  Au Cours du tango 79
Güiraldes, Don Manuel 72
Güiraldes, Ricardo 70-6, 97, 100; *72*
  Raucho 72, 73; *73*
  'Tango' 73-6
Guy, Donna 39

habanera 40, 41, 42, 46, 54
Hernández, José
  Martín Fierro 20; *20; 40*

Ibarguren, Don Carlos 88
Isabel, Princess of Spain 68, 72
Israels, Mrs Charles H. 92
Italian immigrants, Argentina 21, 35, 36, 50; *118*

Japan, tango in 195; *193*
jazz 70, 180, 194-5

Karaslavov, Georgi S. 181
Keeler, Ruby 184
Kern, Carlos 59
Kinney, Troy and Margaret 70, 84

La Ñata Gaucha *see* Maizani, Azucena
Lamarque, Libertad 141, 150, 156
Lanvin, Jeanne 182
Larreta, Enrique 94, 95, 96, 101; *94*
Laura *see* Montserrat, Laurentina
Laurenz, Pedro 157; *119*

Le Pera, Alfredo 125, 126, 136, 180
Lehár, Franz
The Ideal Wife (Tango Queen) *99*
Linder, Max 99
Llosas, Juan 104
Logatti, Lorenzo 59, 99; *99*
Lomuto, Francisco 119
London, tango in 61, 81-2
López Buchardo, Alberto 72
Lucile 182
Lugones, Leopoldo 50
lunfardo 37, 64, 132, 137
Lyaz, René 135
Lynch, Ventura 44-5
lyrics 37, 117, 132-9; censorship 137, 156

Madame Lucile *see* Lucile
Maffia, Pedro 119
Magaldi, Agustín 128
Maglio, Juan 58, 60-1; *61*
Mainchin, Madame 80
Maizani, Azucena 139, 141-4, 151; *141*
mambo 184
Manzi, Homero 144, 156
Marchi, Baron Antonio de 61
María de Buenos Aires 158; *142, 143*
Mariani. Luis *138*
Marino, Alberto 128
Mario, Luis *see* Carnelli María
Maroni, Enrique Pedro 134
Mary, Queen of England 85
Mascarilla *see* Filiberti, Juan
mazurka 40, 43, 45; 46, 54, 88
Mayakovsky, Vladimir
'Tango with Cows' 98
maxixe 70; *68*
Mecklenburg-Schwering, Anastasia, Grand Duchess of 86, 92
Mederos, Rodolfo 113
Megata, Baron 193
Méndez, José 152
Mendizabál, Rosendo 12, 50, 51, 58, 72; *50, 51*
Mercure de France 87, 88, 90, 96
Merello, Tita 141, 150
merengue 184
Merry de Val, Cardinal 90-1
Michael, Grand Duke of Russia 84-5
microphone, advent of 120
milonga 40-1, 44, 45, 51, 54
milongueros 152
milonguita 117
Mistinguett 68; *68*
Molar, Ben *149*
Montevideo 54, 63
Montserrat, Laurentina (Laura) 48
Mora 191
Morton, Frederic 180
Mrozek, W.
Tango 181
Munch, Edvard 179; *179*
Muñoz, Carlos *see* Púa, Carlos de la
musical instruments for tango bands 62, 120, 146 *see also* bandoneon, violin cornet

Nacional café *see* Buenos Aires
Nacional record company 124
National Geographic 193
Narova, Cecilia *186*
National Tango Day 148
Nava, Arturo de 123; *54-55*
Nazis, tango and the 180
Nélida *see* Rodríguez, Nélida
Nelson *see* Avila, Nelson
'new tango' (*el nuevo tango*) 157
New York, tango in 91-4
Nicholas II, Tsar of Russia 86, 96
Nieso, José *119*
Nieves, María 154-5; *190*
Noailles, Anna de 69

Orcaizaguirre, Jorge 182
orchestras 120, 146, 150, 157; *120, 121 see also* bands, *orquestas típicas*
organ grinders 51; *55*
Orquesta del Tango de Buenos Aires 160
orquestas típicas 60, 68, 101; *121 see also* bands, orchestras
Orquesta Típica Tokio 193

Pacino, Al 175; *170*
Pacho *see* Maglio, Juan
Paramount films 125
Paris 23, 61, 67-9, 72, 76, 79, 87-91, 101, 104, 194
Apollo dance hall 101
Argentine community 94-7, 100, 101; *95*
El Abasto club 101
El Garrón club 101
Magic-City dance hall 80, 101
Maxim's restaurant 73, 77
Palais de Glace 76
society 68-9, 79-80, 124-5
payadores 41, 123
Pereya, Luis *188*
perigundines 47, 57
Perón, President Juan Domingo 155-6
Petróleo *see* Estévez, Carlos
Piazzolla, Astor 143, 148, 157-9; *159*
Pichetti, Professor 90
Pichuco *see* Troilo, Aníbal
Pius X, Pope 90-1; *90*
Pizarro brothers 101
Plebs, Milena 143; *6-7, 183, 190, 191*
Poiret, Paul 69, 79, 90, 194; *80, 81*
polka 40, 43, 54, 84, 88
Poli, Manolita 140
Polito, Juan 147
Ponzio, Ernesto 58, 59
Portalou, Ludovic de, Marquis de Sénas 77
porteños 39, 44, 50, 61, 62
Pourtalès, Comtesse Mélanie de 76
Prague, tango in 193
Pringué, Gabriel-Louis
Trente Ans de dîners en ville 68
prostitution 38-9, 47, 48, 118
protest songs 137, 145
Púa, Carlos de la 132-3
Pugliese, Osvaldo 128, 160; *160*
Puglisi, Cayetano 119
Punch 84

quebrada 46, 50
Quinteto Nuevo Tango 158
Quinteto Real 157
Quiroga, Rosita 141

radio, popularizing tango 150
Ramos Mejía, Sebastian (El Pardo) 47
Ratcliff, Susana 113
Ray, Roberto 128
Razzano, José (El Oriental) 64, 115, 123-4; *123, 138*
RCA Victor records 125
record companies 59-60
Reid Andrews, George 43
Reyes, Alfonso 96
Ricardo, José (El Negro) 124
Richardson, P.J.S.
History of English Ballroom Dancing 84-5
Richepin, Jean 88-90
The Tango 88, 90; *81, 88, 89*
Rinaldi, Susana 129; *143*
Rio, Delores 184
Rivero, Edmundo 128
Roca, General Julio Argentino 21
Roccatagliatta, David (Tito) 58
Rodríguez, Gerardo Hernán Matos 63, 134, 147; *134*
Rodríguez, Nélida *186*
Rodríguez, Pablo *140*
Rodríguez de Gobbi, Flora 63, 67
Rodríguez Molas, Ricardo 41
Rogers, Ginger *184*
Rohan, Duchesse de 69
Rome, tango in 87
Romero, Manuel 17, 141
Rongalla, María *see* Vasca, María la
Rosendo, A. *see* Mendizábal, Rosendo
Rostand, Maurice 69
Rovira, Eduardo 157
Rubia Mireya *see* Verdier, Margarita
Ruffo, Titta 123
Rufino, Roberto 128
Ruiz, Floreal 128
rumba 184
Russia, tango in 86; *87*

Saborido, Enrique 59, 67, 140
Salaverría, José María 97
Salgán, Horacio 157
salones de baile 115
Santamaría, Elvira 182
schottische 40
Sciarreta, Vicente *119*
Schwarzenegger, Arnold 184; *184*
Schwerin-Löwitz, Countess 86
Sénas, Marquis de *see* Portalou, Ludovic de
Sentis, José *134*
Sexteto Mayor 160
shoeshine parlours *33, 60*
SHOWS
Façade (ballet) *174*
Fous des Folies 189
Sunshine Girl, The 82
Tango Argentino 51, 182; *183, 186-7, 188, 191*
Tango Princessin 86
Tango, Tango 190
Tango X 2 (Tango Para Dos) 143; *5, 6-7, 173, 190, 191*
Simara, Bernabé (El Indio) 80
Simone, Mercedes 141, 150; *140*
singers 128-9; women 140-4
Sketch, The 84
smooth tango 50, 51
SONGS
'Aguas tristes' (Sad Waters) 144
'Al mundo le falta un tornillo' (The World Has a Screw Loose) 137
'Anclao en Paris' (Stranded in Paris) 146
'Apache argentino, El' *188*
'Balada para un loco' (Ballad for a Madman) 158-9
'Bartolo' 63
'Bizcochito' (Little Biscuit) 144
'Brisa, La' (The Wind) *57*
'Bueyes, Los' (The Oxen) 132-3
'Callecita de mi barrio' (Lane of my *Barrio*)133, *133*
'Cambalache' (Junk Shop) 136-7
'Canción de Buenos Aires, La' (Song of Buenos Aires) 17, 141
'Carretero, El' (The Driver) 123
'Casas viejas' (Old Houses) 145-6
'Choclo, El' (The Corncob) 59, 67; *59*
'Chorra' (Thieving Woman) 145
'Cuando llora la milonga' (When the Milonga Weeps) 141
'Cumparsita La' (The Little Carnival Procession) 63, 147; *134*
'De amor propio' (Vanity) *115*
'De mi barrio' (From my *Barrio*) 133
'Dejáme entrar, hermano' (Let Me Come In, Brother) 141-4
'Don Juan' 59
'En esta soledad' (In This Solitude) 144
'En tu olvido' (In Your Oblivion) 144
'Entrerriano, El' 51, 72; *50*
'Esta noche me emborracho' (Tonight I'm Getting Drunk) 141, 145; *139*
'Felicia' 59
'Gacho gris' (Grey Hat) 133
'Giuseppe el zapatero' (Giuseppe the Shoemaker) 133
'Gringo, El' 135
'Infanta, La' 68
'Inspiración' *190*
'Irresistible, El' 59; *99*
'Lagrimas' (Tears) *56*
'Linyera' (The Vagabond) 141
'Lita' *see* 'Mi noche triste'
'Mal de amor' *134*
'Malevaje' (Underworld) 141; *138*
'Malevo, El' (The Hoodlum) 141
'Marne, El' 101
'Melodía de arrabal' (Song of the Arrabal) 136
'Mi noche triste' (My Sorrowful Night) 64, 124, 133-6; *56*
'Morocha, La' 59, 67, 140, 141
'Milonga sentimental' 144
'Milonguero triste' (Sad Milonguero) 148
'Milonguita' *117*
'Oh! Fraulein Greta!' 104
'Orchids in the moonlight' 184
'Padre nuestro' (Our Father) 141
'Pan' (Bread) 137
'Pensado en tí' (Thinking of You) 144
'Pero yo sé' (But I Know) 141
'Picardia' *117*
'Por una cabeza' (By a Head) *131,170*
'Qué vachaché?' (Go on with You) 145; *136*
'Quejas de bandoneón' (A Bandoneon's Complaints) 148; *186-7, 189*
'Responso' (Dressing Down) 147
'Rodríguez Peña' 55
'Se va la vida' (Life Goes By) 141
'She's a Latin from Manhattan' 184
'Talar, El' 51
'This is How to Dance the Tango' 65
'Ultimo café, El' (The Last Coffee) 136
'Ultima curda, La' (The Last Binge) 148
'Volvé negro' (Come Back, Negro) 144
'Volver' (The Return) 180
'Yira, yira' (It Turns, It Turns)144
Spain, tango in 87
Spitalnik, Ismael 150
sports and social clubs, dance venues 153, 154, 156
Stampone, Atilio 147, 157, 160

tango a la francesa 97
tango agringado 135
tango americano see *habanera*
tango andaluz 42, 51, 54
tango bands *see* bands, orchestras, *orquestas típicas*
tango criollo para piano 51, 52, 54
tango discreído 145
tango liso see smooth tango
tango songs *see* **SONGS**
tanguistes and *anti-tanguistes* 87-91
Tania (Ana Luciana Devis/Discépolo) 117, 141; *137*
Tanturi, Ricardo 128; *129*
Taylor, Julie M. 176-7, 178
tea dances 74, 77, 79, 82, 86, 91
theatres as tango venues 154
Thelma, Linda 63; *62*
thés dansants see tea dances
Times, The 82, 84
Tito *see* Roccatagliatta, David
'traditional' school of tango musicians 119-20, 146, 147
Troilo, Aníbal Carmelo (Pichuco, El Gordo) 128, 129, 147-8, 157, 158; *138, 148*
turkey trot 70, 83

Uchalova, Eve 193
Undarz, Bernardo (El Mocho) 152

Valdés, Silva 97
Valentino, Rudolph 101; *100, 194*
Vardaro, Elvino 146
Vargas, Angel 147
Vasca, María la (María Rongalla) 48, 59
Verdier, Margarita (Rubia Mireya) 48
Verdu, Quintin *104*
Verón, Pablo *189*
Viejo Tanguero 44, 47, 50
Villoldo, Angel 59, 63, 67, 140; *19, 59, 99*
violin cornet *119*

Walton, Maurice and Florence 85, *85*
waltz 40, 84, 88, 171
Wells, H. G. 98
Whiteman, Paul *119*
Wolfe, Elsie de 91-2
women singers 140-4
women's orchestras 121; *121*

Zeminova, Milena 193
Zerrillo, Roberto 119
Zola, Emile 88
Zotto, Miguel Angel 143; *6-7, 183, 188, 190, 191*
Zotto, Osvaldo *191*